Ndi-Igbo of Nigeria

Identity showcase

Ndubisi Nwafor-Ejelinma

Order this book online at www.trafford.com
or email orders@trafford.com

Most Trafford titles are also available at major online book retailers.

Printed in the United States of America.

ISBN: 978-1-4669-3892-2 (sc)
ISBN: 978-1-4669-3893-9 (e)

Trafford rev. 08/13/2012

www.trafford.com

North America & international
toll-free: 1 888 232 4444 (USA & Canada)
phone: 250 383 6864 • fax: 812 355 4082

Reviews

"One of the merits of this book is that it provides an invaluable compendium of the history and culture of the Igbo people of Nigeria. It is addressed both to the many general readers for whom the Igbo nation is of persisting cultural interest and to specialized readers and researchers who wish a wide knowledge of the Igbo heritage. It will also be of special interest to several readers, particularly those who have had bias and preconceived primitive notions about the Igbo people".

Dr. P. Amuchie.

"I have never read a more exciting book. The depth of scholarship, the flowery and command of language and manipulation of humor, the wide spectrum of coverage, all make the 'Identity Showcase' very compelling and a pleasure to read. Once you start reading it, you can't stop until it is done. It is an amazing literary treasure."

Dr. Ken Amalu

"This book is a masterpiece in concept, scope, exposition, depth of details and in delivery. The historical and cultural details are testimonies of an eye witness with a powerful and urgent message. The Showcase is a classic in it's own right. This is one book every Igbo man and woman should be proud to read, possess and treasure."

Dr. Iky Ifedi.

Contents

Acknowledgement

I owe great gratitude to my 'Editorial Staff', dear friends who read, corrected and edited the manuscript and gave it shape and form: Professor Paul Achike, Prof. Nnaemeka Echendu, Dr. Ebiringa Ebegbulem, Dr. Paul Amuchie, Dr. George Ibekwe, and Dr. Steve Okeke. And very importantly I acknowledge the technical expertise of Mr. Joseph Udoh, the computer 'wizard' who gave the manuscript the final structural touch-up. Special thanks to Rev. Awowole who designed the book title cover.

To special and dear friends and relations who sustained me in my winter days in California: Mr and Mrs. Ike Mbaelu, Dan Mogbo, Ebere and Ugochukwu Anakwenze, Dr. Ejike Onyeador, Dr. and Grace Okpara, Prof. and Mrs. Eyiuche Udeze, Solomon Egbuho, Attorney Solomon Kanu, Mr. and Mrs. Robert Anyanwu: ***Okuko anaghi echefu onye kworo ya odu n'udumiri.***

I salute and honor my sweetheart Chinwe Ayanamiru, my wife, the springboard of my life. After God she is the greastest being in my life. A woman of God with a heart of gold. I salute all our five great children.

I most humbly and respectfully acknowledge my teacher, mentor and friend Prof. Chinua Achebe. I thank God for granting me the tutelage under this great master.

And greatest of all, I remain infinitely thankful and grateful to the Almighty God for granting me the grace to share this knowledge with the world.

In Memoriam

This book is dedicated to the memory of my dear friend **Ugochukwu Boniface Anakwenze (RIP)**

To all Biafrans who were massacred in Northern Nigeria

To all **Biafran Soldiers** who lost their lives in the struggle
Your sacrifice has not been in vain.

> ***"Better to die fighting for Freedom,***
> ***Than to live and languish***
> ***In perpetual fear and mysery."***
> **(Butte Kitto)**

To
Ikemba Gen. Odumegwu Ojukwu
Whose dream will surely come to pass.
Another you
Will never be.

Foreword

"This 'Identity Showcase' is a document based on extensive research among the Igbo-speaking people in Nigeria's seven southern states, It is a real treatise on all facets of Igbo Identity.

It is so far the most comprehensive and authentic resource on that subject because, it covers in great detail: the Igbo States geo-political origins, touching on local government demographics, vital Igbo institutions and traditions: Kola-nut culture, name and food culture, Igbo relationships and dynamics of traditional governance.

The Showcase includes an amazing documentary on the greatest patriarchs and patriots who are the embodiment of Igbo identity and philosophy. It throws a powerful searchlight on the Biafran phenomenon, and closes with the epitome of Igbo patriotism as personified by Gen. Odumegwu Ojukwu. Nothing in contemporary Igbo history or literature has come close to this. Finally, the catalogue of over 4800 traditional Igbo names is a monumental achievement.

This book should be a 'must read' because it is an authoritative reference and resource. And more importantly, it has potential to slow down the alarming pace of loss of Igbo authentic identity especially in the diasporas."

Dr. G. Ibekwe.

List of illustrations

Introduction

MOTIVATION:

Several factors both remote and immediate motivated putting this "**Showcase**" together. Our people say: ***"awo anaghi agba oso ehihie na nkiti"***.(the frog does not run around in the noon day for nothing). One of the most primary factors is: to provide pertinent **information** and **knowledge** for Ndi-Igbo in the first place, and for other interested readers**.** That great and very famous newspaper '**The West African Pilot'** founded by Dr. the Rt. Hon. Nnamdi Azkiwe (of blessed memory) had its motto as: ***"Show The Light And The People Will Find The Way"*** and indeed it did show the light and the entire West African sub-region found their way to political awareness and national independence.

The Old Testament Prophet Hosea said in Chapter 4 verse 6: ***"My people perish for lack of knowledge".*** This aphorism is an all time truth. Lack of knowledge (a euphemism for stark ignorance) is a state of mental, intellectual and moral bankruptcy. It is a very dreadful disability, which like leprosy, is very crippling and dilapidating. It manifests itself so prominently that any and every one can see and recognize it. In social gatherings lack of knowledge makes one dejected and a miserable laughing stock. There is nothing as shameful and embarrassing as the lack of knowledge of one's linguistic and cultural identity and heritage. The Igbo terms for such folks are: "***onye nzuzu, onye iberibe, onye apari, onye ihurihu, onye efulefu, ofeke".***

People in this cultural deficiency class are like lost luggages without any identity tag or label. We see this every day among our youths in the diaspora, teenagers who have no knowledge of where they hail from. What most of them claim to know is that they come from Africa, but have no knowledge of the geographical location of Nigeria their home country on the map of Africa, nor the precise location of the Igboland on the map of Nigeria.

An overwhelming percentage of them have no knowledge of the culture of their home state, name of their home town, and absolutely no knowledge of their village. But most of these children can exhibit an amazing knowledge of all the characters and sequences of **Harry Potter's** novels, the names and careers of great movie stars, the names and statistics of all the football and basketball stars and the major league matches.

Unfortunately, quite often, we the uncritical adults always blame our kids for their cultural ignorance. But children cannot know what they are not taught. It is not the school teacher who will educate our children about Igbo identity and cultural heritage. This type of knowledge is the responsibility of the home, that is parents. There are many homes where both parents are Igbo, (even from the same village) and yet their children cannot speak one word of Igbo language, and cannot count the first ten numerals (1 to 10) in Igbo. This cultural tragedy is not a thing of pride, it is not a status symbol. Rather it is holding the door wide open for the cultural enslavement to our children. And very sad to say, the Igbo are the only cultural and ethnic group both in Nigeria and in the diaspora who are consistentenly putting our children in this tragic harms' way. In Igbo name culture the names ***Afamefuna / Afamefule; Amaechina / Uzoechinna,*** have now become a ridicule of their intended linguistic and cultural meaning and essence. If a twenty-one year old college student whose name is ***Amaechina*** does not know the name of his father's village, nor can he count Igbo numeral one to twenty, who does not know that both the father and the student are "***ndi iberibe; ama ha echiela".*** Let us be courageous enough to tell ourselves the truth, and stop making inexcusable excuses.

It was high time to wake up to the responsibility of rescuing our children from this state of cultural and identity homelessness by providing and seriously inculcating in them the basic knowledge of who they are and where they come from. Otherwise, the next generation would be completely lost like a twig in the ocean waves. Lethargy, indifference, ineptitude, or procrastination is not an option. This responsibility is a moral, cultural and political obligation.

In summary therefore:

- This book aims at providing some basic answers to the yearnings and desire of our people for some documented educational resource material for use in helping our children and youths to study and appreciate the value, beauty and wealth of their cultural heritage.
- There is a great dearth or scarcity of written literature in Igbo on the issues and topics treated in this work;
- This is also an attempt to provide information and resource literature for the peoples of the world to see and know some of the unchartered waters of the Igbo world;
- This work is also an attempt to disabuse the minds of people especially in the western world, and some of our kit and kin, who have drunk the unwholesome waters of ignorance, prejudice, pre-conceived opinion and mis-information regarding the Igbo world;
- In a way also, it will attempt to help set some records straight regarding some historical inaccuracies that have been maliciously or ignorantly bandied or floated around by some distractors of Ndi-Igbo who distort facts and paint the Igbo blacker than they are, or undermine their accomplishments on the national and international scene;
- This would also serve as an attempt to preserve and promote some vital aspects of Igbo cultural identity and heritage which seem to be fast fading into obliviom.
- And finally, this book hopefully will encourage parents to begin to salvage and inculcate Igbo identity and cultural pride in their children. The best and most qualified teacher to teach Igbo children Igbo heritage and identity are Igbo parents, the home, not the classroom. As long as a father is Igbo, the child is an Igbo child in spite of the political jargon of citizenship by assimilation. Okereke Kalunta Nwodo could be an American citizen by political naturalisation, but no white man, Asian, Mexican, Spanish, Japanese or British goes by that name. The

great and immortal Africanist Dr. Emman James Kwegyir Aggrey (1875-1927) of Gold Coast now Ghana, made a powerful, incisive and indictive statement at his doctorate convocation ceremony at the University of Columbia in 1914: "He who is not proud of his color and his tongue is not fit to live."[1]

Ignorance of one's cultural heritage and identity is not a status symbol, it is a tragic bondage. Best put, it is a status symbol of self inflicted intellectual and cultural slavery.

Chapter One

Who Are The Igbo?

HISTORICAL ANTIQUITY AS IDENTITY

1. PREAMBLE:

In his dissertation Max Gbanite (2003) postulated as follows: "The Igbo are the most ardent Nigerians anywhere in the world today." Studies by experts have shown that four out of every five Africans outside Black Africa are Nigerians; and statistics provided by experts in demography and ethnography confirm that three out of every four are possibly Igbo. Some historians and cultural anthropologists have also postulated that the Igbo nation is probably a "lost tribe of Israel", although there has not yet been any conclusive or definitive anthropological or historical evidence to substantiate this hypothesis. However, what has remained constant and incontrovertible is that no study has been able to provide a proof of the migration of Ndi-Igbo from any where on this earth. And whereas every other ethnic or linguistic group or tribe that inhabits Nigeria today can trace their source of migration or origin, the Igbo arguably are the only group that were there before others. For instance, every body knows where the Hausa came from. Everybody knows where the Yoruba migrated from. There is also historical evidence of where the Bini people came from—a migrant clan of the Oduduwa hegemony. There is also historical evidence of where the Efik and the Ibibio came from. But there is no historical evidence that Ndi-Igbo originated from any where else. Postulates on this issue are mere spectulatives and lack conclusive anthropological, ethnographic and historical authentic evidence.

Ndubisi Nwafor (Ph.D. Thesis Ibadan, 1983) in his series of investigations and interviews about the historical origin of the Igbo:

- ***"We did not come from anywhere, and anyone who tells you we come from anywhere is a liar. Write it down."***
  (Mazi Mathias Ugochukwu Ekeanyanwu, an elder (about 95 years old) of Mbaise, 1982)

- ***"Indeed, no historical question arouses more interest and disputation among the present day scholars than the inquiry where did the Igbo come from?"***
  (Prof. F. Isichei: A History of the Igbo People, 1976.)

- ***"The speculation among some scholars and archeologists that the Ibo (sic) might have been the biblical lost tribe of Israel, who after contact with ancient Egypt were pushed southwards as a result of Arab invasion of North Africa, does not seem to hold much anthropological evidence."***
  (G.T.Basden, Niger Ibos, London, 1966)

Prof. Herskanin (1978) also refutes this theory and argues that there has never been found any archeological or anthropological evidence to substantiate this assumption, nor is there any linguistic or cultural evidence of linkage, to allow of any benefit of doubt.

Prof. Dike (1977) "Although the Igbo are by nature very adventurous people, they were never nomadic."

****"To suggest that Ndi Igbo migrated from anywhere is like the kind of fairy tale and foolish talk which some European scientists are trying to teach children that God Almighty did not create the world, that the earth came to being as a result of an accident in the planetary system, or that monkeys and apes are the ancestors of humans."***

(Chief Z.C.Obi, (late) The Onu n'ekwulu Igbo, First National President of Igbo State Union: an interview 1979)

- ***"Since God created the world, my great great grand ancestors lived and died here. We were not told that they met anybody here, or that they drove anyone from this place. The only creatures they fought with in the very early days were elephants, tigers and gorillas, and some monstrous reptiles."***
  (Chief Titus Okeze Ugwueke Nnamani of Nsukka, an interview, 1982)

- ***"When God created the earth, He planted Ndi-Igbo in this very place. This is the ancestral home of Eze Nri the main stem of Igbo."***
  (Ichie Eze Nri Ugochukwu Udedike Akuozo, an interview 1981)

- **Archeological evidence of antiquity:** The great and renowned Igbo scholar and anthropologist Prof. **Afigbo 1981:4:** "scientific analyses and data obtained from archeological findings show that Early Igbo appear to have first occupied the Awka-Orlu plateau area, often referred to as the Igbo heartland four to five thousand years ago". **(in C. Aniakor and H. Cole; 1984)**

Also very significant, one of the most recent and authentic historical documentation of the antiquity of the historicity of the Igbo in their homeland is the time line published in **Peoples of Africa, by Cavendish, 2001:**

900	1300	1400-1500	1861-1910
Igbo-Ukwu art Culture florished	Yoruba kingdom of Oyo founded	Bini kingdom at the height of power	Nigeria brought under British rule

So far, since no one has been able to prove or come up with any historical evidence of the migration of Ndi-Igbo, nor is there any substantial scientific or anthropological evidence that contradicts the antiquity of the Igbo in their homeland, the history of their origin stands out as a very credible and remarkable cultural and historical identity.

However, there is a little exception and explanation that needs to be established with regard to the historicity of the Igbo of Onitsha and the Igbo of the Delta State. The reference being made here is that of the Igbo of the ancestral stock of the renowned general Ezechima—and his descendants the stock of **Umuezechima.** History has it that they actually originated from the Igbo heartland east of the Niger, but that their spirit of adventure and exploration took them across west of the Niger. Their first known permanent settlement west of the River Niger was known and called **Igbuzo**-meaning **Igbo bi n'uzo**,—the Igbo living abroad. Eventually their restless spirit of adventure and exploration took some of them further westwards as far as the fringes of the old Bini Empire. There they established permanent settlement for a good while. It was there that their leader and hero Chief Ezechima built fame, fortune and a strong administrative and militia command. It was there that they came in contact with aspects of Bini culture especially with regard to local administration and chieftaincy affairs. Time past, history rolled by, the small immigrant kingdom under the command and control of Chief Ezechima enjoyed peace, power and prosperity.

But in the process of time, history took a new and very different turn when a very powerful monarch Oba Esigie ascended to the throne of the Bini Empire, (1540-1550). The new Oba saw the Umuezechima clan as a foreign and intrusive element and a potential danger within his domain. The new Oba demanded tribute, homage and absolute loyalty from all the chieftains in his empire. By some arrogance and political posturing Chief Ezechima did not consider himself and his people subject to the high handedness of the new Oba and would neither concede nor capitulate. Oba Esigie saw Chief Ezechima as a rebellious vassal and a dangerous political toothache, so he determined to take punitive and decisive military action against the Umu Ezechima clan. For a brief while Chief Ezechima and his people put up some resistance. Unfortunately, the overwhelming military power of the Bini Empire forced Umuezechima to withdraw and retreat. To ensure that Chief Ezechima and his people will not re-organize, regroup and return to constitute any potential danger, the Bini army drove and pushed the retreating clan beyond the territorial fringes of the Bini Empire.

Umuezechima continued their flight and their retreat, tracing their way back eastwards from whence they came. According to an Imo proverb: ***"Uzo onye gara mbu anaghi eghi ya anya", (***a road or route one has passed before is ususlly not very difficult to trace.)

The retreat was painful, slow, irksome and tortuous, and naturally some families and groups detached and established camps and settlements along their flight en-route. Steadily as they retreated towards the Niger, their number and moral stamina continued to dissipate. But the very tough and heroic ones continued doggedly because ***"oso ndu anaghi agwu ike", (***the race for life is never given up because of tiredness or fatigue), until they got as far as to Asaba and settled along the west banks. The last diehards and the most tenacious continued the retreat and crossed over to the east banks of the Niger in order to ensure absolute safety, ***"maka adi amama"***, and settled at the place now known as Onitsha.

But unexpectedly, for a good while, they encountered a lot of opposition and hostility from the Obosi indigenes. There are historical records and documents of the frequent confrontations, skirmishes and litigations with the Obosi people. But that is not the thrust of the present thesis, nonetheless, it becomes relevant in the context of historicity and identity. The false claim that the Onitsha people and the Ika Igbo people of the present Delta State/ Anioma State originated from the Bini stock, is a mis-history, misconception and a historical fallacy. That hypothesis has no authentic historical evidence. Even the name alone of their great legendary progenitor Ezechima and the lineage name Umu Ezechima both are clearly, distinctly, culturally and linguistically Igbo, and not Edo.

However, these brave "returnees" from the fringes of Bini Empire had learned and assimilated some rich cultural attitudes and customs from their contact with the Bini people. ***Onu taa akwu, eze ga ebu nmanu,*** if the mouth eats palm fruit, the teeth will have evidence of oil. This is very evident especially in some aspects of the chieftaincy tradition and culture of the Onitsha, Oguta, Asaba, Ogwashi, Issele-Ukwu, Osomali people, to mention just a few.

COMMENT:

The heroic adventures and saga of the clan of Umu Eze Chima, go to confirm the veracity in a popular Igbo axiom ***"Agaracha must come back."*** meaning, travelers and adventurers will eventually return to their ancestral home. There is no place like home. The Israeli experience is a case in point. After many centuries of political persecutions, dispersals and migrations, they came back to be resettled in their patriachial homeland—Cannan now Israel.

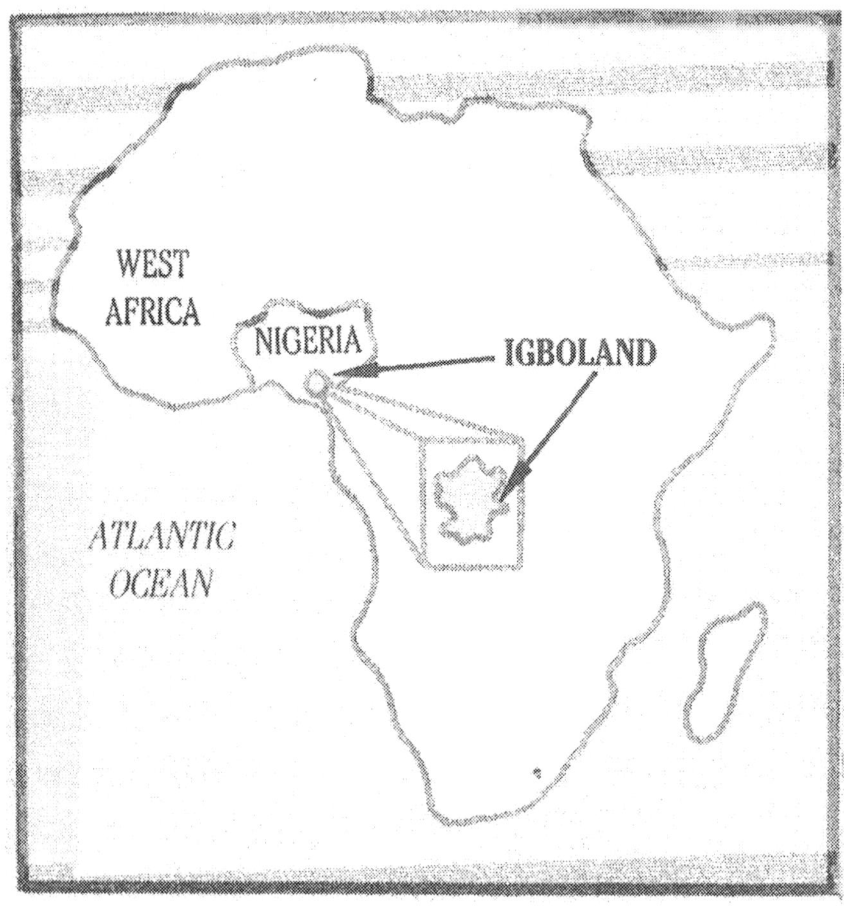
WEST
AFRICA
NIGERIA
IGBOLAND
ATLANTIC
OCEAN

Chapter Two

Geographical and Political Identity.

- **National boundaries**
- **Cultural neighbors**
- **Igbo States Table of names and dates.**

The Igbo speaking people of Nigeria number more than fifteen million, a population greater than that of many Western nation states. The Igbo rank as one of the largest ethnic and homogenous group on the African continent. Mbaise clan in Imo State for example has the highest population density in Africa. Population density is calculated on the basis of the number of persons who live per square mile area. Mbaise women folk are blessed with prolific fecundity, and their husbands appreciate and reward this in the cultural celebration of "**ewu ukwu**"—a goat for the womb that has produced seven children. And this is a great pride and a great prize.

In the past, this was an identity of the Mbaise clan, as it was with the ancient Hebrews. Then number was power, security and the cornerstone of prosperity. But now economic imperatives, advancement in education and other social factors such as mechanized agriculture, local and national security provided by the police and other law enforcement agencies, have radically affected and changed the number factor in the population equation. New and modern trends have positively underscored the point that it is quality

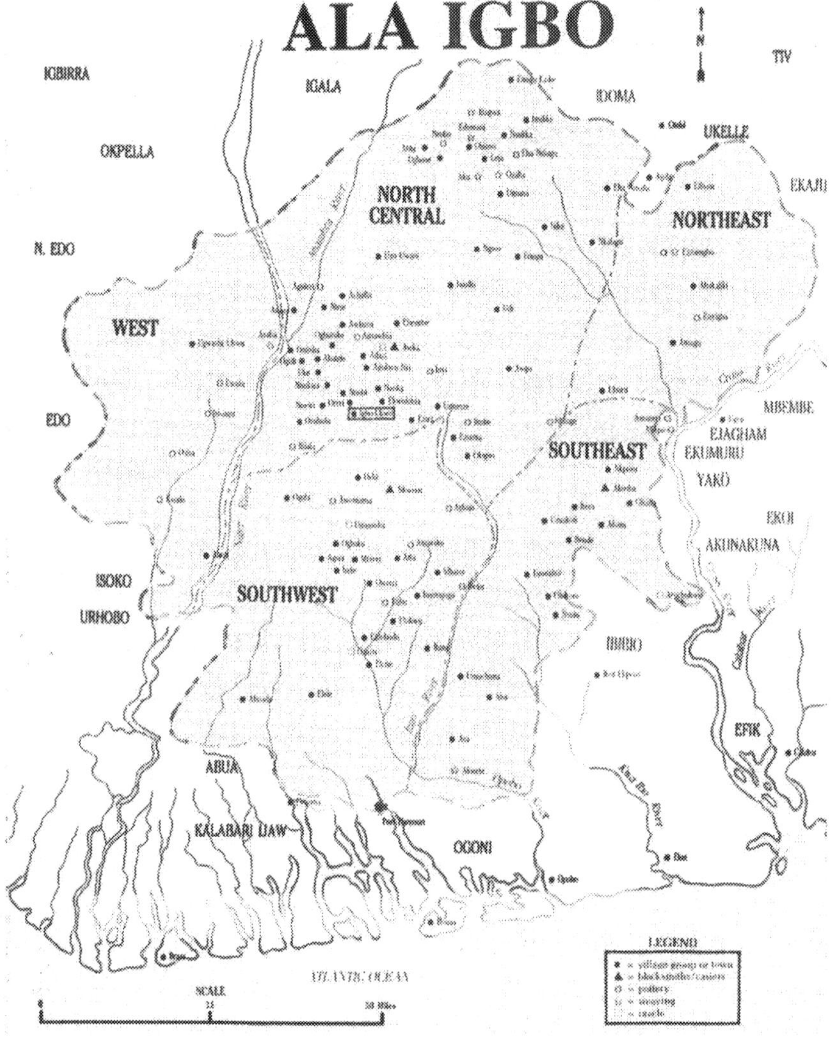
ALA IGBO
N
IGBIRRA
IGALA
IDOMA
TIV
OKPELLA
UKELLE
NORTH CENTRAL
NORTHEAST
N. EDO
WEST
EDO
MBEMBE
EJAGHAM
SOUTHEAST
EKUMURU
YAKO
EKOI
AKUNAKUNA
ISOKO
URHOBO
SOUTHWEST
IBIBIO
EFIK
ABUA
KALABARI IJAW
OGONI
LEGEND
SCALE

and not quantity, and this paradigm factors in everything including population and child breeding. The Igbo awareness and acceptance of this new population paradigm can be seen in some traditional names, idioms and proverbs***: 'iri ka nnu'*** ten could be better and more powerful than a thousand.

Geographically, Ndi-Igbo live in a vast land area in the southeastern part of Nigeria. This vast land area stretches from the tropical rain forest in the south to the tropical savanna grassland in the north. Their neighbors in the north are the **Igala and the Idoma** tribes. In the west their neighbors are the **Okpella,** the **Edo,** the **Isoko** and the **Urhobo**. To the south their boundary neighbors are the **Kalabari,** the **Ijaw** and the **Ogoni** people. Their neighbors in the eastern flank are the **Ibibio,** the **Ekoi,** and the **Nembe** people.

The Igbo country can be divided into five physio-geographical regions: the North Central, Northeastern, Southeastern, Southwestern, and the West.

Political metamorphoses: How Ndi-Igbo got to where they are now.

> The story of the "Unification" of Igboland is more bizarre than the story of how cassava became garri. For many decades Ndi-Igbo were subjected to wallow in the Nigerian political wilderness with no definite ideological framework or coherence. In the process of time and history under the British colonial administration, Ndi-Igbo were in the fore front of Nigerian political struggle for national emancipation. Their national spirit of patriotism was unmarched.
>
> In educational development, commerce and industry Ndi-Igbo were head and shoulder above other Nigerian tribes. Their spirit of enterprise and adventure are phenomenal and took them to every nook and corner, every town and village in Nigeria and beyond. They survive and make remarkable progress wherever they plant themselves, or wherever fortune or misfortune force them to reside.

Unfortunately, these natural endowments enshrined by nature in the spiritual and physical make up of the Igbo race, turned the hearts and minds of their sister tribes against them. In the eyes of the others Ndi-Igbo are very selfish, very greedy, very aggressive, too ambitious and 'too forward'. This was the genesis of 'Igbophobia' (fear of Igbo domination) in the Nigerian political cosmos.

That was why during the rough and tumble of Nigerian political evolution, Ndi-Igbo became a common target. All other regional government administrations and power structures earmarked the Igbo for discrimination, disenfranchisement and deprivation. In the dark days of Nigeian political instability Ndi-Igbo saw pepper and they saw fire. They saw storm and tempest.

They were subjected to frequent and terrible ethnic cleansing, slaughter and genocide in the hands of their northern neighbors in the cattle country. They went through the sharp and bloody sword of Islamic jihad. They saw pogrom and suffered holocaust. Ndi-Igbo were visiously attacked from three cardinal points: from the North, from the West and from some other tribes in the Eastern flanks, including some misguided Ndi-Igbo of *Mba Miri* who promulgated the bogus, malicious, vindictive and reprehensible **"Theory of Abandoned Property."** which some other governments bought and swallowed hook, line and sinker.

But, it must also be mentioned that in some cases, some "uneducated" and "loud mouthed" Igbo elements attracted too much attention to themselves, by making too much noise in other people's lands, and by stepping roughly on other people's cultural sensitivities.

The Nigerian political quagmire began with the so called British **Amalgamation of Northern and Southern Nigeria in 1914.** These were two extremely different and incompatible entities that should never have been forced or forged into any kind of union. But it was a ploy and administrative strategy of the British colonial government to keep and maintain selfish control over that big chunk of territory in the West African sub-region.

The second phase was the beleaguered Federal regional system introduced in 1954. Soon after that, the fractionalization and balkanization of the regions into states ensued with unforeseen but very harsh and unsalubrious consequences. The political upheavals, tantrums and outbursts that followed as a result of all that include:

- the inequitable distribution of the "national cake" revenue derivation and allocation;
- the reckless and illogical concentration of vital federal institutions in the most bizarre manner, e.g., the location of the central oil refinery in the North, the central command and control of all the units of the military: Army, Navy, Air Force and major military installations and headquarters in the North, just to mention a few.
- the illogical and disproportionate award of federal appointments;
- the vexed and irreconcilable census figures that weighted heavily in the favor of the Hausa Fulani oligarchy incumbency;
- the marginalization and disenfranchisement of Ndi-Igbo in the entire national equation and in the scheme of merit;
- the brutal pogrom and selective genocide unleashed on Ndi-Igbo in 1966, and

- finally, and the last straw that broke the camel's back was the reckless effrontery and bravado with which the Gowon government repudiated and abrogated the Aburi Accord for a peaceful resolution of the bloody Nigerian crisis. For readers who may not be familiar with the Aburi Accord, and to refresh the memories of those who might have forgotten some details, we will attempt to state it in brief because it is a relevant part of Igbo political identity. The Aburi Accord was the agreement signed at the end of the political peace conference held in Aburi in Ghana by the warring parties—Nigeria and

> Biafra. The conference was held in Ghana and presided over by the Ghanian President Lt. General J.A. Ankrah. The venue was chosen because of the fact that the safety of the Eastern Nigerian delegates led by the Governor of the Eastern Region Colonel Emeka Ojukwu could not be guaranteed anywhere in the western or northern parts of the country. A strong and reliable secret intelligence revealed a very well coordinated plot by the Gowon junta to apprehend and assassinate Ojukwu and all the Eastern delegates if they came to any conference. But they did not know that "***nwamadi ha nagbarizu onwu kara ha wuru dibia".*** (the person they are plotting to destroy by secret plot has greater inteligence than the secret conspirators).

The bitterness and fear of Igbo leadership (Igbo-phobia) has been the obsession and nightmare not only of the cattle Hausa-Fulani blood thirsty jihadists, but also the obsession of a few misguided ego-eccentric radical "tribalists" and "patriots" in other parts of the country.

It will be recalled that Chief the honorable Jeremiah Obafemi Awolowo and a few die—hard political demagogues planned in 1962, to wipe out Azikiwe and all the NCNC parliamentarians in the Federal House of Representatives in Lagos. The plot was to blow up the Federal House of Parliament with very high power dynamite explosives. Unfortunately for them, the nefarious plot leaked and the Chief was apprehended, tried and sentenced to ten years imprisonment with hard labor: (another senior accomplice in the bloody plot fled the country) Following was the sentence record verbatim:

"At the conclusion of the judgement by Chief Justice Sowemimo, Chief Awolowo was sentenced as follows:

- 1st. Count—10 years I.H.L. (Imprisonment with Hard Labour) Treasonable felony, contrary to section 41(b) of the Criminal Code.
- 2nd. Count—5 years I.H.L.
  Conspiracy to commit a felony, contrary to section 516 of the Criminal Code
- 3rd. Count—2 years I.H.L.

Conspiracy to effect an unlawful purpose, contrary to section 518(6) of the Criminal Code.
Date: September 11, 1963"
(Thanks goodness the trial Chief Justice was not an Igbo man)

Now back to where we left off from the Aburi Accord:

The agenda of the Aburi Meeting was:

1. Re-organization of the Nigerian Armed Forces
2. Adherence to the Constitutional Arrangement
3. Issue of displaced persons within Nigeria

The delegates were:—

1. Chairman: Lt. Gen. J. A. Ankarah of the Ghana National Liberation Council as host and presiding
2. Lt. Col Yakubu Gowan, head of the Nigerian delegation.
3. Major Mobolaji Johnson—Governor Lagos State
4. Col. Robert Adebayo—Governor Western State
5. Lt. Col. Hassan Katsina—Governor of Northern State
6. Lt. Col. Odumegwu Ojukwu—Governor Eastern State and—leader of the Eastern delegation
7. Lt. Col. David Ejoor—Governor Mid-West State
8. Commodore J.E.A. Wey—Governor Rivers State
9. Alhaji Kam Selem—Inspector General of Police
10. Mr. Omo-Bare

- The Article of the Accord: (Verbatim) Executive authority of the Federal Military Government should remain in the Supreme Military Council, to which any decision affecting the whole country shall be referred, the matter requiring determination must be referred to the military governors for their comment and concurrence.
- Specifically, the Council agreed that appointments to senior ranks in the police, diplomatic, and consular services as well as appointments to super-scale posts in the federal civil

service and the equivalent posts in statutory corporations must be approved by the Supreme Military Council.

- The regional members felt that all the decrees passed since January 15, 1966, and which detracted from previous powers and positions of regional governments, should be repealed if mutual confidence is to be restored.
- But things fell apart and hell was let loose: The Accord reverts to discord.

On their return from Aburi, in response to the Accord, the federal government with the instigation of the Hausa-Fulani oligarchy persuaded Gowan to immediately promulgate Decree No. 8, in total defiance of the Aburi Accord. The Accord finally broke down. Things fell apart. The Eastern delegates were left with no option than to cry foul, and to declare loud and clear "ON ABURI WE STAND", otherwise "to your tents O Israel." Col. Odumegwu Ojukwu was mandated by the Eastern Consultative Assembly to assume the office of Head of State and make the famous and historic Ahiara Declaration on May 29, 1966.

Easterners were forced into a tight situation of survival and self defense—the secession, and the declaration of Repblic of Biafra. Consequently, as a reprisal, a vicious and bloody war was unleashed on the East, with all the fury and military might of Nigeria, and the collision of Britain, Russia and Egypt 1967-70. In fact, the Aburi Accord could have prevented the tragedy that ensued and engulfed the country for three bloody years had the British High Commisioner Francis Cumming-Bruce and Elbert Matthews, the US Ambassador not prevailed on Gowan to disregard the crisis saving Accord. The Aburi Accord would have secured a quasi-confederation with self-autonomy for each region pending the return of normalcy. It was their fear that if the rebellious East was not crushed and dismembered, the imperial powers would subsequently lose their control of the abundant natural resources that were in the Biafran territory.

- Furthermore, although the breakdown of the Aburi Accord was the most immediate cause and the last straw that broke the camel's back, there were other deep-rooted and diverse socio-cultural and fundamental causes. The feudal Islamic

> Hausa-Fulani in the north were traditionally ruled by an autocratic, conservative Islamic hierarchy consisting of some thirty-odd Emirs who, in turn owed their allegiance to a supreme Sultan. This Sultan was regarded as the source of all political power and religious authority, that must be obeyed and never questioned.

The Yoruba political system in the southwest, like that of the Hausa–Fulani, also consisted of a series of monarchs called the Obas. The Yoruba Obas, however were less authocratic and formidable than the Emirs in the north, and the political and social systems of the Yoruba accordingly allowed for greater upward mobility based on acquired rather than inherited wealth and titles.

In contrast, the Igbo in the Southeast lived mostly in autonomous, democratically-organized communities, although there were monarchs in some of these ancient kingdoms such as in Nri, Arochukwu, Nnewi, Onitsha and Ohafia. Unlike in the other two regions, decision making among the Igbo resided in the general assembly in which every man could participate—a system usually refered to as **"Ohacracy"** ***Oha na eze***—government by the people.(see Chinua Achebe **'Things Fall Apart'** Chapters Four, Six and Ten).

Traditionally the Hausa-Fulani commoners had contact with the political system only with and through their village head who was designated by the Emir or one of his subordinates, and did not view political leaders as amenable to influence. Political decisions were to be obeyed without question. Thus this highly centralized and authoritarian political system elevated to positions of leadership persons willing to be subservient and loyal to superiors, the same virtues required by Islam for eternal salvation. A chief function of this political system was to maintain Islamic and conservative values, such as the **notorious sharia law,** which caused many Hausa-Fulani to view economic and social innovations as subversive or sacrilegious.

But above all, and most importantly, the most fundamental difference between Ndi-Igbo and the cattle Hausa-Fulani are the religious tenets and philosophy. Islam advocates intolerance and militancy. The religious principle and motto of Islam is: "Accept the

Koran or have the sword." One of the basic doctrines of Islam and the Koran is that anyone who is not a Moslem is an infidel. It goes further to enjoin that if a committed Moslem kills an infidel, that beastly and barbaric act of murder earns the murderer a straight ticket and visa to paradise, where he will further be rewarded with the prize of seven virgins. So right from infancy their children are subjected to heavy dosage of indoctrination of hate, intolerance, violence and murder. By the time they become teens, they have become die-hard fundamentalists, and very obsessed with the desire to kill and destroy. By adulthood they have developed an insatiable appetite for sadism, barbarism, and adepts in decapitation and arson. (see pix of Christians worshipper burned alive in Jos recently)

On the other hand, the Igbo are predominantly Christians (about 96%). Christianity teaches and enjoins tolerance, love, patience, long suffering, kindness, hospitality to strangers, and compassion for the unbeliever. Jesus' teaching on love: "***love your enemies, bless those who curse you, do good to those who hate you, and pray for those who spitefully use you and persecute you.***" (St. Matthew 5: 44; St. Luke 6:27; 28: 32-36) And above all, the 6th. Commandment in the Christian Holy Bible enjoins: "***Thou shall not commit murder***" (Exodus 20: 13), and being Christians the Igbo dread sheding of human blood because it is a deadly sin which God will not forgive and which will condemn the perpetrator to everlasting hell fire.

A practical demonstration of this was how the government of the Eastern States under the leadership of Gen. Odumegwu Ojukwu (himself a profound Christian) handled the issue of the pogrom committed against Easterners by the northerners. The International Red Cross estimated that over 600 thousand Easterners were slaughtered and over 200 thousand were maimed. Even when lorry and truck loads of these victims were being brought back home, Gen. Ojukwu ordered that no northerner residing in any part of the Eastern States should be harmed. He ordered for their safe passage and provided military and police escorts for all northerners returning to their home states. Now the difference is clear, who and what the Igbo are, and why the Moslems fundamentaly do not like the Igbo.

The pros and cons and the events of the civil war are not the thrust nor the main issue of this presentation. However, the mention of it becomes necessary as it constitutes a vital historical milestone and reference point in the context of the history and identity of Ndi-Igbo. Moreover, it makes a lot of history and testimony about the character, ethical, moral and spiritual values and disposition of Ndi-Igbo.

As far as history is concerned, the story of how Ndi-Igbo of the present seven states evolved, was not just a political process of evolutionary development, it was a political nightmare. It is a tale full of sound and furry, full of hate, full of heroism and patriotism, full of pride of success. But as luck would have it, Ndi-Igbo finally arrived as an "ethnic block" of seven states.

The ugly face of genocide:

1. **Economic genocide**:
   Seizure of physical assessts: Immediately after the Nigeria-Biafra war, the first atrocious act of the Gowan junta was to systematically exterminate Ndi-Igbo, those who survived the war by economic strangulation. It was a well planned economic genocide of a whole race of people in order to accomplish what guns, bullets, bombs and blockade could not achieve. For instance in Port Harcourt all economic assets and institutions of Ndi-Igbo were declared 'A**bandoned Property'** and forfeited to the indigenous local inhabitants and the state governments.
2. **Fiscal and bank assets**:
   At the end of the bloody civil war, all financial resources and accounts of Ndi-Igbo in Biafra were seized, embezzled or reduced to twenty pounds sterling. This atrocious act was designed to reduce every surviving Igbo man and woman to the status of poverty and beggary. With that stroke of malicious vindictiveness, all Igbo millionaires and industrial tycoons were reduced to ground zero. But the Igbo belief that ***onye chi ya egbughi, madu apughi igbu ya,*** (translated literary—if your God does not kill you, no one else can kill you), and that ***ihe na etiri ngwesi egwu di na ime ala.*** (what

plays the music for the dancing bird is inside the ground) The rate and resilient speed with which the Igbo recovered from that economic genocide, dazed their enemies and still amazses the rest of the world.

3. **Intellectual genocide:**

Many years after the civil war, Igbo children and youths who were not even born at the time of the civil war, are still being subjected to the most reprehensive kind of intellectual apartheid and obnoxious discrimination. The federal government policy of the notorious **quota system for admission into federal government colleges and other tertiary institutions** is a case in point**.** To substantiate this, let us take a look at the following unedited excerpt by Chief Olu Sanu, a former Nigerian Ambassador to China, published by the **Punch News Paper of 10/20/2008:** "Nigerian's former Ambassador to China, Chief Olu Sanu, on Saturday, reviewed the state of education in Nigeria and expressed serious concern over the collapse of the sector.

He faulted the current admission guidelines of Federal Government Colleges based on the examination coordinated by the National Examination Council. He said the examination body pegged the cut-off point requirement for candidates from Anambra and other Igbo states at 360 out of 500 because Anambra State produced the student with the highest score of 429. According to his report, "Any student who scores below 360 points in Anambra, Imo or Abia State will not gain admission to a Federal Government College, whereas, in the same report, the highest score in a state in the North was 165 points and the cut-off point for that state was 100." Thanks to God the Ex-Ambassador Mr. Sanu is not an Igbo man expressing a crazy tribal sentiment and insinuatory fabrication.

To deprive or deny a generation of youths the right to education and knowledge on account of their tribal or linguistic background, is tantamount to intellectual apartheid. It is like depriving an infant baby of breast milk: ***Onye sepuru nwata***

onu n'ara, choro ya onwu." (a person who prevents a baby from sucking breast wants that baby to die of starvation).

To deny and deprive a youth of the vital means of livelihood and access to good life, is equivalent to amputating a person's arms and rendering the victim miserably and hopelessly incapacitated: ***Onye e gbujisiri aka abuo, wu odi ndu onwu ka nma.*** (if a person's two hands are amputated, the person is as good as dead) This was the basic agenda and design of the perpetrators of the so called federal character policy in education and admission. It is worse than apartheid, It is Igbo-phobic. It is sadism. It is extremely divisive. It is enthroning mediocrity. It is like demobilizing a motor vehicle by removing the battery. What they are saying to the brilliant Igbo youths loud and clear is "Y**ou don't belong here".** This is not your country.

In the cattle country the hatred of the Igbo by the northerners is endemic, it runs in their religious, social and political fabrics. This venom of Igbo-phobia has always been the attitude and mentality of the cattle Hausa-Fulani hegemony from day one of the concept of Nigeria as a political and a geographical entity. It has never changed, it may never change, and nothing has been able to change it. Does this statement sound insidious, inflammatory, unpatriotic, naïve, stinks with tribal bigotry? Just wait until you read the following undoctored excerpt from the horses' mouth, **Government Gazetet, Kaduna, 1964**:

In 1964 during a debate in the Northern House of Assembly, the bitterness against Ndi-Igbo was legislatively proclaimed and their physical elimination officially discussed and legally sanctioned Here are a few excerpts from the Government Gazzette, Northern House of Assembly 1964:

- MALLAM BASHARI UMARU: "I will like you sir, as the Minister of Land and Survey, to revoke forthwith all Certificates of Occupancy from the hands of the Ibos resident in the region, (Applause)

- MR. MEGIDA LAWANTA: "In fact it is quite a long time that we in our part of this region have known the Ibos and I do not think at the moment there is any Ibo man owning a roof in Igbirra Division. I am appealing to the Minister to make life more difficult for them"
- ALHAJI YUSUFU BAYERO: "Mr. Chairman, I will like to appeal to the Minister of Establisments and Training if he will appeal to the Minister of Local Government about some employees who are Ibos and are working under some Native Authorities here. I cannot see why they should be in our region. We are sure that they are the poorest people in the country".
- ALHAJI USMAN LIMAN (Sarikin Musawa): "What brought the Ibos into this region? They were here since the Colonial Days. Had it not been for the Colonial Rule there would hardly have been any Ibo in this Region. There should be no hesitation about this matter. Mr. Chairman, North is for Northerners, East for Easterners, West for Westerners, and the Federation is for all. (Applause)"

To all these demands for drastic action against Ndi-Igbo, the Chairman of the House and Premier ALHAJI SIR AHMADU BELLO, K.B.E ., The Sarduana of Sokoto replied "It is my most earnest desire that every post in this Region, however small it is, to be filled by a northerner." (Applause)

- ALHAJI MUSTAFA ISMAILA ZANNA DUJUMA (Minister of Establisments and Training): Mr. Chairman, Sir, since 1960 this Government had laid down a policy:. First NORTHERNERS, second EXPATRIATES, and third, NON-NORTHERNERS. Mr. Chairman, Sir, I have noted very carefully all the speeches made by all the members in this Honourable House and I am ready to put all up to my Government for their views, and I hope my Government will give them consideration . . . I think these two things are the major things I have to answer now. One is on scholarship, and the other is how to do away with the Ibos."

- ALHAJI IBRAHIM MUSA GASHASH, O.B.E., (Minister of Land and Survey): "Mr. Chairman, Sir, I do not like to take up much of the time of this House in making explanations, but I would like to assure Members that having heard their demands about Ibos holding land in Northern Nigeria, my ministry will do all it can to see that the demands of Members are met. How to do this, when to do it, all this will not be disclosed. In conclusion, you will see what will happen soon. (Applause)."

Thereupon Alhaji Mustafa Dujuma, Alhaji Musa Gashash and other Northerner leaders proceeded to plot "how to do away with" Ibos, and the world was soon to see what would happen. Under the influence of these leaders, Northern Nigerian Local Government Authorities abruptly terminated the appointments of Igbos in their services, prematurely terminated their contracts, suddenly withdrew their Certificates of Occupancy of residential plots and business premises, and actually expelled some from Northern Nigeria, and ruthlessly subjected others to verbal and even physical attacks and threats of total annihilation and seizure of their assests and properties.

Shortly, too, the N.P.C., the party in power in Northern Nigeria, published a highly scurrilous booklet entitled "SALAMA: Facts Must Be Faced". This document launched a vicious and inflammatory attack on Ibos. Indeed it was contrived to inflame the feelings of Northern Nigerian masses to such an extent that on the flimsiest pretext and as soon as the signal was given, the masses would pounce upon Ndi-Igbo and massacre them with ruthless brutality. It did happen from time to time.

Simultaneously, in Western Nigeria, a booklet titled UPCAISM was published by the government. In it was displayed photographs of stores and shops run by Igbo traders in Lagos and Western Nigerians were incited to accept the inflammatory lie that the Igbo "strangers" had expropriated Western Nigerian land and the fruits thereof. The government of Western Nigeria, like their counter part in the North, organized and conducted very malicious and incisive campaigns of hate against the Ibos. The Igbo were callously dislodged from their merited positions in Western Nigeria and in Federal agancies and institutions. Even business firms were urged to remove Igbo indigens from, or to refuse to appoint them to positions in their various establishments." (This excerpt was culled from: "The Genocide Papers" ***Ekwe Nche***, by Political Action Committee Organization, USA, 1996).

Some time in 1997 the Ikemba, Gen. Odumegwu Ojukwu was the guest of honor at a Town Meeting organized by the Igbo Cultural Association in Los Angeles, California USA.

One topic that generated a lot of interest was the identity of Ndi-Igbo. In his contribution the Ikemba drew parallels between the anti-Semitism against the Jews in Europe and what he called Nigerian political Igbo-phobia. He opined that there seem to be a cosmic connect or correlation between the two races because the Jews are every where, dynamic and are prosperous in everything, just as the Igbo are every where dynamic and prosperous. He recalled that it was the prosperity of the German Jews and their economic affluence in Hitler's Germany that inflamed the jealousy and envy of the Nazists and fanned the flames of the infamous and heinous holocaust. He opined that the experience of the German Jews has some very identical parallels (i.e the economic undertone) with the Igbo experience in the Nigerian conext.

The Ikemba remarked that the Igbo have very peculiar cultural charismatic identity which touches and rubs off on everything and everybody in their environment. He wondered why it is that "if Hausa and Yoruba fight, it is the Ndi-Igbo that will be killed. If Nigeria and Ghana fight, it is Ndi-Igbo that will be killed. If Cameroun and Nigeria fight it is Ndi-Igbo that will be killed."

A classic example of this anti-Igbo sentiment was the bloody massacre and destruction of Ndi-Igbo and their assets which took place in Kano in February 1956. It happened on a Friday afternoon, a crowd of Moslems were trooping out of the Sabon-Gari Central Mosque after worship. Along the Market Road which was the main traffic highway that ran through the commercial district of the Sabon-Gari Kano. A reckless cyclist suddenly swung right into the middle of the road and stopped to pick up his cap which the wind blew off his bald head. By accident he hit himself against the bonnet of a slow moving taxi cab and fell onto the road. He had no fracture or any serious injuries, but he was disoriented. The cab driver stopped and came out to pick up the fallen cyclist. Immediately a small group of people who rushed to the scene of the accident noticed that the cab driver was not a northerner, was not a Moslem, was not dressed in the Hausa costume, they concluded that he must be a ***nyamiri***—the Hausa derogatory pseudonym name for Igbo people. In the twinkle of an eye the small crowd which gathered at the scene of the accident swelled to an angry violent mob. They attacked the driver, lynched him to death, decapitated him at the scene and set his taxi cab ablaze.

But it did not end there. The violent mob action exploded in size and fury like a dangerous tornado. The rampage, killing and arson spread into the Sabon-Gari main market where the Igbo had stalls, stores, shops and super markets. Big commercial institutions and establishments were looted and burnt down. Even churches and schools were not spared in the arson and rampage.

Ndi-Igbo in Kano city were completely taken unawares. In utter confusion and panic they fled abandoning their businesses, fleeing for safety wherever their instinct took them. For two days Ndi-Igbo and their families were in hiding and Sabon-Gari Market was like a war zone. By the time the Mobile Police and the military were deployed to quell the violence, a total of 49 Igbo including children and pregnant women had been brutally slaughtered and butched in cold blood. Some were slaughtered like goats, some were decapitated like chickens for an offence which no Igbo person committed. Institutions, commercial and industrial facilities that were burnt and destroyed included: two churches, two schools three petrol stations, mechanic workshops, restaurants, merchandise and provision stores, Igbo Town Hall and beauty salons.

At last when the dust had settled, it was discovered that the cab driver was not even an Igbo man. He was a Cameroon national. The defense which the office of the Kano State Attorney-General put up was that "the tragedy was a sad case of mistaken identity", that the cab driver looked like an Igbo man. What a defense for the wicked mob brutality of blood thirsty hounds and the sadistic propensity of the Hausa-Fulani jihadists.

In the Nigerian context especially in the North, to look like an Igbo man is a stigma that carries a death sentence. As the saying goes: if your enemy hates you, that's no news; if your enemy kills you because he hates you that's Nazist mentality; but to kill any one else simply because that person looks like your enemy, is the most heinous and reprehensible atrocity that can only be conceived by a brutish mentality. The Nazists and Facists killed the Jews because they hated them, but the Nazists and the Facists did not kill the Arabs or the Palestenians because they looked like the Jews.

Now can one see what the Ikemba was talking about? Was he just crying wolf? Was he maliciously whipping up tribal sentiment and hatred? Was he just being mischievious and manipulative? It is the typical experience of the Igbo people in their own country Nigreia. Of course that tragic Kano incident of 1956 was not an isolated happen-stance. It is typical for the Igbo in the Nigerian experience: frequent unprovoked lynching, massacre and arson in various parts of the cattle country. That bloody incident was a loud and clear evidence that Igbophobia is neither a myth nor a figmentation in the mind of an insane tribal 'war monger'. It is a political and historic reality. It was like the anti-Semitism in Nazi Germany. A people hated and massacred just because of their ethnicity and their religious belief system. ***(see Appendix-pictures of innocent and defendless christians massacred, butchered, roasted in cold blood by radical and blood thirsty moslems in all parts of Northern Nigeria under the very nose of moslem government authorities)*** That is exactly what the late Eze Akanu Ibiam was saying in his protest letter to the Queen and Her Majesty's government in 1967, Chapter Three hereunder: ("*It is simply staggering for a Christian country like Britain to help a Moslem country militarily to crush anothewr Christian country like Biafra. This is too much for me. This act of unfriendliness, betrayal and treachery by the British government towards the people and the Christian Republic of Biafra who, as Eastern Nigerians, had so much regard for Britain and the British Christian way of life)*

A full and undited text of Ibiam's letter is presented in the next chapter.

In his address to the Annual International Convention of the People's Club of Nigeria on Saturday July 23rd, 2005 at JW Marriott, Washington DC, His Excellency Governor Orji Uzo Kalu of Abia State asked this troubling question:

> ***"What is our sin that we should be so despised and humiliated? I have asked this question several times, and yet nobody has provided the answer. I asked this question at the Igbo Summit in Enugu in 2000. I also asked the same question when I addressed Ohaneze Leaders and Southeast representatives to the National Political Reform Conference in Abuja. I did not fail to ask the question again when the five southeast governors met on Friday, July 15, 2005 in Umuahia. Today I ask once again: "What is our sin that we should be treated like unwanted second class citizens? Can anybody provide me an answer?"***

No one can deny that it was the cumulative effects of those frequent and spontaneous massacres and genocides in Northern Nigeria and the pogrom of 1966 in which over 60,000 Ndi-Igbo were brutally massacred in the most gruesome and hideous manner, coupled with long smoldering pressures of gross political and economic defranchaisement that triggered off the Nigerian Biafra War. Although the war is not the main thrust of the present discourse, nevertheless it factors very significantly as part of Igbo historical and political identity.

Between 1966 and 1991 the Nigerian physical and political landscape underwent a lot of butchering and tinkering and panel beating in the name of states creation, and we all have seen the good, the bad and the ugly. For some it has been a healthy and welcome realization. For some it was a nightmare and mismatch of ethnic incompatibles forced into a political Pandora box. For the Igbo cultural and linguistic groups, it was like manna from heaven, a distant dream come true.

The table below shows the historical cum political datelines and composition of the present seven Igbo states. The Igbo speaking are more than 96% dominant in five of the seven states, In the Delta and Rivers states where they are not the physical dominant majority, they constitute vibrant, cultural and politically conspicuous entities.

State	Capital	Date created	Preceding Entity
Abia	Umuahia	27 August 1991	Imo State
Anambra	Awka	27 August 1991	East Central State
Delta	Asaba	27 August 1991	Bendel State
Ebonyi	Abakaliki	1 October 1996	Enugu State & Abia State
Enugu	Enugu	27 August 1991	Old Anambra State
Imo	Owerri	3 February 1976	East Central State
Rivers	Port Harcourt	27 May 1967	Eastern Region

Administrative composition and demographics of the present Igbo states:

The knowledge of one's social background and cultural heritage is very essential for any body, and this is desparately necessary for Igbo youths. The ignorance of it is not a thing of pride. So it becames apt to include some basic information regarding the administrative and demographic composition of the various Igbo state units. The ignorance of their ethnic background and cultural identity amongst Igbo youths in the United States and all over the diaspora is alarming. Out here in the United States for instance, most Igbo children always claim that they come from Africa, 40% of them have no knowledge that they are Nigerians, rather they know that they come from Africa. Less than 10% of them claim that they are Igbo; less than 1% of them know the name of their home town or village. From critical investigation and from relevant statistical studies, none of them has the faintest knowledge of their home local government area. This is the basic knowledge (Igbo Cultural Heritage) that the Igbo Cultural Association of Los Angeles California started inculcating in Igbo youths during their Annual Igbo Children's Summer Camp in Los Angeles which was started 1996.

For this the reason it is considered necessary to include some basic information and foundational knowledge regarding the demography of the respective local government areas of the Igbo states as a useful educational source material at such and similar social activilies and festivals.

- Note of caution: Please note that the statistical figures provided hereunder as Demographics may not be exactly accurate or current by the time this publication gets out from the press to the public because Nigerian histo-political demographics and figures are as changeable as the political climate.

Abia State:

Popularly referred to as "God's own country", Abia State is one of the most peaceful states of Nigeria, and has been a "haven" for foreign investors. The state's population has grown rapidly since its creation.

The capital of Abia state is Umuahia, although the major commercial city is Aba, formerly a British Colonial government outpost. In the days of the defunct Eastern Region and the East Central State, Aba town was famous as the power heart-beat of Igbo land—the legendary ***Enyimba*** town. In the good old days of Azikiwe and NCNC (National Council of Nigeria and Cameroon) politics, whenever the party needed to re-charge or energize its political batteries and mobilize for strategic national objectives, the Igbo took their national convention to Aba the 'radical' ***Enyimba town.***

Demographics

Abia State was created on August 27, 1991 from part of Imo State. She was one of the nine constituent states of the former Niger Delta region. The name "Abia" is an acronym of four of the state's most densely populated regions: Aba, Bende, Isuikwuato, and Afikpo. (ABIA)

Presently Abia State is made of 17 Local Government Areas:

1. Aba - North
2. Aba - South
3. Arochukwu
4. Bende
5. Ikwuano

6. Isiala-Ngwa North
7. Isiala Ngwa South
8. Isiukwato
9. Ukwa East
10. Ukwa West
11. Obingwa
12. Ohafia
13. Osisioma Ngwa
14. Ugwunagbo
15. Umuahia North
16. Umuahia South
17. Umunneochi

Anambra State:

Anambra is often referred to as the "***Light of the nation***". Anambra possesses a history which stretches back to the 5th. Century AD., as revealed by archaeological excavations at Igbo-Ukwu, Nri and Ezira. These findings revealed a greater number of details on the ancient kingdom of Nri, which held sway in the area of Anambra River basin from c. 948 AD to 1911. The old Anambra State was created in 1976 from the defunct East Central State, and its capital was Enugu. The capital of the New Anambra state is Awka,

Awka town was the ancient and traditional foundry of Igboland, the land of smiths and carvers. Awka was very famous for their master smiths and manufacture of dane guns (egbe cham). In the pre-colonial era, Awka smiths held the sway in iron works and wood architecture.

Demographics:

Statistics show that Anambra State has the highest number of JAMB candidates going after the limited number of spaces in Nigeria's tertiary institutions, and naturally the greatest and most victims of the infamous ***"quota system"*** and the so called federal policy of **"priority for the disadvantaged areas".**

Nnewi town is often referred to and popularly known as the ***"Taiwan of Africa***". Whatever mechanical or automobile part you do not find at Nkwo Nnewi motor parts market does not exist any where else in the Nigerian auto industry. A member of a Japanese trade mission visiting Nnewi was reported by a local news media to have said: ***"just describe it, they will fabricate it and it will be the original."*** (Sun Rise Saturday 13, 1978)

History has it that the former **Onitsha Main Market** built in the early 1950's was the largest and most ultra-modern shopping complex in the West African sub-region. The engineering and architectural layout was magnificiently imposing, the entire large and extensive area was top covered, the internal electrification and communication devices were superbly hi-tech, the internal underground drainage systems were the best and most functional. The Onitsha Main Market was the pride of Nigeria. But unfortunately, much of it was destroyed by the the Nigerian soldiers during the Nigeria Biafra War.

Nri was historically the most ancient kingdom in Igboland. Nri was acclaimed and most revered as the ancient seat of wisdom and governance.

Anambra State is composed of 21 Local Government Areas:

1. Aguata
2. Awka North
3. Awka South (State Capital)
4. Anambra East
5. Anambra West
6. Anaocha
7. Ayamelu
8. Dunukofia
9. Ekwusigo
10. Idemili North
11. Idemili South
12. Ihiala
13. Njikoka
14. Nnewi North
15. Nnewi South
16. Ogbaru
17. Onitsha North
18. Onitsha South
19. Orumba North

20. Orumba South
21. Oyi

Ebonyi State.
Demographics

Ebonyi State is made up of 13 Local Government Areas, 95% of which are Igbo speaking, and 5% non-Igbo speaking. The state capital is Abakaliki, but Afikpo is the largest city. Other major towns include: Edda, Onueke, Nkalagu, Uburu, Onicha, Ishiagau, Anagari and Okposi. Ebonyi was one of the six states created in 1996. Ebonyi was created from the old Abakaliki Division of Enugu State and the old Afikpo division of Abia state. Ebonyi is called the "salt of the nation" for its huge salt deposit at the Okposi and Uburu salt Lakes. The 13 LGAs are as follows:

1. Abakaliki (State Capital)
2. Afikpo North
3. Afikpo South
4. Ebinyi LGA
5. Ezza North
6. Ezza South
7. Ikwo
8. Ishielu
9. Ivo
10. Izzi
11. Ohaozara
12. Ohaukwu
13. Onicha

Enugu State.

The famous "Coal City State", Enugu has a very strong mystic flavor of destiny for being the "capital of the Igbo country". It was favored to be the historical and political capital of Ala-Igbo. It was the capital city and administrative headquarters of the fomer Eastern Region. Later Enugu became the capital of the former East Central

State, then it also became the capital of the Old Anambra State. And finally Enugu metamorphized to be the capital of the new and current Enugu State. (itching to be renamed Wawa State)

Enugu has so many social institutions to boast about in the history of Nigeria. Popularly known as the famous Coal City, it was the home of the famous Enugu Rangers Football Club, the home of the most famous Catholic Seminary—The Bigard Memorial Seminary (BMS) established in 1924, was the largest and most illustrious Catholic Seminary in the world. Enugu State was also the home of the first indigenous university in Nigeria—the University of Nigeria, Nsukka (UNN).

Enugu State is composed of 17 Local Government Areas:

1. Aninri
2. Awgu
3. Enugu East (State Capital)
4. Enugu West
5. Enugu South
6. Ezeagu
7. Igbo-Etiti
8. Igbo-Eze North
9. Igbo-Eze South
10. Isi-Uzo
11. Nkanu East
12. Nkanu West
13. Nsukka
14. Oji River
15. Udenu
16. Udi
17. Uzo-Uwani

Imo State: Population about 4.8 million.

Popularly referred to as "The land of Hope", Imo State came into existence on February 3, 1976, during the military regime of General Murtala Muhammed. The state is named after the Imo River. Part of it was chopped off to create Abia State, and later another chunk of it was split to form Ebonyi State. In fact this state has undergone more political and demographic surgeries than any other.

Demographics:

The major cities and towns include: Owerri, Nkwerre, Orlu, Okigwe, Oguta, Mbaise, Emekeuku, Orsu, Amaigbo and Mbano. The state is rich in crude oil, natural gas, and is blessed with very fertile agricultural lands.

Owerri was the first home of thre Shell 'Darcy Oil Company. Some enthnographers and anthropologists affirm that the people of Owerri clan are some of the most liberal minded, hospitable and happy-go-lucky in Igboland. They live together happily in large clusters of family groups and homesteads, thus leaving vast and extensive arable land arears for community agriculture and industrial development, unlike in Anambra State where large community lands are virtually non-existence.

Imo State has three senatorial zones namely:

1. Okigwe—with 6 L.G.As
2. Orlu—with 12 L.G.As
3. Owerri—with 9 L.G.As

Local Government Areas	Head Quarters
1. Abor Mbaise	Aboh
2. Ahiaazu Mbaise	Afor Oru
3. Ezinihite Mbaise	Itu
4. Ihite Uboma	Isi Nweke
5. Ehime Mbano	Ehime
6. Ideato North	Urualla
7. Ideato South	Dikenafai
8. Ikeduru	Iho
9. Isiala Mbano	Umuelemai
10. Isu	Umundugba
11. Mbaitoli	Nwaorie

12. Njaba	Nneasa
13. Ngor Okpalla	Umuneke Ngor
14. Nkwere	Nkwere
15. Nwangele	Amaigbo
16. Obowu	Otoko
17. Oguta	Oguta
18. Ohaji Egbema	Nmahu Egbema
19. Okigwe	Okigwe
20. Onuimo	Okwe
21. Orlu East	Omuma
22. Orlu West	Mgbidi
23. Orlu	Orlu
24. Orsu	Awoidemili
25. Owerri Municipality	Owerri
26. Owerri North	Orie Uratta
27. Owerri West	Umuguma

Delta State

The capital of Delta State is Asaba.The state has a population of about 3.1 million.

Delta State is one of the most heterogenous among the the Igbo states. It is composed of diverse peoples and numerous languages. The major ethnic groups are: the Igbo, Urhobo, Izon, Isoko, and the Itsekiri. It was created August 27, 1991, from the defunct Bendel State. Bendel State was formerly known as The Midwest Region, and eventually it gained a state status in 1963 from the former Western Region.

At the inception of Delta state it was made up of 12 political divisions called local government areas—LGAs. This was later increased to 19 in 1996. Presently the state is made up of 25 LGAs. The state capital Asaba, is a very strategic nodal town at the west bank of the Niger, and at the head of the Niger Bridge which was built at a cost of six million pounds sterling in 1965 by the Julius Berger Construction Company.

Demographics:

The 25 LGAs are: (the first ten being the Igbo ethnic groups)

1. Asaba, the state capital
2. Aniocha North
3. Aniocha South
4. Ika North
5. Ika South
6. Ndokwa East
7. Ndokwa West
8. Oshimili North
9. Oshimili South
10. Ukawni
11. Bomadi
12. Ethiope East.
13. Ethiope Weat
14. Isoko North
15. Isoko South
16. Okpe
17. Patani
18. Sapele
19. Udu
20. Ugheli North
21. 29 Ugheli South
22. Uvwie
23. Warri North
24. Warri South
25. Warri South West.

Rivers State.

Rivers state usually referred to as the "Oil well" of Nigeria, was created by an emergency military decree on May 27, 1967, primarily as a reprisal move to traumatize and frustrate the birth and development of the Republic of Biafra. In other words, Rivers State did not evolve from any logical, constitutional, democratic or demographic rational or process. As a result of the mad hurry and lack of social judgement, a very heterogegous conglomeration of diverse peoples and languagues were hurriedly forged together, and forced into a most awkward and absurd political mismatch Pandora box. But that political mess is not the thrust of the present discourse.

Demographics.

Rivers State is made up of 23 LGAs, namely:

1. Abua-Odual
2. Ahoada East
3. Ahoada West
4. Andoni
5. Asari-Toru
6. Bonny
7. Degema
8. Eleme
9. Emoha
10. Etche
11. Gokana
12. Ikwerre
13. Khana
14. Obia-/Akpor
15. Ogba/Egbema/Ndoki
16. Ogu-Bolo
17. Okirika
18. Omumma
19. Opobo/Nkoro
20. Oyigbo
21. Port Harcourt (Capital city)
22. Tai

The Igbo speaking elements in Rivers State include: Ahoada, Ikwerre, Etche, Eleme, Emoha, Opobo, Akwete, Omumma, and Egbema. All these had their ancestral roots in Imo State and other parts of the Igbo heart land. The political saga of King Jaja of Opobo is one eloquent testimony. King Jaja of Opobo was an indigen of Nkwere in Imo State. Historians and cultural anthrolopogists affirm this position.

Cultural Index:

The Igbo are the most adventurous and the most widespread ethnic group that can be found in every nook and corner of Nigeria, and in fact in most countries of the world. Wherever they decide to settle principally for business reasons, they establish homes and permanent settlement. They invest their time, talent and resources to develop the place. Ndi-Igbo are reputed for investing in multi-million capital businesses: estates, banks, hotels, hospitals, tourist industries, educational institutions, churches, super markets, community halls, and cottage industries outside and beyond their home states—all over Nigeria and in foreign lands.

From their business headquarters in the diaspora they make regular pilgrimage to their ancestral home in Igboland for family and social reunions, festival celebrations, vacations and holidays. Thus, the Igbo are unlike every other Nigerian ethnic groups who do not establish permanent homes nor invest in capital commercial projects outside their cultural environment. This might sound clannish or smack of tribal bigotry to say that no other tribal group has any substantial commercial or industrial investment in any part of Igboland. Any "doubting Thomas" is hereby challenged to check it out and prove the contrary.

Also, noteworthy is the fact of the character of the Igbo spirit of nationalism in the Nigerian context. For instance, in the then Eastern Region and the former East Central States there were scores of institutions and street names of Western and Northern personages and towns: Lagos Street, Ibadan Street, Kano Street, Ilorin Street, Kaduna Street, Ilesha Street, Ondo Street, Zaria Street, Sokoto Street, Warri Street, Lokoja Street, Saduana Street, Benue Street, Abeokuta Street; Fulani Street. Institutional names such as Awolowo Hall, Bello Hall in University of Nigeria Nsukka, Fafunwa College of Education, Herbert Maculey House, just to mention a few. But there was no where out there in those other regions and states with street names of Igbo personages or streets of Igbo town names. Except in Lagos the Federal Capital, check it out. Like the Igbo idiom: ***"ihe anya huru, ama anaghi agba ya"***—what the eyes sees, cannot be an object of controversy.

Unfortunately, for a long time, the Igbo center of interest abroad led to the neglect of their homeland. This was a lesson which they have learnt in a very hard way—the bitter lesson of the Nigerian Civil War (1967-90), the bogus and obnoxious decree of ***"abandoned property".*** Yes, Ndi-Igbo learned their lesson in a very hard way and have since made a serious u-turn—from their open nationalistic character **"anywhere na home."** But since after the civil war, charity now begins at home—**"aku lue uno"; (**the prosperity abroad has come home**), Nwamonoh—(**the child that honors his home/roots).

With this new social awareness of home first and best, the fire was kindled and that resulted in tremendous and unprecedented physical and structural developments which mushroomed and blazed like wild fire all over Igboland. Edifices, private mansions, commercial centers, cottage industries, banks, hotels, entertainment and recreation centers and industries, markets and supermarkets changed the entire physical and social landscape and skyline of towns and villages. The indomitable resilience of the Igbo identity became very manifest after the civil war. Towns and institutions that were maliciously destroyed or completely obliterated by vandals in Nigerian military uniforms during the bloody civil war were quickly replaced with structures of ultra modern architectural finesse. Places like Onitsha, Nkpor, Ogidi, Awka, Enugu, Abakaliki, Owerri, Aba, Abagana, Umuahia, Nsukka, Port Harcourt, Okigwe, Aguleri, Asaba, Uguta, just to mention a few that were badly hit, now look much better and as if nothing did ever happened. According to a British journalist who visited the war torn zones—Onitsha, Enugu, Aba, Owerri, Umuahia, five years after the civil war (1975) made this observation: "Nothing can surpass the resilient spirit of the Biafran people".

The Igbo can thrive in any human environment because of their tremendous capacity for adaptation and their tenacious indomitable and dynamic spirit. Their doggedness and tenacity in competition, their shrewd business acumen always overwhelm and baffle their business competitors. Their amazing capacity of resilience in the face of misfortune and disaster is phenomenal. It is their amazing spirit of survival and their capacity to adapt to inimical and hostile situations and circumstances that a British merchant sailor noted in his journal: "***The Jaja Saga",*** Colonial Office Gazette, London,

1936). It was about how an Ibo (sic) slave boy rose to the rank of a naval commander of crude war canoes and defied the Royal British military expedition in the Niger Delta. More about this character is in the subsequent chapter.

The characteristic **ubiquitous nature** of the Igbo which has been mentioned earlier, is remarkable. They are found every where on the globe, some times in places where you will least expect to see a black person. "Any where in the world you go and don't find an Igbo person, that place must be uninhabitable. You should find your way out." Prof. Ijeh Amobi, Black Studies Journal, University of Indiana, 1991.

Chapter Three

The Heroes of Igboland:

The Icons of Igbo national and international identity.

Ikenga is the Igbo cultural symbol and icon of excellence, accomplishment and personal achievement. It is a carved wooden motif in concrete physical form. But in the abstract, it is a philosophical, moral and spiritual concept believed to be latent, dynamic and propelling for survival, achievement and excellence. When somebody is hard working, rich and prosperous, the Igbo will say that his Ikenga is alive and active. When somebody is lazy, unambitious and unproductive, the Igbo will say that he has no ikenga or that his ikenga is dead. The word "**ikenga**" itself is a linguistic coinage from the phrase—**"ike m ga"** meaning let my strength, my power prevail, be productive, outstanding, remarkable. In the Igbo traditional society when one's efforts yield outstanding or remarkable results, he praises his ikenga, and may commission a traditional craftsman or sculptor to carve an ikenga motif which he would proudly display in his **"obi"**, his living room.

The Igbo hero displays his ikenga just as an athletic champion would display his trophies and medals, just as a doctor or any proferssional would display his certificates and diplomas or licence of authority in his office or sitting room. By nature Ndi-Igbo are very adventurous and achievement oriented people. "*In the Igbo country, age was respected, but achievement was revered.*" (Achebe, Things Fall Apart, 1994, p. 8)

This spirit of achievement and excellence is made manifest in several different ways in the lives of many Ndi-Igbo at the local, national and international scenes. The Igbo have produced famous heroes of great renown in various fields of human endeavor. Some of these include men who rose from obscurity to fame, men and women who excelled and towered like colossus above their colleagues and contemporaries, stood above like giants among their equals. Many Igbo men and women have left their footprints not on the ordinary sands of time, but on the granite rock of ages and on pages of history.

Ala Igbo has produced men and women of 'timber and caliber' who have been rated and acclaimed as icons and their accomplishments have "immortalized" them and become historical milestones and reference points. Some of them have passed to the great beyond. But some of them are still here with us, gracing this earth with their aura and greatness. They are proud icons of Igbo identity.

According to Max Gbanite: "the Igbo are the most ardent Nigerians anywhere in the world today. Since the conception of Nigeria as a nation, the Igbo have played very prominent roles in shaping and reshaping its history and destiny, and will continue to play significant roles in whatever becomes of the future of Nigeria."

Below are select examples of Igbo heroes who have held the mantle of leadership and whose achievements and accomplishments have made national and international headline news in history.

1. Equiano, Olaudah
2. King Jaja of Opobo
3. Owele, His Exellency, Dr. Nnamdi Azikiwe
4. Sir Louis Philip Odumegwu Ojukwu
5. Gen. Johnson Thomas Umunnakwe Aguiyi-Ironsi
6. Emmanuel Ifeajuna
7. Sir Francis Akanu Ibiam
8. Prof. Kenneth Onwuka Dike
9. Ben Chuka Enweonwu
10. Dick Tiger
11. Dr. Chike Obi
12. Dr. Jaja Anucha Wachukwu
13. Prof. Zulu Sofola

14. Prof. James Ezeilo
15. Prof. Chinua Achebe
16. Chief Emeka Anyaoku
17. Cardinal Francis Arinze
18. Chief Augustine Ilodibe (aka Ekene Dili Chukwu)
19. Chief Chiadikobi Phoebe Ajai-Obe (SAN)
20. Chief Mrs. Janet Mokelu
21. Dr. Michael Okpara
22. Dr. Alvan Ikoku
23. Dr. Enoch Oli
24. Chief F.C.Ogbalu
25. Mazi Mbonu Ojike
26. Dr. K. O. Mbadiwe
27. Ikemba Gen. Chukwuemeka Odumegwu Ojukwu.

- **Equiano Olaudah**: (1745-1797) aka Gustavus Vassa the African.

  An "Up From Slavery" Saga

  Equaino is an epic, a saga, a legend, a historical phenomenon, a classic exemplary of the Igbo spirit of survival even in the most inhuman circumstance. Equiano is the saga of a slave boy who by dint of hard work and an incredible determination, rose to the status of celebrity and international fame. He was an Igbo boy kidnapped in childhood and sold into slavery and was taken to the New World—America. He eventually earned the price of his own freedom by carefully trading and saving. Eventually as a seaman, he traveled the world, including the Mediterranean, the Caribbean, the Atlantic and the Artic. Coming to London, he became involved in the movement to abolish slave trade, an involvement which led him to writing and publishing several historical memoirs and documents.

  According to **Peoples of Africa, Vol. 7, p.387,** published by Marshall Cavendish 2001: ***"Slaves were rarely able to speak out about their lives. But in 1789 Olaudah Equiano published the story of his life." As a boy, he had lived happily with his family in Igboland, a land "uncommonly rich and fruitful." When he was eleven, African slave dealers***

kinapped him and his sister. They were taken to the coast and put on a ship. As the ship crossed the Atlantic, the air became unfit to breathe and many of the slaves fell sick and died. In North America Olaudah was sold to a plantation owner. Later he was sold to a new master in England, where at the age of 21, he was able to buy his freedom. He married an English woman, became active in the movement to abolish slavery, and wrote his life story."

This Igbo slave boy became the first and greatest African in recorded history, not only of his century, but beyond. His greatness and accomplishments could be comparable only to that of the biblical Joseph, the Hebrew slave boy who rose from slavery to become the Prime Minister of Egypt. According to the popular Igbo proverb: ***'Chi ya muanya, ikenga ya di ire. (*** His chi is alive and awake, and his ikenga is active, fast and furious).

- King Jaja of Opobo. (1821-1891)
  This is another saga, another epic and another legend, of an Igbo slave boy who rose from slavery and achieved the greatness and power which petrified the British colonial government. Born in Igboland (around Nkwere), and sold as a slave at the age of about 12, this gifted and very enterprising youth eventually became one of the most powerful chieftains in the West African sub-region. Astute in business and politics, he became so wealthy and powerful and gained control of the palm oil trade which was the basic trade and economy in the Niger Delta region. He built a formidable commercial empire—'Palm Oil Trade kingdom'. He built a merchant navy of war canoes with which he protected and controlled the booming oil business. For a good while, Jaja continued to regulate trade and levy duties on British traders to the displeasure and anger of the British Royal Niger Merchant Company.

  Then was the era of gunboat diplomacy, and the superior British merchant navy rose to the occasion. But Jaja was unyielding and fought like a wounded lion. There were bloody skirmishes. But during a lull, Jaja was treacherously lured into a meeting ostensibly for peace talks with the British Consul onboard a British warship. There he was arrested and deported into exile to St. Vincent Island far away in the West Indies. Four years later he died allegedly en-route back to Nigeria. The circumstances of his death is still shrouded in suspicion. Although his captors claim innocence, but according to Prof. Ola Rotimi: *"if the witch cried in the night, and the child died in the morning, who does not know that it was the witch that killed the child."* (Kurumi 1971). And as the Igbo idiom states: "onye ahuru ukwu ya n'ubi jii, ma onye zuru jii n'ubi", (***the footprints found in the farm belong to the thief that stole the yams.)*** **And a Ghanaian proverb says:** ***"since the pot is the custodian of the soup, the pot must know what happened to the fish in the soup."***

Speaking to news reporters on the occasion of the celebration of King Jaja in Opobo Town, Chief Bellgam Pepple, high Chief of Opobo clan, emphatically restated the popular opinion of his clan: "Britrish can deny from now till kingdom come, na British kill King Jaja." (Eastern Nigerian Outlook, February 15, 1958)

King Jaja was the first victim of foreign territorial intrusion in West Africa. He is an icon of Igbo identity.

The Owelle Dr. Nnamdi Azikiwe, (aka Zik of Africa, 1904-1996)

For the economy of time and space, the life, history, achievements and accomplishments of this great African colossus can best be encapsulated in very graphic form, because his firsts and greatests will make volumes. Here is a graphic profile of the greatest and most flamboyant African politician and statesman:

- He was the father and beacon light of Pan African Liberation Movement, towering head and shoulder above all his contemporaries.
- Zik was the first African to lecture in Political Science at Lincoln University, USA. 1932-1934.

- On his return to Africa he founded the first of five groups of newspapers, **The African Morning Post** in Accra Ghana in 1934.
- In Ghana, Dr. Azikiwe beame a mentor to Kwame Nkrumah, the Premier of that British colony and who later became the first President of the first independent African country, 1957.
- First Nigerian Governor General of Nigeria.
- First President of Independent Republic of Nigeria.
- Founder and publisher of **The West African Pilot Newspaper**—(1937) the first and most circulated newspaper in the West Africa sub-region ***"which became a fire-eating and aggressive nationalist paper of the highest order, which ignited and fanned the flames of nationalist movements in sub-Sahara Africa."*** (London Observer, 1959)
- Founder and chief executive of **African Continental Bank**, the first indigenous bank on the African continent.
- Founder of the **University of Nigeria, Nsukka, (UNN) 1960,** the first indigenous university on the African continent, (courtesy University of Michan, USA).

  A comment: In a jubilant emotional outburst a respected chieftain and business tycoon—Chief Ihekweaba of Nkweree (of blessed memory) at the inauguration ceremonies of the University declared: "***Ndi ala anyi, unu ahula ugbua, na ihe ahu umu anyi na achoga n'ala bekee, Nnanyi Azikiwe ewetalaya n'ala anyi. Bido ugbua gawa, onye obula neziga nwa ya ala bekee igagu univasiti, na akwara onwe ya over coat."*** (our countrymen, you have all seen now that the golden fleece which our youths go to seek overseas, that our hero Azikiwe has brought it to our homeland. So from now on, any one who sends his child to overseas university, is wasting his money superfluously buying an oversize coat).
- Dr. Azikiwe towered over the affairs of Africa's most populous nation, attaining the status of a truly national and international hero, who came to be admired across regional and ethnic lines and divides (New York Times, 1966.)

- Although Dr. Zik was always known as a great and famous politician, statesman, great scholar, a media guru and a great pioneer, there are other aspects of his greatness that many people seem to have not much knowledge about. For instance, that he was a great sports enthusiast and a celebrated sports champion. His sporting accomplishments and accolades include:

  i) Welterweight Boxing Champion, Storer College, USA (1925-27);
  ii) High Jump champion, Howard University Inter-Scholastic Games USA (1926);
  iii) Gold Medalist in Cross Country, Storer College, USA (1927);
  iv) Back-stroke Swimming Champion and No. 3 swimmer in Freestyle Relay team, Howard University, USA (1928);
  v) Gold Medalist Mile Race Inter—Collegiate Athletic Association Championships at Hampton Institute Virginia, USA (1931);
  vi) Gold Medalist in 1,000 yards Inter-University Games, Brooklyn USA (1932);
  vii) Soccer Captain, Howard University, USA, (1930-32);
  viii) Zik entered to compete in the One Mile Race to represent Nigeria in the A.A.A of Great Britain 1939, but was rejected on the technical grounds that he dropped his foreign name "Benjamin" in his entry listing, thus Zik became a victim of cultural discrimination in international atheletics.
  ix) In Nigeria Dr. Zik founded, promoted and sponsored many sporting and athletic clubs: boxing, cricket, soccer, swimming and tennis.

In all, Zik of Africa was not just a political colossus, a brilliant intellectual giant, a celebrated and most distinguished statesman, but he was also a magnificiant embodiment of brain and brawn, prowess and agility, a celebrated athletic power house. No other Nigerian leader has come close to all these amalgam of accomplishments.

He deserved all the accolades of honor as a primus inter pares, **Ogbuefi Nnanyelugo, Eze Nwakaibeya, Onwa netiliora.** May his mighty and gracious soul continue to Rest in Perfect Peace.

Sir Louis Philipe Odumegwu Ojukwu: KBE; (1908-1967) aka LP

1. **Transport Tycoon:** Founder and CEO of Nigerian National Freight and Haulage Transport system. He created the first and largest national trucking and haulage company, carrying and hauling Nigerian agricultural produce from the hinterlands and farmlands to the ports of export in Port Harcourt and Lagos. It was called the Ojukwu Transport Company. (O.T.C.).
2. He was the first African millionaire, the first Nigerian to invest in the London Stock Exchange.
3. His vast financial empire included vast estates, holdings, and subsidiary companies in Lagos and Port Harcourt, making him the richest Nigerian landlord.
4. He was the first President of the Nigerian Stock Exchange. In recognition of his vast financial empire, and his tremendous contribution to the economic development of Nigeria, the British Colonial Government honored and decorated him with the knighthood: Knight of the British Empire—KBE.
5. He was the President and financier of the ACB, and a host of other companies.

He was the father of Ikemba Gen. Odumegwu Ojukwu. He died in the early days of the Nigeria-Biafra War.

Gen. Aguiyi-Ironsi, GCON, MBE, IDC, MUD, (1924-1966)

Johnson Thomas Umunnakwe Aguiyi-Ironsi was born to Mazi Ezeugo Aguiyi on March 3, 1924, in Umuahia Ibeku, present day Abia State, Nigeria.

He became Nigeria's most brilliant and distinguished soldier, the first African military officer to command a United Nations Peace Keeping Operation in Congo, Leopoldville.

Military career: Aguiyi-Ironsi enlisted into the Nigerian Army on February 2, 1942. Excelled in military training at Eaton Hall, England and also attended Royal Army Ordnance Corps before he was commissioned as an Infantry Officer in the rank of Lieutenant on 12 July 1949. He soon returned to Nigeria to serve as Aide de camp to John Macpherson, Governor General of Nigeria, and later assigned the Equerry to Queen Elizabeth 11 during her royal visit to Nigeria in 1956, the assignment for which he was sent to the Buckingham Palace to train.

During the Congo Crisis of the 1960s Ironsi led the 5th. Battalion of the Nigerian Army to Leopoldville provinces. His unit proved integral to the peacekeeping effort, and he was soon appointed the Force Commander of the United Nations Operation in the Congo. Ironsi distinguished himself as a very brilliant soldier and commander by scoring very strategic and amazing victories with his units.

After his international assignment Ironsi returned to Nigeria in 1964 and was eventually promoted to the rank of General officer Commander (GOC) of the Nigerian Army, on February 9, 1965 thus becoming the first Nigerian to hold the highest military rank in the country. During the bloody crises that preceded the Nigeria Biafra War, he was appointed to act as the Military Head of State by the Supreme Military Council. Although his tenure as Military Head of State was very short lived, he attempted very hard to implement plans for the unification of the country that was fast falling apart.

But, unfortunately and ironically, in his quest for a peaceful resolution of the bloody coups and counter coups of 1966, and for remedy for a United One Nigeria, he was killed in Ibadan along side his host Lt. Col. Francis Adekunle Fajuyi the military governor of the Western Region, by Hausa soldiers on July 29. He lived and died a brave soldier.

Emmanuel Ifeajuna: Commonwealth Gold Medalist

Ifeajuna distinguished himself as one of the finest Nigerian athlete and the best High Jump athlete at the British Commonwealth

Empire Games in Vancouver Canada 1954. He won the only Gold Medal for Nigeria at that international sports festival. He set a new Commonwealth record in that event. Ifeajuna was killed in 1967 during the Nigerian Biafra War.

Sir Francis Akanu Ibiam, (1906-1995), M.D., G.O.C.N.,LLd., KBE.,

The Eze Oha of Afikpo.

He was the first Nigerian and first African missionary medical doctor in history.

- Dr. Ibiam's career as an educationist came to the fore and he was appointed the first African Principal of the Hope Waddell Institute, Calabar in 1958. This was the famous Comprehensive institution that became the training ground and alma mater of some of Nigeria's most distinguished statesmen, medical doctors, engineers, theologians and university professors. The late Dr. Nnamdi Azikiwe was one of products of that famous institution. Igwe Kenneth Orizu 111 of Nnewi was also one of the products of that great institution.
- Dr. Ibiam was the first African President of the World Council of Churches—1961-1970.
- Founder and Honorary President, Student Christian Movement of Nigeria.
- In recognition of his Christian missionary achievements, his amazing spirit of philanthropy and other accomplishments, the British Home Office decorated him with the knighthood of the British Empire—KBE in 1951, and KCMG, in 1962.
- But in 1967 Dr. Ibiam dropped his English name Francis and returned the insignias of his knighthood of the British Empire with these words: "***I consider it illogical and immoral to wear the insignia of your knighthood in view of the dangerous weapons you give to the Federal troops to eliminate me and my people.***"

Hereunder is the full and unedited text of Eze Akanu Ibiam's Protest Letter to Her Majesty Queen Elizabeth 11. This is necessary because it is a monumental historical document that very eloquently expresses the political mentality, the cultural disposition and the spiritual character of a true traditional and unadulterated Igbo statesman and patriot, an image that is not easy to find in the context of Nigerian ethnography. No amount or kind of description or paraphrase in human language can adequately convey the solemnity, the gravity, the political immensity and the emotional intensity of the import and essence of Ibiam's protest letter. And very importantly, this document has very compelling historical, moral and inspirational values. In context, it is a brilliant political exposition on some high water marks of the Nigeria-Biafra war and a sagacious indictment on the infamous and shameful role of the British government in the Nigeria-Biafra War. The entire letter reads:

> "*Your Gracious Majesty, I am deeply and humbly constrained to present you with this letter. For many years, indeed throughout my mature life, I had been a proud but disinterested admirer of the United Kingdom of Great Britain and Ireland and her peoples. The history of Your Majesty's country is replete with heroism, discoveries which were near miracles, and institutions of higher learning of the most outstanding character and achievement. Britain though insular and small in size and capacity, had centuries ago proved conclusively, to the world that for any community and nation to reach the acme of greatness and respectability, it is not quantity that counts but quality and the type of people who make up the nation.*
>
> *British Christians had the privilege and honour of evangelizing not only a part of Africa, my own continent, but also a greater part of the rest of the world. Her missionaries, men and women, left home and kindred and comfortable life, to spread Christianity far and wide in areas of the world, where for better description, life was anything but civilized in the Western sense of the word, civilization. They endured lack of scientifically purified water, electricity or gas light. They trekked long miles of single-file roads, endured our moist heat and*

drenching rains, the nuisance of mosquitoes, and sand flies and other indigenous African insects. In their early days of missionary venture, they imported tons of tinned foodstuffs and cared nothing for their lives so long as they could preach the Gospel and its Good News, heal the sick, and bring education and enlightenment to the people. The result of this effective humanitarian service, supported financially, morally, and prayerfully by the Churches way back in their homeland, has borne exceedingly abundant fruit, and for us in Biafra (formerly Eastern Nigeria), their work has, by the grace of God, made our homeland as much a Christian country as any other reputed countries of the world.

Despite annoying treatment meted to me and my fellow African students now and again in certain quarters, I was highly impressed with the religious life of the people of Britain, particularly in Scotland, where I lived and studied in the University of St. Andrews for seven years in one of the coldest part of the United Kingdom. Altogether, I resided in Britain for ten long years. And having seen their homeland and lived in this Christian atmosphere in which they grew up, the self denial and self sacrifice of the Christian missionary came home to me very forcibly. I drew much inspiration from their splendid example, and my understanding and realization of the full meaning and significance of the Christian life dawned on me with great sense of joy and thankfulness.

After taking my medical degrees, therefore, I offered my services to the Foreign Mission Committee (now the Overseas Council) of the Church of Scotland, Edinburgh. I joined the Church of Scotland Medical Service, Calabar Mission, Nigeria, and served the mission and its offspring, the Presbyterian Church of Nigeria from February 1, 1936 to January 31, 1967. With the consent and approval of the Overseas Council, I was on leave of absence without pay during the last five years, December 1960—January 1965 of my missionary service, while I was Governor of Eastern Nigeria. As the only Nigerian among a group of some seventy European Missionaries for twenty-five years, the going was in the main, stiff at various times, I felt most frustrated and unhappy. For although

Missionaries inspired me without knowing it themselves, I regret to say that, by and large, they did not encourage me. Such a situation did not bother me, however, because I was inwardly happy to serve my people in this unique capacity, and I was not going to quit, come weal, come woe, until, like other missionaries, I had served my turn for thirty yeas or reached the age of sixty. If European missionaries, I argued within me, could leave their well-ordered homeland and ease of life, more or less, and where they could make a name for themselves academically or otherwise, and came to my homeland where amenities of life in the European background were hardly existent, I did not see any reason why I, an African, could not follow their footsteps and serve my own people in my own country under the conditions which call for naked hardship and self sacrifice

In the 1949 New Year Honours Awards, Your Majesty's revered and late father, His Majesty King George VI, graciously conferred on me the honour to be an Officer of the Civil Division of the Most Excellent Order of the British Empire (O.B.E) for services to the Church and state. Again, in the New Year honours, 1951, he conferred on me the dignity to be a Knight Commander of the Civil Division of the Most Excellent Order of the British Empire (K.B.E) for selfless service to the Church and my country. I happened to be in London at this time as a special guest of the British Council, and when I was invited by a Buckingham Palace Official to present myself before His Majesty to receive the insignia of Knighthood, I begged permission to have them conferred me on my return home to Nigeria. I did receive the insignia and certificate at the hands of His Excellency the then Governor General of Nigeria, Sir John Macpherson, but I had the distinction and singular privilege of receiving the accolade from Your Majesty's august person during your Majesty's Royal and memorable visit to Nigeria in February, 1956.

On the attainment of independence and sovereignty of Nigeria on October 1, 1960, Your Majesty was graciously pleased to appoint me as the Governor of Eastern Nigeria on the recommendation of the Honourable Premier of Eastern Nigeria with the assent of His Excellency the President of the Federal Republic of Nigeria. In August 1962, Your Majesty conferred on me the dignity of being a Knight Commander of the Civil Division of the Most Distinguished Order of St. Michael and St. George (K.C.M.G.)

For these great honours and special recognitions, I am humbly grateful to Your Majesty and to your Majesty's Britannic Government. They are a happy reflection of the importance of Africa and her people before God and man. Howbeit, I must renounce all of them at this time. I do so to register the strongest protest at my command against Your Majesty's Government of United Kingdom and Ireland for supplying military equipment and arms to Nigeria which has waged a senseless and futile war of aggression against my country, the Republic of Biafra. My objection and protest are directed solely and entirely to the British Government because I believe that the staunch British friends of Africa, particularly the CHURCH, and informed British public opinion will deplore this unkindly act of British Government to the Republic of Biafra. With the highest sense of responsibility, therefore, and bearing clearly in my own mind the moral issues which are at stake, my own stand thereat, I return the insignia and paraphernalia of my title to Your Majesty's Britannic Government through the British High Commissioner who is resident here in Enugu—the capital city of the Republic of Biafra.

During the months of May, July, August, and September, 1966, Northern Nigerian soldiers and civilians planned and committed the most atrocious crimes against Eastern Nigerians—now citizens of the Republic of Biafra. Sadistically, brutally, and in cold blood, they murdered and slaughtered thousands of my brothers and sisters who were then living in Northern Nigeria and other parts of the former and defunct Federal Republic of Nigeria. They killed innocent children, helpless women, and defenseless men without any reason or rhyme. They entered churches and hospitals and slaughtered them in cold blood. And most unbelievable and yet only too true, they massacred women in actual ***LABOUR and their***

unborn babies. *They plundered, looted, assaulted and raped women and burnt down the homes of Eastern Nigerians and left them naked, wretched and destitute. The International Red Cross put the number of slaughtered Easterners at 40,000. That was in deed a very conservative figure.*

The most painful brutal and unsoldierly act of all was that these Northern Nigerian soldiers killed their superior officers, including and especially His Excellency the Military Governor of the Western Nigeria, Lt. Col. Francis Adekunle Fajuyi, and his guest and comrade, His Excellency, the Head of the Supreme Military Council and Commander of the Armed Forces of the former Republic of Nigeria, Major-General J.T.U. Aguiyi-Ironsi, both of them of blessed memory. On July 29, 1966, they were kidnapped by Northern Nigerian soldiers and ruthlessly killed after torturing them. It must be stated here that the late Major-General J.T.U. Aguiyi-Ironsi, an Eastern Nigerian at that time, went all out to build up ONE UNITED AND STRONG NIGERIA through a unitary Government Administration, but paradoxically and ironically, he met a cruel and untimely death for that very reason. It is very strange, therefore, that Her Majesty's government should be futilely waging a war of aggression against Biafra in her impossible bid to force Biafra back into this very same union—One Nigeria from which she had been so purposely and systematically forced out. Be that as it may, our kit and kin fled Northern Nigeria, Western Nigeria and Lagos and returned to their homeland of Eastern Nigeria, the only place they could have protection. In the process, Eastern Nigeria was left to cater for at least two million refugees, and she has done and is doing so with commendable achievement. Eastern Nigeria did not retaliate in any way, for we do not kill strangers within our gates, and being humble and sensitive Christians, we refused to commit murder, contrary to the commandment of God, particularly as we believe that two wrongs can never make a right. Northern Nigerians in Eastern Nigeria were therefore collected together and escorted safely by train across the border to their own section of Nigeria.

In the succeeding months, Hausa/Fulani controlled Lagos Government of Nigeria purposely, directed, and inexorably forced Eastern Nigeria out of the Federation, and our Military Governor with advice and consent of the Consultative Assembly had no other choice but to declare Eastern Nigeria a free, independent and sovereign state to be known as the Republic of Biafra. This happy and historic occasion took place on May 30. On July 6th, Nigeria attacked Biafra in her mad wish to force Biafra to return to the Nigeria federation. Having killed over 40, 000 of us in their land and seized our property worth millions of pound sterling, they have now come to kill more of us in our own homes and make the rest of us slaves to the Hausa/Fulani feudalists and Moslems

The people of Biafra are, therefore, fighting a war of LIBERATION AND SURVIAVAL. We adamantly refuse to be colonized by the Hausa/Fulanis of Northern Nigeria or by any other people in the world. Moreover it is an ardent desire of the Hausa/Fulani and Moslem Northern Nigeria to subjugate Biafra and kill Christianity in our country.

Your Majesty, the British officials in Nigeria are fully aware of all these. They know that we are injured and deeply grieved people and had been cruelly treated by our erstwhile fellow citizens of the Federal Republic of Nigeria. The British officials not only knew the crux of the matter, but they also encouraged Northern Nigeria to carry out and execute their nefarious plan against us. They are angry with Biafra because Biafra categorically refused to remain as part of the Nigerian federation and political unit only to be trampled upon, discriminated against and hated, ruthlessly exploited and denied her rights and privileges, and slaughtered whenever it suited the whims and caprices of the favored people of Northern Nigeria. To add insult to injury, Your Majesty's Britannic government, instead of being neutral in our quarrels or finding ways and means to mediate and bring peace to the two countries, has now taken upon herself to supply military aid to Nigeria to help them defeat and subjugate Biafra.

It is simply staggering for a Christian country like Britain to help a Moslem country militarily to crush another Christian country like Biafra. This is just too much for me, Your gracious Majesty, this act of unfriendliness and betrayal and treachery by the British government towards the Christian people of the Republic of Biafra who, as Eastern Nigerians, had so much regard for Britain and her Christian people.

In the circumstance, Your Majesty, I no longer wish to wear the garb of the British Knighthood. British fairplay, British justice, and the Englishman's word of honour which Biafra loved so much and cherished have become meaningless to Biafrans in general and to me in particular. Christian Britain has shamelessly let down Christian Biafra.

I love the Republic of Biafra very dearly and pray that, by the grace of God, she may remain and continue to grow and live and always act like a truly Christian country for all times.

I am, Your Majesty

Yours Most Respectfully
(AKANU IBIAM)
(Biafran Voice, Nov. 15, 1967)

- **A Sainthood Model:** In the history of Nigeria, the best example and model was Eze Dr. Akanu Ibiam. He was a great doctor but preferred to be a missionary. He used his salaries and all official emoluments due to him to give scholarships to indigent students in his school. He did not build or own any personal or private house of his own, but was contented to live with his family in his mother's old three bedroom house in the village. He never had a personal bank account. In fact it was when the governorship of the defunct East Central State was imposed on him, that the government built a **state house** –a modest four bedroom bungalow for him in his village. For most Nigerians this sounds like a fairy tale. Ibiam was a saint indeed. He spent all his life doing good, like his master

Jesus. He was an epitome of Christian morality and humility. A proud icon of Igbo identity.

May his great and saintly soul continue to rest in perfect peace.

Prof. Kenneth Onwuka Dike, (1917-1983),

Father of Modern African History

Kenneth was born on December 17, 1917 in Awka, Eastern Region, Nigeria. He studied in Achimota College, Ghana, Fourah Bay College, Sierra Leone, Duraham University in the United Kingdom, and in the University of Aberdeen, Scotland. And finally at King's College, London, where he obtained his Ph.D. in 1950, Professor Dike was one of the first wave of Nigerians appointed to the academic staff of the University College, Ibadan. He rose through the ranks to become the first Professor of History. He was actively involved in the conception and birth of the University College Hospital, (UCH) Ibadan.

- He was the first Nigerian Vice Chancellor of the nation's premier university, University of Ibadan, (formerly U.C.I— Univrsity College Ibadan). 1958 to 1962.
- Founder and President of the Historical Research Council for Africa.
- He laid the foundation stone for research in African History, and pioneered a lot of research projects and programs and a lot of scholarly publications in African history.
- In 1973 he was appointed the First Mellon Professor of African History at Harvard, (USA) Here Dike spent the greater part of the last decade of his life teaching and research.
- He returned to Nigeria in 1980 to take up the position of first President, Anambra State University of Science and Technology, a position he held until his death in 1983 at the age of 67 years.

It is very significant and worthy of note that it was during his tenure as the Vice Chancellor of the University of Ibadan (UCI), that the International Institute of Tropical Agriculture (IITA) was born. The IITA under the auspices of the United State Department of Agriculture came to Nigeria to establish an ultra-modern agricultural Research Plantation at Umudike (Umuahia) in then Eastern Region. It was Prof. Dike who insisted that the project –IITA should be located in Ibadan in order to be a resource and research center for the Faculty of Agriculture of the University of Ibadan. That was the Igbo man's spirit of true nationalism—nation before tribe. No other Nigerian of any other ethnic group or tribe could have been so magnanimous and selflessly nationalistic. For the true Igbo, Nigeria came first before tribe. That was then when things had not fallen apart, that was then when the truism was true "One Nigeria", that was then when tribalism and the demon of Igbophobia had not yet been conceived in their mother's womb. That was then when ***"monkey thought that every bush na home."*** But now according to an Imo proverb, ***"agbisi gbaa otile, ya amuru ako."*** (meaning when the black ant (agbisi) stings the buttock, the body learns a hurtful lesson). But the truth of it will for ever remain a memorial in the annals of Igbo nationalism.

Now take a look at this statistics of the demographic composition of IITA top management and administration personnel published by the Institute of International Demographics of Research Institutes in 1989:

1.	Whites including Europeans and Americans:	40%
2.	Yoruba:	31%
3.	Igbo:	8%
4.	Asians, Indians, Australians:	16%
5.	Others: of African stock:	5%

No one is trying to blow one's own trumpet, or to fan the embers of tribal sentiment because that will be very unscholarly, intellectually indecorous, sociologically an indefensible impropriety, politically unpatriotic and unpalatable as some neighbors of Ndi-Igbo would definitely want to construe it. However, it will also be very naïve and disdainful for anyone to ignore or connive at very concrete hard historical facts and figures based on international research and published by a United Nations Organization FAO foundation for education and research institutions in Tropical Agriculture.

And it sounds extremely pathetic and incomprehensible that when this great Nigerian scholar, statesman and the grand architect and patriarch of IITA in Ibadan died many years later, in appreciation of Prof. Dike's hard work and contributions in the development of the university and the social infrastructures of the city of Ibadan, the Federal government decided to immortalize his name by naming the street connecting the university (U.I) and the University Teaching Hospital (UCH) **Kenneth Dike Avenue.** Hell was let loose. Some political thugs and tribal demagogues never let it happen because Professor Kenneth Dike was not ***'a son of the soil'***. Each time the sign post of the street name was erected, it was uprooted and destroyed within 24 hours. This was repeated over more than a dozen times, for many months, until the federal government gave up the fight. Only a very fickle minded person will tend to believe that those thugs and demagogues were acting without some local political engineering and instigated by tribal bigotry in high quarters. An Igbo proverb says: ***nwa nnaya dugara oshi, n'eji ukwu agbawa uzo.*** (a child whose father sends him to rob, will have the boldness to kick open the door with his feet).

The present author of this publication was a personal eye-witness to these events, he was then a lecturer at the University of Ibadan. An Igbo proverb says: ***"onya laa, apa ya ga di"*** (a sore/injury will heal, but the scare remains)

Ben Enweonwu, (proper original name—**Benedict Chuka Enweonwu, (1918-1994),** Father of Nigerian Art.

- A product of Ruskin College, Oxford. Benedict Chuka Enweonwu was Nigeria's greatest artist—painter and sculptor, and the first African artist to train at Britain's most famous Colleges of Arts—Goldsmith College, London, 1944, Ruskin, Oxford, 1946, and Slade School of Fine Art, 1944-46.
- He was the first African to collate African Art History. His essays are prophetic as they did 60 years ago.
- Ben Enweonwu was the first African artist whose works of art appeared at public exhibitions, galleries and art fares in most world capitals and museums more than those of any other African artist. His works have appeared in

several international art exhibitions: London, Paris, Lisbon, Copenhagen, Frankfort, Belgium, Smithsonian, San Francisco, Greece and Italy, and are still gracing the National Museum in Lagos, Nigeria.

One of his most magnificent works of art is the effigy of **The Risen Christ** at the entrance gate of the Chapel of Resurrection, University of Ibadan. Enweonwu's other professional and illustrious career include:

Art Teacher in various institutions: Government College, Umuahia, Mission College, Calabar 1940-1941; Edo College, Benin City, 1941-1943; Art Advicer to the Nigerian Government from 1948 to 1990; Cultural Advisor to the Nigerian Government, 1968-1971; Visiting Professor of Art Institute of African Studies, Howard University; Washington DC; appointed Professor of Fine Arts, University of Ife, 1971-1975; Art Consultant to the International Secretariat, Second World Black and African Festival of Arts (FESTAC), Lagos, 1971. He also served as Art Advisor at the Royal Anthropological Institute, London. He was decorated Member of the Royal Academy of Arts, London.

Dick Tiger: (1929-1974) World Light-Heavy Weight Boxing Champion,

Real name—Richard Ihetu, was another example of the dynamic and enterprising spirit of Igbo character. He was born in Amigbo town in Orlu. He rose from obscurity to world fame, from picking and collecting empty bottles and cans along streets and from dustbins in Aba, where he was nicknamed "Onye ololo" (scavenger of empty bottles) to become a multi-million dollar world champion, business tycoon and philanthropist.

Tiger became the first ever African boxer to win world titles in two divisions: Bantam weight and the Heavy weight divisions.

Here under is a graphic profile of Tiger's brilliant boxing career:

- WBA Middle Weight Champion: 23 October 1962-7 Dec. 1963
- WBC Middle Weight Champion: 7 May 1963-7 December 1963

- World Middle Weight Champion: 21 October 1965-25 April 1966
- World Light Heavy Weight Champion: 16 December 1966 - 24 May 1968
- Ring Magazine Fighter Of The Year: 1962
- Ring Magazine Fighter Of The Year: 1965
- Inducted into the International Boxing Hall Of Fame USA: 1965. The first African to achieve this honor and title.

A brief summary of the brilliant boxing career of Dick Tiger shows that he had a total of 81 professional fights, and he won 60 of them with TKOs.

In recognition of his brilliant and illustrious boxing exploits in Britain, Her Majesty's government decorated him with the knighthood of MBE—Member of the British Empire. But as a result of the role of the British government played in the Nigeria Biafra War, Dick Tiger renounced all association with Britain and returned his insignia of knighthood to the British Queen.

He died of liver cancer on December 14, 1971 at the young age of 42. He was/is an icon in the Igbo Nation Hall of Fame.

Dr. Chike Obi, (1921-2005), (nickname Dr. Chiak)

Prof. Emeritus, Mathematics. In the political arena he was known as '*Oku nagba ozara,* (Fire hurricane of the desert)

Born Chikeze (Chike) Edozien Obi in Onitsha Anambra State, educated in various parts of Nigeria before reading mathematics as an external student of University of London. Immediately after his first degree, he won a scholarship to do research study at Pembroke College, Cambridge, (UK) followed by a doctoral studies at Massachusetts Institute of Technology, Cambridge, USA. becoming in 1950, the first Nigerian to receive a Ph.D. in mathematics**.**

Following is a profile of his illustrious academic and professional career:

- The first mathematician ever to resolve the mathematical theory of **Non Linear Differential Equation of the Second**

Order, an area in science and mathematics where the best geniuses in the world have always dreaded to tread.

- He made enormous contributions on the world scene in the areas **of Pure and Applied Mathematics.**
- **He** was a full-time Professor at the University of Lagos (UNILAG)
- **The World Encyclopedia of Mathematics** rates that Nigeria produced the three greatest Mathematicians on the African continent: Prof. Chike Obi, Prof. James Ezeilo, and Prof. Adegoke Olubumo, and Chike Obi is rated the greatest of the greatest.
- He was a Visiting Professor of the University of Rhode Island USA, the University of Jos, Nigeria, and the Chinese Academy of Sciences.
- Chike Obi was decorated with Nigeria's highest honor—Commander of the Order of the Niger (CON), and a Fellow of the Nigerian Academy of Science (FNAS).
- He was a man of many parts: Mathematician, university professor, politician, author and a very dynamic social revolutionary. In the political arena he was known as Oku nagba Ozala, the fire hurricane that consumes the desert.
- **Obituary:** The President General of Ohanaeze Ndi-Igbo, Dr. Dozie Ikedife lamented: "***He was an icon and a pride not just to Nigeria and Africa, but also to the world of Science and Mathematics. By his demise the world has lost one of its brightest gems***"

Dr. Jaja Anucha Nwachukwu, "Ugo Ngwa" (1918-1996)

He was a brilliant and distinguished Orator, and a celebratted Elder Statesman.

Dr. Jaja Anucha Nwachukwu, was the Ideh 1 of Ngwaland, Abia State:

- First African Laureate (Gold Medalist) in Oratory of the famous Trinity College, Dublin, Ireland. His professional colleagues called him "**the Golden Voice of Africa**"
- He was the founder and organizing secretary of the Dublin International Club.

- He was the first indigenous Speaker of the Nigerian House of Representative. from 1959-1960. Wachukwu replaced Sir Frederick Metcalfe of Great Britain. Notably, as the First Speaker of the House, Wachukwu received Nigeria's Instrument of Independence, the Freedom Charter, on October 1, 1960 from Princess Alexandria of Kent, Her Majesty the Queen of the United Kingdom's representative at the Independence ceremonies.
- First Nigerian Ambassador and Permanent Representative to the United Nations, his friends and colleagues at the United Nations acclaimed him as "very versatile, brilliant and very eloquent."
- He was the first Nigerian Minister of Foreign Affairs in which office his contributions and accomplishments were phenomenal.
- In 1957 he was elected leader of the Nigerian Federal Delegation to the Commonwealth Parliamentary Association Meeting to India.
- He was elected Principal Secretary of the Igbo State Union 1948-1952.
- He was decorated with several chieftaincy titles in recognition of his immense philantrophic contributions in Ngwaland.

Prof. Zulu Sofola, (1935-1995)

(Real full name—Nwazuluoke, nee Okwumabu, but her Theatre name was Zulu by which she was internationally known)

Zulu Sofola, born by Igbo parents in Issele-Ukwu, Delta State, and married to an Ijebu Yoruba Professor Tunde Sofola.

* She was Nigeria's and Africa's first and most celebrated female playwright and dramatist.
* First Nigerian and African female to earn a Ph.D. in Theater Arts.
* First female Professor and Director of Theater Arts in Nigeria.
* In her life time Zulu was the most versatile and prolific female playwright on the African continent. At the time of

her untimely and sudden death in 1995, Zulu had more than twenty plays in her repertory.

Many of her plays have been produced in universities and theatres all over Europe and America. (The present writer was her student at the University of Ibadan)

Chief Mrs. Janet Mokelu.

Pioneer Freedom Fighter and frontline Political Activist

She was the first female parliamentarian and member of a House of Representatives in the history of Nigerian politics. She was a very dynamic pioneer nationalist and played very significant role in the fight for Nigerian independence. She was the woman leader in the NCNC—the major political party that won independence for Nigeria.

Chief Phoebe Chiadikobi Ajayi-Obe, SAN

Mrs. Phoebe Chiadikobi (nee Erine, of Okija, Anambra State) married to Dr. Ajayi-Obe a Yoruba. She is a very brilliant attorney and is regarded in very high official quarters as the most brilliant female lawyer in her generation. In recognition of this, she was awarded the highest legal honor of distinction – Senior Advocate of Nigeria—SAN in 1989, making her first and most distinguished female lawyer in Nigeria.

Prof. James Okoye Chukwuka Ezeilo: "Father of Mathematics"

Prof. James Ezeilo was born in Nnanka in Aguata LGA. He is a product of DMGS Onitsha. He earned B.Sc. Lond. First Class Hons. Maths, 1953; M.Sc. Lond; 1955; Ph.D. Queen's College, Cambridge, 1959.

* The World Encyclopedia of Mathematics rates Prof. James Ezeilo as one of the three greatest Mathematicians on the African continent, along with Prof. Chike Obi and Prof. Olubummo.

- In addition to that, Prof. Ezeilo is regarded by scholars all over the world as the "**The Father of Mathematics in Nigeria.**"
- He was a pioneer in the use of Leray-Schauder degree type arguments to obtain existence results for periodic solutions of ordinary differential equations.
- Prof. Ezeilo has published more books and articles in mathematics than any of his colleagues and contemporaries both in Nigeria and in Africa.
- He was one time Vice Chancellor of the University of Nigeria, Nsukka (UNN).
- He is a Distinguished Member of the World Council of Mathematicians.

Chinua Achebe, Prof. Emeritus.

Chinua was born in Ogidi, Anambra State of Nigeria. Product of Umuahia Government College and University College, Ibadan.

- Achebe is celebrated and reputed to be the greatest African novelist.
- In Nigeria he is the first and greatest.
- His best classic—**Things Fall Apart** is acclaimed a world classic, and has been translated into more than fifty different languages, a feat that no other African novelist has so far achieved. More than three million copies have been sold in the United States since it was first published here in 1959. Worldwide, there are over eight million copies in print in fifty different languages.
- Achebe's books can be found in every university and college library in Europe and America. In fact his novels are the basic texts in Black and African Literature in all Institutes and Departments of African Studies all over the world.
- Achebe is an icon and universities all over the world feel very highly honored to hear him speak.

  An Aside: The present writer was his student at the high school, and has personally been a beneficiary of the fame and celebrity of this great icon in 1987, in my capacity as a Visiting Professor at the University of Kansas.

During my first week as a Visiting Professor in African Studies at the University of Kansas, the Head of Department learnt from me that Achebe was not only my High School teacher, but that I was very familiar with the cultural environment and cosmos of ***Things Fall Apart,*** which coincidentally was the recommended text for the graduate class I was going to teach.

The Head of Department jubilantly exclaimed **'eureka'** that he has found the man who will teach and speak with the authority of first hand experience. During the first two lectures he sat in my class and listened with wrapped attention and excitement. Convinced and excited that he has indeed found a teacher with the authority of first hand experience of **Achebe** and on ***Things Fall Apart,*** he arranged with the Faculty Dean and the Vice Chancellor for me to give a public lecture on Achebe for a handsome honorarium. The deal was sealed. The stage was set. Fliers and posters went out all over the campus.

Two weeks later it happened. The university auditorium was jammed to capacity, over 2,500 enthusiastic audience from the university community and environs. At the end the lecture was adjudged a huge success by the university authorities and by the local press and media.

That was how this great icon, an international literary giant, his fame rubbed off on me. It was an experience I have always cherished.

The following are a few of his numerous literary works:

- Things Fall Apart, 1958
- No Longer At Ease, 1960
- The sacrificial Egg and Other Stories, 1962
- Arrow of God, 1964
- A Man of The People, 1966
- Chike and the River, 1966
- Beware, Soul Brether, 1971
- Girls At War, 1972
- How the Leopard lost his claws, 1972

- Christmas in Biafra, 1973
- Morning Yet On Creation, 1975
- The Drum, 1977
- The Flute, 1977
- Literature and Society, 1980
- The Trouble with Nigeria, 1983
- The World of Ogbanje, 1986
- Anthills of the Savanna, 1987

Chief Emeka Anyaoku: Commonwealth Secretary General, 1990-2000.

Born Eleazar Chukwuemeka (Emeka) Anyaoku on 18 January 1933 in Obosi, Anambra State. He attended Merchants of Light School in Oba, and later the University College Ibadan where he obtained an honors degree in Classics. Later he attended specialist courses in the United Kingdom and in France. The case study of Chief Anyaoku is a typical example and a testimony that the Igbo is capable of rising to the highest echelon of human endeavor. His brilliant resume is the picture of an international genius—top and above his equals.

- In 1966, he was posted as Director to Nigeria's Permanent Mission to the United Nations in New York.
- The first Nigerian, the first African to be elected to the highest office in the British Commonwealth of Nations, Secretary General 1990-2000. The Commonwealth is a world organization of 53 sovereign nations which links many former colonies of the former British Empire.
- At the 1989 Commonwealth Heads of Government Meeting (CHOMG) in Kuala Lumpur, Malasia, Chief Anyaoku was elected the third Secretary General. He was re-elected at the 1993 CHOMG in Limassol, Cyprus, for a second 5 year term of office.
- Under his stewardship, the obnoxious and hideous apartheid policy of the White minority government of South Africa was peacefully dismantled. This was a feat and a monumental accomplishment.

- Also under his leadership and guidance, the Commonwealth Secretariat launched a variety of important initiatives in sustainable economic and social development programmes including the Commonwealth Fund for Technical Co-operation (CFTC), the operational arm of the Secretariat which reinforced the benefits of the co-operation and mutual assistance among member nations.
- Chief Anyaoku is a tall and beautiful eagle feather on the cap of Ndi-Igbo **"Anyaoku wu eze nwakaibeya ma na ala Igbo ma na ala bekee." (**Anyaoku is greater than his peers both in all Igboland and in the European world.)
  (Late Governor Sam Mbakwe, Imo State)

Cardinal Francis Arinze: (b. 1932)

His Eminence was born i**n Eziowele, Idemili L.G Anambra State)**

Former Prefect Emeritus of the Congregation for Divine Worship and Discipline of Sacraments. He was also Cardinal of Velletri-Segni. He was one of the principal advisors to the late Pope John Paul 11, and was considered ***papabile*** before the 2005 papal conclave.

Like his countryman and tribesman Chief Emeka Anyaoku, Cardinal Arinze is another eloquent testimony that on a level playing field of equal opportunity, Ndi-Igbo can achieve the highest office in any human organization, and can reach the top where no other Nigerian or African has ever been.

The profile of his brilliant and illustrious career and accomplishments is an eagle feather for Ndi-Igbo.

* Arinze became the youngest Roman Catholic bishop in the world when he was ordained to the episcopate on 29 August 1965, at the age of 32.
- He was the first native African to head his diocese of Onitsha, succeeding Archbishop Charles Heerey, an Irish missionsry.
- At the age of 53, he was among the youngest in the College of Cardinals
- In 1985, Arinze was at the Vatican full-time, moving quickly through the Vatican hierarachy.

- In 1999, he was awarded Gold Medallion for his outstanding achievements in the Inter-Faith religion.
- He was the first African prelate to head a major Vatican office.
- In 2005, top Vatican analysts rated Cardinal Arinze as one of the four top most "papabili"—popeable men who have the qualifications to hold the top office of the church.
- At 70, Arinze became the Prefect of the Congregation for Divine Worship and the Discipline of the Sacraments, a post which put him in charge of liturgy, and number four in the Vatican hierarchy.

Negrophobia in the Vatican.
Cynics, racial bigots, and catholic redheads:

According to an official correspondent of the **Catholic Observer, October 2003**:

"The Vatican has a thing about color. There is white cassock for the pontiff; scarlet cloaks for the cardinals; navy and gold for uniforms for the Swiss Guards; yellow for the flag—and soon, we might know whether there is white smoke for a black pope."

It is an open secret that even among some Conclave Cardinals there are cynics and racial bigots who cannot conceive the idea of "white smoke for a black pope." Cardinal **Ratzinge**r a top Vatican king maker acknowledged that racism could have prevented an African succession, and that there were still "great misgivings in the West about the Third World".

Bowing out when the ovation was highest: Not waitng to be sidelined a second time, His Eminence at the height of his glory and accomplishments, submitted his retirement letter to the Pope some time in December 2009. That was a very strategic and maginficient move of wisdom and dignity, ***makana ijele nmanwu na akataka adi azo ogbo.***-(ijele the king of masquerades and lesser masqurades do not contest for the dance arena). Reliable Intelligence sources revealled that His Eminence was persuaded to remain in the Vatican, but he determined and decided to return to Eziowele his village and spend the rest of his life among his own kit and kin as a religious and cultural icon. Once again, ***'agaracha must to return back'.***

Chief Augustine Ilodibe: (alias Nwa Fada, 1932-2007)

Founder and CEO of Ekene Dili Chukwu group of Companies

- A business and Transport guru, who revolutionized public transport system, and laid the foundation of modern air-conditioned luxury bus service in the West African sub-region. Before the arrival of Ekene Dili Chukwu Transport System, the popular means of passenger transportation available were: **gwomgworo, molue, bolekaje, the pick-up bus.**
- Ekene Dili Chukwu introduced the first national luxury bus transport network: north to south, and east to west, with well-equipped offices and maintenance stations in major towns and cities throughout Nigeria.
- His efficient and effective transport administration greatly improved passenger comfort and safety. Passenger comfort also included TV network on the bus, so that passengers could watch World News, TBN and local news. Passenger safety also included well-armed security escorts on board and so passengers could afford to sleep with both eyes closed if they wanted.
- Ekene Dili Chukwu is the only transport organization in West Africa that had the humanitarian component for low and discount fares for college and university students and members of the Nigerian Youth Service Corps (NYSC).
- He was a great philanthropist per excellence, and many indigent students benefited from his generosity and benevolence.
- His transport company was the first to introduce efficient and reliable time schedule—departure and arrival time-table, akin to the air and rail transport systems.

- Ekene is a glowing testimony of how an Igbo man can rise from obscurity and became rich and famous by dint of hard work and honesty, not by 419.

Dr. Dozie Ikedife, President General of Ohaneze Ndi-Igbo Worldwide, in his funeral oration lamented that: "Nigeria has lost a vital economic pillar and institution, that will be impossible to replace. The best chapter in the history of road transport in West Africa has closed."

Dr. M.I. Okpara: b. 1920

Michael Iheonukara Okpara was a great political leader and Premier of Eastern Nigeria during the First Republic (1959-1966). He was extremely dynamic, patriotic, bubbling with zeal and enthusiasm, and faithfully loyal to his party leadership and political philosophy. He was Dr. Azikiwe's number one right hand man and trusted companion and friend. He was a very lucky survivor of the January 1966 military coup d'etat, because ***nwa amadi ahu, aka ya di ocha, chi ya muanya di ire,*** (this hero has clean hands, his (chi) guarding angel is alert and powerful).

He was an Igbo from Ohuhu, near Umuahia, born in 1920, the son of a peasant laborer. He attended Uzuakoli Methodist College, won a scholarship to read medicine at the old and famous Yaba Higher College, graduated and set up a private medical practice in Umuahia. But the political blood in him was hot, fast and furious. He joined the Zikist Movement, the militant wing of Dr. Zik's NCNC and later became the national secretary of the movement. After the shooting of rioting workers at the Enugu coal mines (1949), Dr. Okpara was arrested and detained by the colonial government for allegedly organizing and inciting the workers for political ends. But he was later released.

Dr. Okpara was elected to the Eastern House of Assembly in 1952. Between then and 1959, he held various positions and offices in government including—Head of Civil Service, Minister of Health, Minister of Agriculture, and finally, Premier of Eastern Region.

In recognition of his immense contributions in Igboland, many health and agricultural institutions and universities have been named after him: Dr. Michael Okpara University of Agriclture, Dr. Michael Okpara Medical Center, and the famous social center The Okpara Square in Enugu, In 1964 he was decorated GCON (Grand Commander of the Order of the Niger), the country's highest award of honour and merit in recognition of his services to the country. You deserve a 21 gun salute!!

Dr. F. Chidolue Ogbalu: (1927-1990)

Popularly known and called FCO, and officially regarded as the "Father of Igbo Language and Culture", was born in Abagana in Anambra State. He was a lifelong teacher who devoted his life to the development and improvement of the study and teaching of Igbo language. In fact no person dead or alive has contributed so much in the area of Igbo language orthography than FCO. He will always be remembered as the founding father of The **Society For The Promotion of Igbo Language an Culture—SPILC**.

This great honour he achieved at the young age of 22 years. He established a very powerful publishing institution—**The Vasity Press** in Onitsha, which immediately became the most popular Publishing House for very many books in novel literature, history, geography, and comics for secondary schools in those days.

In 1978 The Department of Igbo Language and Culture was started, with the opening of Anambra State College of Education at Awka, with F. C. Ogbalu as the Head of Department. In September of the same year, another Department of Igbo was established at the Federal Advanced Teachers College, Okene, Kwara State.

FCO taught Latin and Economics at DMGS, Onitsha, and at St. Augustine's Grammar School, Nkwerre, the two most famous and oldest CMS grammar schools in Igboland. But most importantly, it will always be remembered that it was the success of one of his SPILC seminars (which I was privileged to participate in) at the University of Ibadan in 1979 was influencial in the establishment of the Department of Igbo Language and Linguistics at the University of Nigeria, Nsukka.

His very busy and active life was cut short by an automobile accident at the age of 63.

Dr. Enoch Oli:

Late Dr. Enoch Ifediora Oli will always be remembered as the second Igbo graduate of Oxford University, after Mr. Alvan Ikoku. He was the founder and first principal of Merchants of Light Secondary School, Oba, 1946, one of the oldest grammar schools in Igboland. Before then, Mr. Oli had served as Vice principal at DMGS, Onitsha, and also at Okrika Grammar School. The Merchants of Light was modeled as an extention of those two CMS grammar schools.

Mr. Oli also served in government as a cabinet Minister in the Ministry of Education and Social Services in the then Eastern Nigeria. One of the distinguished products of the Merchants of Light School is Chief Emeka Anyaoku, First African Secertary General of the British Commonwealth of Nations.

Dr. Kingsley Ozumba Mbadiwe: (KO) (1917-1990)

"The Man of Timber and Caliber". KO was the most flambouant, exuberant, 'superlative' 'bombastic' indefatigable political demagogue on the Nigerian political scene in the immediate post independence era. He hailed from Arondizuogu. He was one of the seven brilliant young men who were inspired and encouraged by Dr. Zik to sail to the United States "in search of the Golden Fleece." in December 1938. The others in the group were: Mazi Mbonu Ojike, Otuka Okala, Dr. Nnodu Okongwu, Engr. Nwankwo Chukwuemeka, Dr. Okechukwu Ikejiani, Dr. Abyssinia Akwaeke Nwafor Orizu, and George Igbodebe Mbadiwe. KO always referred to this group as the "Seven Argonauts"

On his return from the US in 1948, KO undertook an exhibition tour of the country with a movie he had done in the US, he tagged the tour "Operation Greater Tomorrow".

The movie was a promotion of African Arts and Science. In 1951 he joined the NCNC and in 1952 he was appointed Federal Minister of Natural Resources. Thereafter, in quick succession he held various federal ministerial positions. In fact no other Nigerian politician has held so many different portfolis at different times as KO. He was Minister of Lands, Minister of Trade and Commerce, and Minister of

Aviation. As if those were not enough, he was appointed the first and so far, the only "Ambassador Extra-Odinary and Plenipotentiary" of the Federal Republic of Nigeria.

As the Minister of Aviation he structured the Nigerian Airways partnership with the Pan American Airways and took the exotic acrobatic Atilogwu dancers and two royal trumpeters from Kano on the maiden flight from Lagos to New York which he tagged "Operation Fantastic".

At the beginning he was one of the strongest pillars in the NCNC political party and the next to Dr. Zik in political stature. But some how along the line, he derailed from the Igbo political mainstream in 1958, and formed his own party—the DPNC—(Democratic Party National Congress) and structured alliance with the NPC (Northern Peoples Congress). When that failed, he renegaded and allied with the Action Group.

Above all, KO will always be remembered for his flair and appetite for coinage and usage of jaw breaking bombastic words. He was the originator of the phrase "**men of Timber and Caliber"** which became his trade mark. One political historian had this to say: "K.O. Mbadiwe was a flamboyant man who thought only in the superlative."

Mazi **Mbonu Ojike: The Boycott King (1914-1959)**

A Son of the Soil of Arondizuogu, Ojike was one of the finest and unequivocally the most dynamic political activist that Nigeria has ever had. He was fiery, exuberant, eloquent, very uncompromising and very militant in his pride of Africaness.

A profile of his life and career is a catalogue of dynamic accomplishments.

- He was a college scholar at the famous Teacher Training College, Awka, and also taught there after graduation.
- He initiated himself into a dynamic political activism when he led his fellow younger teachers on a strike to end a discriminatory treatment by the Ministry of Education.
- Eventually he left for America as a member of the 'seven Argonauts', studied at Ohio and Chicago universities, obtaining B.A; and M.A.

- He returned to Nigeria in 1947 and plunged into the mainstream of 'Militant Nationalism'. He rose fast through the ranks of political echelon, and was rewarded with important political and ministerial appointments including:
    - Advicer to the NCNC Delegation to the 1949 constitutional conference,
    - Deputy Mayor of Lagos, National Vice President of NCNC, Eastern Nigerian Minister of Works, Eastern Regional Minister of Finance, General Manager of The West African Pilot, etc.

- He will always be remembered as the economist who introduced the PAYE tax system in Nigeria when he was the Minister of Finance.
- His greatest impact was psychological and intellectual, he ignited the fire of cultural awareness, national identity and intellectual re-orientation. He coined the now famous phrase "Boycott all Boycottables", which earned him the title "The Boycott King". He led by example, consistently wearing Igbo dress and outfits to every where: office, parties, and international travels. He insisted on serving palm wine instead of whisky, champagne or beer at his official receptions and parties.

This firebrand political heavy weight, social reformer, exubrant Africanist, eloquent traditionalist was very untimely snatched by death in 1959. O***nwu atu egwu*** (death has no fear), ***Onwu aso anya,*** (death is no respecter of persons), ***Onwu ama eze*** (death has no respect for the great and famous)**.,** ***Onwu ama egbu.*** (death is very insensitive). Mazi Ojike left a lot of legacies for Ndi-Igbo. May his great soul rest in perfect peace!

Alvan Ikoku (1900-1971)

Born in Arochukwu on August I, 1900 in present day Abia State, was educated at Government School and Hope Waddell College, Calabar. Lectured as a senior Tutor at St. Paul's Teacher Training College, Awka in Anambra State.

- While teaching at Awka, Ikoku earned his University of London degree in philosophy in 1928, through its external program, thus making Ikoku the first Nigerian to earn a university degree as an external candidate.
- In 1931 Ikoku established one of the earliest private secondary schools in Nigeria: the Aggrey Memorial College, located in Arochukwu.
- In 1946, he was electeded to the Eastern Nigerian House of Assembly and assigned the Ministry of Education.
- Ikoku gave Nigerian teachers a powerful trade union identity when he formulated the NUT—Nigerian Union of Teachers which became the foundation of the official policy on education.
- Upon retiring from government politics, he served on various educational bodies in the country. He was a member of the Governing Board of Directors of West African Educational Council (WAEC); Member of Council of University of Ibadan; Chairman Board of Governors of Aviation Training Center.
- 1965 he was awarded honorary Doctorate in Law at a special convocation of the University of Ibadan.
- In recognition of his immense contributions and accomplishments in the development of education, the Federal government established the Alvan Ikoku Federal College of Education, Owerri, and also his commemoration on a bill of Nigerian currency, The Ten Naira note.
- He died on November 18, 1971. He was a great icon and a great hero whose name will continue to ring loud and clear in the the Igbo world Hall of Fame.

Chapter Four

Symbols and Paraphernalia of Status and Distinction

- Title tradition
- Animal paraphernalia
- Archtechural motifs
- Arts and Crafts
- Yam culture

Title Tradition

In most human societies and civilizations there are always ranks and statuses and hierarchies and echelons. An Igbo proverb says that all fingers are not equal. The great English writer and novelist **George Orwell** states in his novel **Animal Farm:** ***"All animals are equal, but some are more equal than others."*** In the American Constitution: ***All men are born free and equal before the law,*** but we know that some are in authority over others. Also there is the axiom: "some people are born great, some achieve greatness, and some have greatness imposed on them." But in the context of Igbo identity, it is the greatness that is achieved by dint of hard work, perseverance, and diligence that the Igbo respect and adore and strive for.

In Chinua Achebe's classic novel **Things Fall Apart,** Chapter Three, he describes a very rich man:

> ***"There was a wealthy man in Okonkwo's village who had three large barns, nine wives and thirty children. His name was Nwakibie, and he had taken the highest title which a man could take in the clan"*** (Achebe, First Anchor Books Edn. 1994)

In Igboland, there are social levels, there are ranks, there are echelons, and they are all based on ability, achievement, and endowments. In Igboland age is respected, but achievement is very much revered. Every achievement is celebrated, and this desire to be celebrated is innate and inherent in their spirit, in their moral fiber, and indeed in the Igbo cosmos. The traditional Igbo person does not just struggle to survive, he struggles to excel. This is referred to as the spirit of ***Nwakaibeya, and ikenga.*** Modern Western science of genetics will say that it is in the Igbo genes or in their DNA. Unfortunately, most of the neighbours of the Igbo often misconstrue this inate cultural propensity and Igbo ethos of drive for excellence as greed, selfishness, avarice, and aggressiveness, especially when they are outclassed and out witted in business enterprises and competition.

> Some how, the word **IGBO** as a name seems to have a cosmic connotation when the acronym is put under a linguistic microscope:
>
> **I**: I
> **G**: go/get ahead
> **B**: before
> **O**: others
>
> It is this natural propensity to achieve, to excel and to get ahead of others that propelled those great and "immortal" **Men of Timber and Women of Caliber** in Chapter Three above, to reach for the skies, and carve their names in gold and granite as icons.

In the traditional society title taking was the ultimate and highest ambition for most able bodied men. Ozo was the highest rank. It was the Igbo knighthood title. The Ozo man becomes an **Ichie,** that is he becomes a living ancestor: a custodian of the people's moral, spiritual, cultural and social values and heritage. It automatically elevated one above his peers and contemporaries. He walked high and tall, he spoke with airs of dignity and authority. When he cleared his throat to speak it was a signal for respectful silence. When he spoke, people listen with respect, and he was not to be interrupted or contradicted. He had absolute social immunity He was above any form of verbal or physical insult and assault. It was a sacrilege to physically or verbally assault an Ozo man or his wife.

A classic example in **Achebe—Things Fall Apart:**

> ***"Only a week ago, a man had contradicted him at a kindred meeting without looking at the man Okonkwo had said: "This meeting is for men". The man who had contradicted him had no titles. That was why Okonkwo had called him a woman".***
>
> The Ozo man in his full ceremonial regalia with all the paraphernalia is a spectacle to behold, like a British knight or a Christian bishop.
>
> Ozo is the highest but not the only title of achievement status among the Igbo. Before the invasion of Igboland by the Europeans, and before the Western currency systems were introduced in Igboland, the people were mainly agrarian. Yam was the main cash crop and the capital economic yardstick. It was basically a yam economy. A man's wealth was measured by the size of his yam barns, and achievement and titles were taken according to a man's yam power or the yam status of a man.

Symbols and icons of distinction:

In Igboland there are certain cultural symbols and paraphernalia that are used to denote rank, status and achievement. These symbols and paraphernalia compel attention, respect and reverence. Most of them carry the weight of authority. Just as in the military, the Police Force, and Aviation profession all over the world. Ranks and achievements are clearly denoted by certain paraphernalia attached to the uniform: strips, medals, colors, and the epaulets. These symbols and marks distinguish them from ordinary civilians and also speak of their level and weight of authority within the organization.

In the Igbo world, the objects used as symbols and paraphernalia of rank, status and distinction include:

Animal paraphernalia:

- **Elephant tusk**: ***(odu enyi)*** this is a very prized ivory ornament. In the traditional society it is one of the most important symbols of the Ozo cult. The Ozo man carried his ivory tusk as his staff of office. It was a traditional exclusive privilege. Sometimes the Ozo people used it as a trumpet in salutation of their colleages, and also in the performance of Ozo cult music, dance and funerals.

  The elephant tusk is used also as jewelry ornaments for neck beads, wrist bangles and anklets, which only the very rich can afford.
- B**uffalo horn: *(mpi atu)*** the buffalo horn is a very prized drinking vessel for the Ozo cult. The Ozo man did not use any ordinary vessel for drinking wine or water. His buffalo horn for drinking cup is very personal and exclusive. No body else dared to use it or toy with it.It is a very distinct status symbol.
- **Feathers:**

  Bird feathers used as status symbols include: **eagle feather, ostrich feather, parrot feather, and the peacock feather.**

  Of all animal paraphernalia, the **eagle feather** is the most recognized symbol of status and achievement in Igboland. The Ozo man flies an eagle feather on his red, white or black cap. It is also a symbol of the rich and the powerful.

  Parrot feather is cult symbol of the dibia cult—the medicine and juju cult symbol.

  Just as the Ozo man can be very easily tingudished by his ivory tusk, so the **eze dibia** can be recognized by the parrot feather on his cap.

Ostrich and peacock feathers are mostly decorative ornaments for the rich who can afford them. They are not specifically cultic symbols, but they are symbols of wealth and material achievement.

Some kinds of bird feathers were also used to fabricate hand fans. Whereas the ordinary man used fans woven from plant leaves and straws, the rich, the powerful and achievers used fans made of bird feathers and animal skin. For instance, a hand fan made of eagle feather or ostrich feather will be way out of the economic reach of the average person.

- **Animal skin**:

  Animal skins used as symbols of status and achievement include: tiger and leopard skin, crocodile skin, buffalo skin, gorilla skin, and ram skin. In the traditional society, a full titled Ozo man does not sit directly on any kind of stool, chair, or whatever. He placed an animal skin on the seat before he sat down on what ever, and rested his feet on an animal skin. His feet did not touch the ground. The cultural significance is to insulate himself from the social contamination of the ordinary person.

  The traditional society Ozo was a very high cult of moral and social purity. For this reason an Ozo man always carried three props on his person: his ivory tusk, skin bag, and his leather mat. In the good old days, the Ozo dignitary always had a page boy who carried the skin bag, the skin mat and his traditional carved cult stool (mpata in the dialect of the Old Anambra State). Also when he sat on his personal seat or throne, he rested his feet on an animal skin, because his feet must not touch the bare floor. It is worthy of note that the more dangerous the animal, the more highly prized the skin of the animal, and so also the more prestigious the status of the owner and user of the skin. Traditionally, monkey skin, gorilla skin and reptile skins are cult symbols of the **dibia cult,** the traditional medicine men.

- **Animal Tails:**

  Among the Igbo, animal tails used as status symbols are horse tail and cow tail whisks. In status ranking, color is the determinant factor. The highest ranking is the white, then the black, then the brown. One of the prominent symbols of distinction and status in the traditional society was the horse tail. Every Ozo man carried it on his person. The Ozo man's wife, his 'looloo' also carried a horse tail on her person especially at social ceremonies and festivals. The animal tails are also used in ceremonial performances.

The rich and the powerful also carried horse and cow tails as costume props and symbols of status.

Architecture and artifacts:

In the traditional society, architecture and artifacts are symbols of status and distinction. Just as in any modern society, the kind of house in which a person lives speaks of the financial status of the owner of the house. Specifically in Igboland, the two most important aspects of status are: the size of the compound and the design on the panels of the front entrance gates. Only the rich and the powerful could afford to have and maintain very large walled compound. Usually the compound contained the man's Obi—his reception front house, and the women's quarters or small individual quarters (apartments). This was the basic outlay of the homestead of the great and powerful, of chiefs and traditional rulers in Igboland.

The front door panels of a rich man's house is an artistic testimony of opulence, grandeur and taste. The door panels are made of special wood—iroko—(orji) or mahogany with various artistic designs, carvings, and sculptural embellishments.

Yam Culture

Yam was the principal economic crop and the yardstick of wealth and currency in Igboland before the Europeans introduced money currency. In other words, it was a yam economy and the power and status of a man was determined by the size of his farm and the size of his yam barn. In Nnewi clan and their neighbouring clans, in addition to the yam, wealth was also measured by number of palm trees and bread fruit trees *nkwu na ukwa.*

There were four traditional yam titles in those days.

- ***Ogbu ji:*** a yam farmer was called **Ogbu ji,** onye na egbu ji, the lowest rank, an equivalent of an freshman/ undergraduate, in the yam economy.
- ***Di ji:*** a very successful and prosperous yam farmer took the title **Di ji** meaning master of four yam barns, an equivalent of the bachelors degree in the yam profession.
- ***Di mkpa:*** If he grew richer and his yam harvest doubled four barns, he was qualified to take a higher yam title—**Di mkpa**—husband man or master of yam barns. His yam harvest—tubers and seedlings were counted in hundreds. A reference of this status is in Achebe **Things Fall Apart:**

  "There was a wealthy man in Okonkwo's village who had huge yam barns, His name was Nwakibie, and he had taken the highest but one title which a man could take in the clan. It was for this man that Oknonkwo worked to earn his first yam seedlings." In other words, in that yam economy, this man was a "money lender" an investment institution.

- **Dunu Ji or Eze Ji** was the highest yam title in Igboland, the equivalent of the modern millionaire, or a Ph.D. in the yam profession. In that economy he was a "Yam Estate Investor", and a multi-million industrialist. His yam harvest was not sold in the open market, they were sold in whole sale in barns to rich yam merchants.

However, time has changed. Economic systems have changed. People's mentality, social and moral paradigms and parameters have changed. The Igbo society has become increasingly diffused and divergent, old ways giving place to the new. So also the concept and meaning of titles and status, like most things and values are constantly under a state of flux and under attack by "modern" ideas and interpretations. For instance, in Europe and America the institutions of marriage and family have been undergoing new and various meanings and interpretations. Among some Igbo elements, title taking has lost the traditional, moral and ethical meaning and values. Nowadays the practice of people ascribing to themselves, and investing on themselves with all sorts of fake aliases and sobriquets is very much in vogue. Secondly, the availability of fake paraphernalia in the open market has seriously eroded credibility and compromised status and integrity. It would appear that by and large, **"419"** has taken over the game. A Mr. nobody you met at the park a couple of months ago in some won out pants and old tennis shoes, the next time you see him in an over size velvet gown with lion and elephant embroidery designs, red cap with a wild duck feather on his head, a twisted carved walking stick, and an imitation plastic ivory beads made in Taiwan round his neck. He holds out a dark skin leather fan with his left hand and expects you to salute him as ***Chief Aka ji aku One of Amaraka, federal capital of Njaba State., or chief Odozi Obodo One of Eke Oha.*** If you ask Chinua Achebe he will tell you that the reason for all this '***magamago'*** is that **Things have fallen apart, and 419 has taken over.** A real Imo man will simply heave his head in sadness and say '***ala aruola'***. This is sacrilege, the world has turned upside down.

Chapter Five

Kola-nut (Oji) culture:

Many Igbo scholars and writers have written much about Igbo kola-nut culture. The mention of it here as an aspect of Igbo cultural identity could, at the surface, sound like playing a very familiar old tune on a cranky grandfather gramophone record. However, there could be some Ndi-Igbo who will want to see it from a different or fresh perspective, as the Igbo proverb says: ***uche bu akpa, onye obula nya nkeya***: (wisdom is like a bag, everyone carries his own). The position we will want to take here is to demonstrate or establish the vital relevance of **oji** in the context of Igbo cultural identity.

The etymology of *oji:* If we formulate the word **oji** into a linguistic acronym and assign meaning to the individual letters, it will read this way:

O: stands for **Omenala.**
J: stands for **jikotara.**
I: stands for **Igbo.**

Put together the paraphrase of the acronym in meaning and interpretation is: ***Oji*** is the institution, culture, tradition or phenomenon that holds or unites all Igbo speaking people. The uniting factor of kola-nut is not just a metaphorical symbolism, it is a true practical reality in form, essence and a daily life experience. For instance, five or even ten or more Ndi-Igbo in a gathering can share one piece of kola-nut. One kola-nut could be cut into as many pieces as there are people present to share it. Even one cotyledon of kola-nut ***otu ibe oji*** could be cut into several bits so that all present can participate in a symbolic social and cultural unity. This is what happens at every social ceremony: marriage, wedding, naming, funeral, house dedication, land deal, reconciliation, town and family meetings, etc. This is a ritual symbolism of unity in practice and reality. It is a typical Igbo identity.

But among other tribes that consume kola-nut the Hausa and the Yoruba, two people don't share one kola—nut. It is one man one whole kola-nut. Although the seven Igbo states have and speak one language, there are dialectical variations and idiomatic nuances even within each state, and even within a local government area. For instance, in general social greetings some say: ***ndi be anyi nno nuu;*** some say-***ndi be anyi unu abiala;*** some say ***ndewo nuo;*** some say ***oha na eze mmama nu;*** some say ***ndi be anyi dalu nuuo;*** some say ***ndi beke anyi unu anwuchula;*** and some say ***ndi ala anyi ya gazie nuo.*** The point being made here is that kola-nut tradition or sharing could differ from one dialecticl zone to another, but its unique primacy or pride of place and useage are the same.

Species of kola-nut:

Oji Igbo: ***Cola acuminate*** **Gworo Oji Awusa:** ***Cola nitida***

At this stage it will be expedient to identify and differentiate the two species of kola, and to denote their significance for the Igbo. Botanically, there are two species of kola-nut namely—***oji Igbo (kola accuminata or atrophora),*** the multiple lobe specie, and the ***oji awusa or gworo—(kola nitida),*** the two lobe specie. The later ***kola nitida*** plant which is the more popular specie, grows in most parts of West Africa, and most luxuriantly in the Yourba west of Nigeria. In those areas it is a very valuable cash crop. But the other specie—the ***oji Igbo or the kola accuminata*** which is generally confined to the Igbo country areas is the less popular specie, but very highly valued by the Igbo for ritual and social ceremonies. This specie is largely grown for local consumption. It is this species that gives the Igbo a very distinct cultural identity.

As has been noted, for the Yoruba kola-nut is a very important economic cash crop that yields substantial revenue. So for the Yoruba the primary relevance of kola-nut is its cash value, although the traditional worshippers also use it for rituals and sacrifice. But for the educated and Christian Yourba, kola-nut has no important social value.

The Hausa on the other hand, consume kola-nut more than any other ethnic group in sub-Sahara Africa. In fact, the only time the adult Hausa man or woman is not chewing or gnawing kola (***gworo***) is when he/she is sleeping or eating food. But always, there is some quantity lodging inside the mouth. Give a Hausa man a kola-nut he will say ***sanu, naagwo de*** (thank you very much) and throw it whole and unceremoniously into his mouth and begin to chew and gnaw it for hours the whole day long. Although the kola plant does not thrive in the northern climate, the Hausa are the greatest consumers of ***kola nitada—gworo***.

The Igbo cultivate kola plant—mainly the ***Oji Igbo*** specie basically for local consumption within Igboland. The Igbo celebrate kola-nut with a lot of respect and cultural formality, across religious and educational boundaries. Whenever and wherever kola is presented, it is received and welcomed with respect and gratitude. It is an important act of hospitality, friendship and acknowledgement.

The host in whatever social context will present kola in a very formal way:

Host: ***Ndi be anyi, oji abiala.*** (our people kola has arrived, here is kola).

Response: ***Oji nno. Onye wetera oji wetara ndu.*** (**k**ola is welcome, he who brings kola brings life). This traditional or formal acknowledgement response to the presentation of kola says it all: that for the Igbo, kola-nut is a very important part of their religious, cultural and social life. Even at the highest level of Christian and church ceremonies such as ordination of a clergy, church or parish dedication, and church weddings, etc; kola-nut is the first item on the reception and entertainment program immediately after the religious formalities and rituals are concluded in the church sanctuary.

The Igbo use kola-nut for various reasons and occasions such as in the following:

- for personal, family and community prayer.
- in sharing kola-nut the Igbo celebrate God and give Him thanks.
- for invocation of blessing.
- for consultation and inquiry.
- to celebrate peace and reconciliation.
- to seal agreement and social contract.
- to celebrate unity and solidarity.
- to celebrate hospitality and friendliness.

In sharing of kola-nut age, rank and relationships can be established.

Perhaps the best epigramic expression of kola-nut in the Nigerian context is:

> **the Yoruba produce it most,**
> **the Hausa consume it most,**
> **the Igbo celebrate it most.**

Essentially, for Ndi-Igbo, kola-nut is not merely for consumption, it is for celebration. Wherever two or more Igbo men meet or are gathered, kola-nut is mentioned or presented. In a traditional setting, kola-nut has well defined format and cultural protocol. It has its own cultural language and oral literature in the presentation, blessing, cutting and sharing. This is why the Igbo of Anambra say: ***ofeke anaghi awa oji,*** meaning a fool or an irresponsible fellow does not break or bless kola-nut.

The anatomy and structure of *oji Igbo:* the significance of size, color and lobes.

Because kola-nut occupies such a high and central position in the cultural and social life of the Igbo, the physical nature and structure of oji have cosmic significations.

The nature and structure of oji include the size, color, and the number of lobes (***ibe oji)*** contained in a kola-nut. Just as the quality of gold is measured by its karat quality and content, the nature and amount of lobes of kola-nut has much relevance in Igbo cosmology.

1. ***oji ugo***: the yellowish color specie of oji, this is very highly prized and esteemed as the 'eagle' or 'king' of kola-nuts. It is the primus inter pares in the oji hierarchy. ***Oji ugo wu eze nwakaibeya:***
2. ***oji ikenga:*** the kola-nut with three lobes, is a symbol of prestige and achievement.
3. ***oji ibe nne/ oji nwanne:*** four lobes—in Igbo cosmology four is a mystic number, a number of completion, eg the four market days that make one Igbo week ***(izu) Eke, Afo, Nkwo, Orie.*** In the days when cowrie was used as the monetary system, cowries were counted in multiples of four. The Mbaise people have a saying about four—***ihe rue na ano, ya a noro. (***When something gets to four, it makes an impact and stops). The nut that has four lobes is a symbol of brotherhood, fraternity and completeness.
4. ***oji uba na omumu:*** (the five lobed) when a kola-nut is split open and it has five lobes, the people rejoice because it symbolizes prosperity and fertility.
5. ***oji agbata ndu:*** (the six lobed) symbol of unity and harmony between the living and the spirit world. Usually the smallest lobe is thrown outside for the unseen spirits, and the people share the other five lobes. The occurrence of six lobes is not very common, it is as rare as ***oji ugo. I***t is a happen-stance phenomenon.
6. ***afa oji: oji gbara agba: (size)*** big and very presentable kola-nut**.**
7. ***aka oji*** : the kola-nut or lobe that is the privilege of the person who breaks the kola-nut, a type of entitlement of respect.
8. ***ihe so oji:*** things or condiments that go with oji. Because ***oji*** itself has a slight bitter taste, there are certain cultural items

that go with it to neutralize the bitter taste of kola-nut. These include:

9. ***ose oji:*** alligator pepper—it is the most common accompaniment and companion of ***oji***
10. ***okwa ose:*** a concoction of ingredients and spices, blended into a paste for eating kola-nut. This is always very much appreciated especially in very formal and important ceremonies such as: town meetings, marriage ceremonies, and child-naming. The ingredients and spices blended into a paste include: crayfish, smoked fish, fried melon—***egwusi*** or groundnuts, pepper, a pinch of table salt, and some other local spices such as ***uzuza***.
11. ***nmanya:*** palm wine and beer and other kinds of liquor go very well with kola-nut, especially with the elite and traditional enthusiasts.
12. ***afufa na mkpru ofe, (mkpuru anara):*** cabbage and garden egg also make very good accompaniment.

Oji Language and idioms: This is one of the cultural aspects of Igbo identity:

Onye wetara oji, wetara ndu: a person who brings/offers kola brings life (wishes every one long life)

- ***Oji na ebu uzo okwu:*** kola takes precedence before any other matter/ issue
- ***A naghi ekwukpo oji okwu:*** no dialogue or business takes precedence over or before kola
- ***Ebute oji ebute okwu***: kola opens the door for discussion and dialogue, when kola is presented, the purpose of the gathering is decleared. In other words, the presentation of kola-nut calls a meeting to order.
- ***Oji nwere nso, nwe usoro*** kola has taboos, protocol and conventional procedure
- ***Oji na akowa ony wu onye:*** kola establishes who's who in any gathering
- ***Oji rue uno, o kwue ebe osi:*** when kola gets home, it will tell where it came from

- ***E ji oji edo agbata***: kola is used to establish peace and reconciliation.
- ***Ebute oji, nwakuche amuta ako:*** During the blessing and sharing of kola, a diligent person learns/ gains wisdom.
- ***A nata oji, a nata akpa uche:*** the occasion of sharing kola-nut is also an occasion of sharing and gaining conventional wisdom.
- ***Ofeke anaghi aghota ije oji:*** a fool doesn't understand the cultural process and the protocols in sharing of kola.
- ***Oji eze di eze n'aka.*** The kola is in the hands of the right/ legitimate person
- ***Oji ugo wu eze nwakaibeya:*** oji ugo is the choicest and most prestigious specie of kola-nut, the king in the oji family.
- ***Oji anaghi ako na akpa nze:*** the bag or house of an elder never lacks kola. This is a very powerful testimony that kola-nut plays very important role in the cultural life of the Igbo.
- ***Ndi Igbo anaghi ata oji ka Awusa, Ndi Igbo n'akwanyere oji ugwu***—the Igbo do not eat kola-nut like the Hausa, the Igbo celebrate kola. The presentation of kola-nut in a social gathering is always a hilarious social drama, culturally therapeutic and a soothing social tonic.
- ***Oji anaghi asu bekee:*** kola-nut does not speak English meaning, no matter the degree or sophistication, elitism or foreign environment, kola-nut culture is so strongly and deeply rooted in Igbo language and culture that it cannot be culturally adulterated. So to attempt to celebrate **oji** in any other tradition or language dosen't make much sense.no matter how good the translation. The cultural idiom and the finesse of Igbo linguistics do not have any parallel or suitable equivalent in English translation. In fact it is even among the educated and the Igbo elite that kola-nut is assuming greater visibility and prominence as an Igbo identity.

The celebrating of kola-nut includes the following procedure:

1. The presentation—***iche oji.***
2. The blessing—***igo oji.***

3. Breaking—***iwa oji.***
4. The sharing—***ikee/ibufe oji.***
5. Social exchanges and nuances—***okwu na njakiri n' eso oji.***

This traditional format in the presentation and sharing of kola is often referred to as **"The Social Drama of Igbo kola Culture" (**Dr. Afam Ebeogu 1988?).

Although it has been clearly stated inter alia, ***oji anaghi asu bekee,*** (oji does no speak English), the presentation that follows below will be presented in English translation for technical reasons: Basically and foremost the celebration of koal is a colloquial tradition, it is formatted and linguistically deeply embedded in the oral genre.

Secondly, to avoid the complexity and conflict of linguistic and literary mis-representation and the controversy of autographical inaccuracy. Thirdly, to avoid the dialectical and linguistic variations and nuances that abound in Igbo language and local idiomatic structures. Fourthly, to avoid any criticism of dialectical bias or prejudice, ***(maka a diamama***), because there is an ocean of difference between the colloquial and the written language. We are also very mindful of the fact that there are some components of the Igbo population that are not very familiar with Igbo language in the written form. Lastly, to afford our readers of non-Igbo origin the ease of literary understanding and appreciation of Igbo oji culture.

Dramatic dialogue in Kola presentation:

In any gathering, whether in a private home or in a public social setting, the host presents the kola, usually in a kola bowl ***(okwa oji)*** or plate. Then the kola dramatic dialogue begins.

Host: This is kola.

Guest(s) Response: Thank you, kola is welcome.

Then there is a look around for the most culturally appropriate person to receive the kola from the host. The qualifications include:

1. Age.
2. Title.

3. Relationship with the host, first by physical proximity of residence or neighborhood, (***onye agbata obi),*** and secondly by sanguinity or blood relationship.
4. The office of stewardship: This seemingly minor duty of serving ***ibu oji, a***mong the Anambra Igbo, is the duty or privilege of a ***"nwadiana".*** In certain settings or cultural environment, this minor service or the duty of carrying round the kola bowl, could be very seriously contentious. It could raise a hail of storm and controversy especially among the Anambara people. Every contestant has to very diligently prove, beyond every reasonable doubt, that his mother has the closest blood relationship with the host more than any other person in that gathering. So it behoves any ambitious contender to be very knowledgeable of some vital relationship details of his mother's background. Among the people of Imo State, this knowledge of one's ***ibenne,*** is very crucial and ignorance of it is regarded as the epitome of foolishness***: onye iberibe, onye apari amaghi na ibenne ya wu mba ukwu.*** (A fool doesn't know that his mother's place is a mighty fortress and life refuge). The lack of the knowledge of one's mother's family background and relationships could be used as taunt and ridicule against such an ignoramus contender.

Sometimes this stage of appropriateness of person alone could take a whole lot of time of explanation, arguments and very heated debate. But all this is relevant and important in order to ensure that full protocol is observed, and that the kola is put in the hands of the most culturally appropriate person. Often times the arguments and the debate could a generate a 'war of words' and vicious sarcastic exchanges. But it is quite a exhilarating drama of serious jokes usually punctuated with classic idioms, proverbs, parables, anecdotes, and very pungent innuendoes.

It is important to state here that one cultural identity of the adult Igbo is that they speak in parables and idioms. There is a popular traditional adage: ***onye aturu ilu o si ka akowara ya, ego ejiri lu nne ya nara iyi.*** (an adult who hears a parable and requests for the explanation, shows that the dowry paid on his mother is a waste). That adult is a very big fool.

According to Chinua Achebe, ***inu bu nmanu okwu ji eri ji,*** (idiom/parable is like the the palm oil which is used for eating yams, in speech words use proverbs like palm oil for eating yam). In fact among the Igbo one yardstick of intelligence and wisdom, is the capacity and eloquence in idiomatic expression. All this is the fun and humor ***(njakiri n'eso oji),*** verbal jabs and exciting punches of humor which only those born and bred in Igbo linguistic culture can understand and enjoy. Anyone who doesn't have the tough skin to absorb the sting, jabs and punches of ***njakiri***, or people who have skeletons and cobwebs in their cupboard, cautiously stay away from the ring side in order to avoid the social 'missiles' and 'bullets' of ***njakiri.*** The high and low gist of **njakiri oji** could be as painful as the sting of ***agbisi***. For the Igbo, this is one aspect of kola culture which gives vibrance, pep and hilarity to any social gathering. It provides a healthy social appetizer for the next item on the program.

It is at this stage of kola-nut presentation that one is exposed to the richness of Igbo oral and linguistic heritage: the various genres of Igbo cultural and linguistics expressions, the manipulation and the dynamics of words and wit, the nuances and the finesse in folklore oratory, the command and excellence in literary performance. It is also here that the socio-cultural values and norms of human relationships all come into full play. A lot of wit and wisdom is thrown and bounced around in humor and hilarity. That is why as was stated earlier ***ebute oji, nwakauche amuta ako (***it is at the presentation and celebration of kola that a diligent person learns and gains more wisdom). In fact for the Igbo, kola-nut is an institution for the study, transmission, promotion and preservation of Igbo oral heritage. It has been and still remains a school for traditional and informal education, albeit in dramatic dialogue.

Stage 2. Blessing: The kola passes from the presenter to the person who is judged the most appropriate person to break it. With the kola now in his hands, all the noisy exchanges of ***njakiri oji*** quickly fades into a hush and respectful silence, ***maka na oji n'aso anya***. (kola-nut demands respect). It is prayer time, the ritual invocation of blessing. It is this second stage of kola-nut drama that shows that the Igbo are very religious and spiritual people. This stage is highly loaded with utterances and philosophy of religious, spiritual, moral and ethical concepts and values.

The performer (that is the person blessing the kola) picks or selects the choicest kola-nut from the bowl, lifts it up to wards the ceiling (sky), with his eyes very focus on the kola, he begins a prayer and invocation in this traditional pattern:

- Acknowledging and thanking the Almighty God (***Chineke bi n'igwe, Olisabuwa.***) for providing the kola through the host.
- Implores God to accept and bless the kola.
- Prays God to pour out His blessings on the host, all the guests and all their families.
- Invokes God's blessing: protection and provision for all present.
- Invokes God's protection against all enemies, ***ndi nmuo an ndi ajoo madu, ndi amosu, ndi obi nsi na ndi obi ojoo, ndi oshi an ndi 419, ndi ocho nga noko, ndi agbata ekee, ndi okwu n' uka, ndi odu chi egbu, ndi abani di egwu.***
- Prays for fertility for humans and livestock, and rich harvest from crops and their businesses.
- Prays for love and unity among the brethren: ***egbe bere ugo bere, nke si ibeya ebela, nku kwapu ya; anu kpawa ibeya kpawa, nke si ibeya akpala, ama ya shie.***
- Prays for good moral behavior: ***Chineke e kwela ka nwa main road biara anyi uwa,*** (nwa main road means a bastard child, child born out of wedlock). This speaks of Igbo moral and family values. In other words, kola-nut is reminding and emphasizing to adults and parents of their cultural and moral obligations and responsibilities to their children and to the society at large. A bastard is a very repugnant and shameful stigma and a taboo in Igbo culture.
- Prays for long life and prosperity for all.
- Prays for the success of the day and the business of the moment.

As the performer utters each statement or phrase of prayer, the people respond in unison amen in the local dialect of the environment. The most common in a mixed audience include: ***isee!, ihaa!, ofor!*** The solemnity of the prayer is so grave and reverential that nothing is allowed to interrupt or distract while the kola-nut prayer is in process. And because of the vital essence and solemnity of kola-nut prayer the Igbo will not allow this cultural awesome task to be performed by a foolish, irresponsible, culturally ignorant, morally bankrupt, inconsequential or worthless fellow ***(ofeke, onye apari, nwa oseaka, onye amakekwu, gagwo, onye ihurihu).***

Kola-nut culture transcends the boundaries of dialect or state, educational, religious, social sophistication, time and place. Both at home and abroad (diaspora) kola culture continues to hold the pride of place, and is a sine qua non in Igbo cultural life. So the veracity of the statement that he who brings kola brings life is very self evident and incontrovertible, because he has caused or provided the occasion for prayer for good health, long and better life.

In the traditional setting, an elder or a titled man begins his day with breaking kola with which he offers prayer of thanksgiving and invokes God's blessings and protection on his household. Kola-nut is offered to most people who call or visit from dawn to dusk. The frequency of this prayer process has no limit. It is repeated as many times as people call or visit, both for formal or informal reasons. During my early teens, I had the privilege of spending some of my holidays at my maternal uncle's house. That uncle was a high ozo title man, an icon in that village. He always sat at his ***obi*** most of the time, People passing by especially the men-folk, usually stopped by to share pleasantries which also involved sharing of kola-nut. One day my curiosity compelled me to start taking count of the number of times my uncle shared kola with people who came and went. The first day I counted eleven. The second day I counted thirteen. The third day I counted ten. That was an average of eleven, so he offered prayers eleven times with kola-nut every day. This did not include the private personal kola-nut prayer he said before his chi and ikenga every morning he woke up. As an adult and as a Christian, my prayer life continues to be challenged by my uncle's prayer habit and frequency. My uncle's example is the same and typical of the traditional Igbo man and exemplifies the religious and spiritual relevance and value of the kola-nut with respect to Igbo religious and spiritual life, and as an aspect of cultural identity.

Oji Igbo versus oji Awusa:

As has been stated hitherto, there are two species of kola-nut. In fact it is believed among heathens that it is a sacrilege to offer ***oji awusa*** to an Igbo dignitary or divinity, and that could incur the anger and visitation of the divinity. ***Igbo anaghi echere ala oji awusa*** (the Igbo do not offer the earth goddess ***oji awusa***.) Oji Awusa is never used in any ritual or sacrifice or in any serious cultural ceremony.

A typical scenario was when His Excellency Chief Alex Ekweme, the Ideh of Aguata, and former Vice President of the Federal Republic of Nigeria, visited Los Angeles in 1997, The Igbo Cultural Association of Southern California received him at a Town Hall meeting. A large bowl of kola-nuts was presented as a mark of high respect for such a dignitary. It was the late Professor Boniface Obichere, who did the presentation of the kola to the distinguished visitor. But it was all **gworo (oji awusa),** large and fresh and quite attractive to the eyes. Every one seemed impressed with the quantity and visual appearance of the bowl of kola-nuts on the high table. But the unexpected happened when it came for the august visitor to pick the choicest kola for blessing and breaking. It was discovered that there was not one ***oji Igbo*** in the bowl, but there were more than forty ***gworo.*** The high title **Nze na ozo Ichie Ekwueme** could not find any oji in the bowl of kolanuts. It was declared that there was no ***oji*** because the Igbo do not use ***oji awusa*** for important cultural and social events, especially one of such magnitude. It was such a great embarrassment to al**l.** Suppressed angry voices rose from the audience from all directions in the hall and the gallery, questioning and castigating the persons who committed this "abominable act". One angry voice of protest said: "***ndia anyuo nsi n'unuka"*** meaning some body has pooed in the church, (in Igbo language and culture this is an expression of the highest insult, indecency and dishonor, a sacrilege).

For about five minutes the hall was enveloped in a thick cloud of suffocating silence, whispers of accusation, finger pointing, shame and embarrassment. The elders and patriots at the high table were scratching their foreheads and eye brows in shame and guilt. The youths were murmuring loud in protest and condemnation.

And because ***anaghi ekwukpo oji okwu,*** meaning no business or discussion can precede kola ceremony), all discussions and business were suspended. Some smart guys were dispatched to rush to downtown to scout for **oji Igbo** and to procure it at any cost, and to bring it with haste, as Chief Zebrudaiah alias 430, would say: "with atomatik speed and alakrity." In the interim, the guest of honor displayed an incredible magnanimity and equanimity of mind in gracious composure, chatting and making "senior joke" with the elders around him at the high table, as if nothing of consequence has gone wrong.

It was a display of the sterling character, dignity and wisdom of a seasoned elder statesman. The incident was a great lesson for all and sundry: ***anaghi eji oji awusa eme omenala.*** (the Igbo do not use ***oji awusa*** in serious cultural ceremony). And more importantly, it was a very significant lesson on the prime position of kola-nut in Igbo cultural life, whether at home or in the diaspora.

Chapter Six

Family Agnates and Institutions: (The Social and Cultural Dynamics)

Umunna
Ikwunne/ Ibe nne
Umuada/ Umuokpu

Linguistically ***umunna*** means generations of people of the same ancestry or lineage, the kindred of a progenitor of family tree. In Igbo social cosmology, ***umunna*** is the nucleus of a village. A conglomeration of ***umunna*** constitute the clan. The word ***umunna*** is a composite of two words: ***umu***—children, and ***nna***—father. Literary translated ***umunna*** means children of the same father. The father in this context is the grand progenitor or the founder of the lineage. In sociological terms umunna is the principal power and governing authority in the family system or institution. The *umunna* is the large umbrella that covers every body in the family structure: man and woman, child and adult. However because the Igbo society is primarily pater-lineal, the executive, legislative and judicial functions, decision-making are the prerogative of the male gender.

All members of this large family unit owe unflinching loyalty and allegiance to the ***umunna***. The action of a member could bring pride or shame to the whole family. This is affirmed by the Igbo proverb: ***otu mkpisi aka ruta nmanu, ozuo ahu onu: (***if one finger is dipped in oil, the oil ultimately spreads and stains the whole body). So in every circumstance ***umunna*** always strive to ensure that members conform to proper code of conduct, acceptable moral and ethical behavior. Deviants and miscreants face consequences of fine (nha), or suspension and excommunication (nsupu / nmapu).

The traditional Igbo concept of family is very much unlike the western concept of family which in the the western definition is "me, my wife and my children". The **umunna** offers and ensures protection to every member from both internal and external attack and aggression. This is exemplified in **Things Fall Apart**—(Chinua Achebe), that was why the people of **Umuofia** went to war when the people of Mbaino kidnapped and killed a young damsel a daughter of Umuofia. (Things Fall Apart, Chapter 2.).

Every umunna functions to defend and protect its members. But if and when a person becomes very intransigent, defiant, confrontational, or constitutes himself beyond the discipline and authority of his umunna, he could be slapped with the heaviest punishment which is usually excommunication or ostracism: total exclusion from all rights and privileges of family membership. If the person happens to die in that situation of excommunication, he also forfeits the rights of funeral and proper burial. In the olden days his remains ended up in ***ajo ofia*** (the evil forest) where his carcass made good meal for vultures, scavenging rodents and reptiles.

The seriousness of the role and authority of the institution of ***Umunna*** is put in very graphic idioms: ***onye karia umunna ya, udele e were ya mee ngwongwo na ajo ofia*** (when a person utterly defies his umunna, vultures will use his carcass for spicy snack). ***Onye umunna ya rere efuola.*** (a person sold by his umunna is lost and beyond redemption for ever). It will also be recalled that during the era of slave trade, it was those black sheep of the family that became the first victims to be disposed of by their ***umunna.***

This sounds very scary but it emphasizes the need for good conduct, order, discipline, responsibility and conformity. This system of social control goes to refute and debunk the obnoxious idea among some Europeans that before the white man invaded Ala Igbo, Ndi-Igbo were a race of unorganized bush people that had no form of governance or administrative structure.

The importance and vital role of the institution of Umunna are very well expressed in some traditional Igbo names:

- ***Umunnaka:*** Ummunna is very powerful, it is the supreme authority.
- ***Umunnanweike***: Umunna has power and authority.
- ***Azuka:*** my people are great for me.
- ***Azubuugwu***: my back—family are my strength and my pride.
- ***Ikwuazom***: my people are my savior and my security.
- ***Umunnakwe***: I will prevail by the grace and goodwill of my family.
- ***Umunnabuenyi***: Umunna is big and as powerful as the elephant.

Igbo family agnates: Ikwu na ibe. :

Traditionally every Igbo person who is the product or offspring of two legitimate parents belongs to four agnatic blocks of relationship namely:

1. ***Umunna***: one's father's male relations
2. ***Ikwunne*** or ibenne: one's mother's home and relations.
3. ***Ikwunna*** : one's father's mother's birth place and kindred.
4. ***Ndi ogo***: in-laws. A man's wife's family and her relations

Umunna: As has been said hitherto, a person's umunna consists of his father and all his father's male relations—brothers and all his paternal uncles. This is an Igbo man's closest ties, his tap-root and backbone. He owes unflinching duty of loyalty, dedication and support to his umunna and all that his umunna stands for. In return he enjoys the protection and security of his umunna. Umunna offers all the moral, material and emotional support a man needs to be a useful and productive member of the group. They stood with and by him in all the events of life and death. They would go to war if he was kidnapped or killed. They organized his ransom if need be. All those privileges and rights were also extended to his wife and children. In the good old days, if a man showed no interest in marriage, his umunna 'compelled' him to marry, or they married on his behalf and impose a bride on him. And as the saying goes: ***madu anaghi efe umunna ya aka n'isi:*** (***a*** man cannot defy or do battle with his umunna), rather a man would sink or swim with his umunna in all circumstances.

Ikwunne/ Ibenne:

Ikwunne or ibenne is one's mother's family/kindred and home village. In effect every Igbo person has two homes: his umunna, his father's home (into which he/she was born), and all his/her father's relations; and his/her mother's family and kindred. Although the Igbo society is primarily patrilineal, and heritage is based on patrimony, the motherland offers certain socio-cultural components which the fatherland does not have and may not be able to afford. For instance, whereas the fatherland could banish or ostracize an intransigent male member, can deny a man of funeral or burial rights and privileges, the motherland forbids any such harsh or extreme punishments to ***umu diana***.(offsprings of their daughter) In other words, the motherland is the safest refuge for any child or adult. The Igbo proverb: ***oso chuwa nwata, o gbala ikwunne ya, (***if a child is driven out and expelled by his family, he takes refuge in his motherland). This is very well illustrated in the situation when Okonkwo the hero in **Things Fall Apart** was forced into a compulsory exile for seven years when he committed involuntary manslaughter:

> "***it's true that a child belongs to its father. But when a father beats his child, he seeks sympathy in his mother's hut. A man belongs to his father when things are good and life is sweet. But when there is sorrow and bitterness, he finds refuge and protection in his motherland."*** (**Things Fall Apart,** chapter 14, p. 134).

Okonkwo's motherland did not just offer him and his large family of three wives and their children refuge and shelter, "***he was given a large plot of ground on which to build his compound, three pieces of land on which to farm***." He had free labor at his beck and call.

He was treated like the chief he was in his fatherland, but with great affection and profound compassion and dignity.

Actually in Igboland, there is no situation or stage in a person's life, from the cradle to the grave that a person's **ibenne** does not play very active and prominent roll. A good child/person is treated and pampered like a sacred cow in his **ibenne.** In Nnewi clan they say: ***nwadi ana wu eke.*** (one is treated like a sacred python) in one's mother's village. Even members of the mother's ***umunna*** don't enjoy the same pampering and indulgence as **umudiana.**

The place and cultural significance of the **Ibenne/ Ikwunne** are very eloquently expressed and reflected in some traditional Igbo names:

***Nneamaka*: mother is a great asset.**
***Nneoma*: mother is a thing of joy and treasure.**
***Ezinne*: mother is amazing.**
***Nnebuka*: mother is a tremendously great.**
***Nneazom*: mother has saved me.**
***Nnebundo*: mother is a great refuge and shelter.**
***Nnebuenyi*: mother has elephantine value.**
***Ugwunne*: mother has gracious value.**
***Nnebunne*: mother is there for me always.**
***Udenne:* I am by the grace of my mother.**
***Ibenne*: salute to my mother's family.**
***Akunne:* a mother's treasure.**

Umuada/ Umuokpu:

The institution or association of ***Umuada*** is an organization that is not found any where else in the Nigerian context or in the Western European world. It is typically and uniquely Igbo, and it is another phenomenon of Igbo identity. The etymology of the word ***Umuada*** is a compound of two words: ***umu*** and ***ada***—literarily it means the daughters of the same father. The word daughters in this context means all female progenies or descendants from a common family tree or progenitor. ***Umuokpu*** as they are called in Amambra State is the same etymological derivative of a compound of two words: ***umu*** and ***okpu,*** okpu means taproot or spine bone. U***muokpu*** means all female progenies descended from the same taproot or from a common progenitor. ***Umuokpu or Umuada*** means the same thing expressed in Igbo dialectical variants. In other words, all females that trace their origin to a common progenitor or father ancestor belong to this family institution. These females grow up and may get married into the same village, or outside into other villages or clans. Those of them who are "lucky" to be married into or around the village of their birth are generally referred to as ***amuru n'uno bi n'uno***—meaning, born and bred and married at home, in the popular Igbo parlance—'**daughters of the soil.'** (the spouse of the present writer belongs to this group). In some quarters they are also known or referred to as ***'Adaejemba' (***this daughter will not leave home, will not go to a foreign land). The ***Umuada*** who marry outside their home village or into other towns and clans, are referred to as ***Umuada bi na mba*** or as they say it in slang ***'Umuada abroad'*** the group of ***Umuada*** who live in "foreign lands".

A joke (war of words) about these two groups: the ***amuru n'uno bi n'uno*** generally express or carry about themselves some airs of pride and superiority, that they are more beautiful and so indispensable that the home village cannot afford to lose them to any "foreign" suitors. They claim that only the ugly ones could be 'disposed' off to foreign suitors, the best are retained at home. On the other hand, the ***Umuada abroad,*** refute this position, that they are the best and the most beautiful ones. They claim that they are the show piece and the pride of the village, the ***'Ada eji eje mba',*** the ones that possess the potentials that can attract and compel the attention and desire of foreign suitors. In other words, they are more marketable commodity than the "rejects" that will forever remain home bound. They call themselves ***ihe oma eji eje mba,*** the pride and treasure which the family is proud to show off in beauty contests. The good ones that go places, while the ugly ones stay home.

Hovever, all these daughters wherever they are (at home or abroad), see and regard themselves as sisters. They organize themselves into a kind of solid and powerful sorority which the Igbo call **Otu Umuada/ Otu Umuokpu.** Back home **Umuada** hold their meetings in any of the three venue systems of their choice:

1. At the obi of their common traditional home (***obi umunna ha dum)***
2. At the residence of the eldest of them all who is usually the chairperson or president of the association: (***n' ulo onye isi ada ha)***, a mark of honor and respect for age and seniority.
3. Some adopt the rotational venue system: ***n' ulo n'ulo be ndi otu ha.***

The primary objectives and functions of the *Otu Umuada* sorority include**:**

- **For mutual solidarity and protection** among their members. Wherever they are **Otu Umuada/Umuokpu** always form a united front to protect themselves from the maltreatment and excesses of abusive husbands. If the case of their member is justified and clearly apparent, **Umuada** can always rally round to give moral, material and physical support in defense of their victimized or suffering member in several ways: they could make appeals to all parties for a peaceful resolution of the conflict or problem. They will intercede and will "fight" for the safety and security of their member. In the traditional society, if **Umuada** takes up arms against a man, it invariably ends in a disaster for the man however highly placed or powerful that individual could be. The popular Igbo idiom regarding confrontation with ***Umuada: Onye n'eche Umuada ogu, ji nne ya achu aja nmuo*** (a man who picks up fight with ***Umuada,*** is offering his mother for sacrifice to the evil spirits). The truth of the matter is that every woman including every one's mother is a member of ***otu Umuada.*** Therefore by extension, to fight ***Umuada*** is tantamount to fighting one's mother and one's sisters. My uncle always said: ***nwoke n'eche Umuokpu ogu n'agwo onwe ya na apiti: (***a man who fights ***Umuada*** smears himself with stinking mud and dirt).
- For their mutual social and economic welfare: ***Umuada*** have financial resources and power which accrue from the entrance fee of new members; their regular membership dues and contributions, fines and donations from various other sources.

They invest their funds in self-help programs such as ***isusu,*** contributions and interest on loans given to their members. By this means, members are empowered to do profitable Small scale business and develop economic strength and independence from stingy and selfish husbands.

- For social and moral control and discipline among their members and in the homes of their brothers and uncles. ***Umuada*** always keep very vigilant eyes over the domestic welfare of their brothers and uncles, and do not hesitate in disciplining any erring wife ***(Ndi inyiom di).***
- For promoting love and unity among the children of their members. In some communities, especially in the Nnewi Local Government area of Anambra State, there is always a big cultural celebration at the end of the year general meetings, which is festivity and merrymaking, It is obligatory for ***Umuada*** to attend with all their children. This is a great forum for cousins to meet, know and socialize with one another
- For promoting and strengthening their cultural roots.

In many communities the ritual of the annual reunion of ***Umuada*** with their home families and village, has tremendous positive cultural effects. The organization of ***Umuada*** is so strong and powerful, and their annual home-coming is so compelling for them to the point of addiction. Many young men who had been "lost" in foreign lands like Lagos, Kano and Jos, are "dragged" home by their wives association of ***Otu Umuada.*** Hitherto, such folks preferred to spend their leave and Christmas holidays "abroad". In the language of an old and frustrated mother: "***ha bi na tanship n'emefusi ego ha ebe ha naeri hotel n'nu bar",*** (they stay in the township wasting their money in hotels and beer parlors).

Umuenem village in Nnewi is a good case study. December 27 of every year is set apart and called **Umuokpu Day**. It is a great festival day for all and sundry—Christians and non-Christians. Every December 27 before noon, ***Umuokpu*** and their entourage of children go to their individual families with gifts to present their children to their maternal grandparents ***Oku Nwokpu (***their off-springs—their human treasures) which they have achieved. The grandchildren bring gifts and presents of cultural value. The boys bring faggots of fire wood, and the girls bring pitchers of drinking water. In return the grandparents bless them with prayer and material gifts. Each grandson is given a rooster, and each granddaughter is given a choice big yam. This is the traditional minimum. In many cases the boys could be given nanny goats, and the girls, young lambs. The ethical and cultural symbolism of these female animals is to inculcate in the children a strong sense of responsibility to care and fend for the baby animals and to nurture them to yield. In subsequent annual visits the children are expected to bring to their grandparents the first off-spring of each of their animals in addition to other traditional presents.

At noon on December 27, the whole village assemble at the village square for agreat merrymaking. Troops of dancers, masquerades, acrobats and musicians come to perform at the square. Men come with kegs and gallons of palm-wine. Women come with pots and basins of delicious traditional dishes. It is always eating and drinking galore. It is always a great cultural return and reunion of ***ndi uno and ndi ofia,*** (home people and people from "abroad"). It is always a day children look forward to receive gifts from their grandparents, and to enjoy the pomp and pageantry of a traditional carnival, and very importantly, to reunite with their cousins. Parents and grandparents also look forward to it for reuniting with their daughters and their grandchildren.

4. ***Otu Umuada*** as a powerful institution of social control and moral discipline:

In Igboland, ***Otu Umuada*** is one powerful cultural organisation of social control. Their power and effectiveness manifest especially in events of traditional marriage, funeral rites and ceremonies. They are so strongly united and unbending in their resolve and determination, that any person in his/her right senses would do every thing necessary to avoid collision and confrontation with them. Their unwritten laws and constitution are like the laws of the Medes and Persians, 'written on rocks'. The traditional parlance in describing the formidable power of ***Otu Umuada*** is***: Onye akpakwana nwa agu aka n'odu, ma odi***

ndu, ma o nwuruanwu translated, no one should mess or toy with the baby of a tiger (cub) whether the tiger is dead or alive.

A case scenario:

This is a true historical event that happened in a village in Nnewi Local Government area of Anambra State around 1986:

There was this rich and well established man (popularly known as ***"Chief Ideh Akajiaku* 1 *of Eko Lagos",*** he lived in Lagos with his wife and their three children. Along the line, his 419 business and flirtatious life style turned his life upside down, and his home into a burning hell. His illicit affairs with a lady secretary in one of his super-market stores resulted into a pregnancy. Some days the "Ideh 1" would not even return home but spent nights and weekends with his sweet sixteen secretary in Five Star hotels. Naturally this agitated his wife and she started to complain and to nag.

But the "Ideh 1" remained adamant and arrogant. He boasted that he was the owner and boss of his house and his booming business. He became very abusive and threatened his wife with violence, repatriation and divorce. One day he arrogantly announced he has decided to bring in the sweet sixteen mistress into the house as a second wife. At this juncture a violent altercation ensued. The "Ideh" went wild with violence, literally mauled his wife mercilessly, battered and bruised her face so badly that she looked like the victim of a ghastly vehicle accident.

A couple of days after he carried out his threat of repatriation. At mid night he stormed into the wife's bedroom with a loaded gun in his hand, yelled in a voice full of terror and finality the ultimatum: "choose between instant death and being bundled back to the village this night right now!" Of course the helpless woman chose life and accepted to be 'deported' to the village. "There is a dandfo bus waiting outside to take you home and I give you thirty minutes to disappear from this house!"

In his very brutish machoism, the man forcibly repatriated his wife and his three children to the village and brought in the sweet sixteen mistress (***nwada***).

Thenceforth, the wife and her three children were abandoned in the village in utter neglect, without any kind of financial support or provision. When the man learned that his own mother had taken over the care and provision of his abandoned wife and children, the man cut off all financial aid and subsistence which he used to give his mother. He also cut off electricity and tap-water from the mansion. His old mother was diabetic and had complications of arthritis. So when all her means of medication and nourishment were abruptly short down, emotional pain added insult to injury.

Every body in the village heard about this pathetic situation, some were cursing out the Ideh and his new mistress to hell and death. Some suspected that ***'ihe nkaa agbaghi aka, nwayi ashawo a ji ogwu'. (***this kind of behaviour is not ordinary, this prostitute of a secretary has used witchcraft and juju on the man). After a protracted battle with illness, depression and neglect, the old woman succumbed and died. The news of the death of the old woman immediately provided ***Umuokpu*** with very powerful weapon and ammunition. They decided to use the occasion of his mother's death to deal squarely with him.

First Umuokpu went to the traditional village head and requested him to advise the police not to interfere on the occasion of the funeral ceremonies. Then Umuada hired a bulldozer and paid the operator to bulldoze down the front walls and the main gate of the man's massive mansion. Finally ***Umuokpu*** blocked the drive way to the mansion with piles and heaps of refuse and rubbish and logs of wood. By the time Chief Ideh Akajiaku arrived in his Mercedez 500XL limousine from Lagos for his mother's funeral, he could not believe his eyes. He rushed to the Nnewi Police station to report and to ask for police escort. The police chief told him that the case was a private family funeral affair and they were not authorized to dabble into such traditional matters. He rushed to the Onitsha Police headquarters to lodge his complaint, but they referred him back to the Nnewi police. At last he gave up and good counsel advised him to go down on his knees and make peace with ***Umuokpu***.

How ***Umuokpu*** dealt with this man will be too sordid, nauseating, gruesome, and horrendous to be included in this discourse. But the conclusion of the matter is: ***odogwu nwoke ahu ji anya ya hu nti ya,*** (That rich and powerful man saw hell with his eyes). The lesson was loud and clear: ***Onye akpakwana Umuada aka n'odu,***

ma ha di ndu ma ha nwuru anwu, no body should mess with the institution of Umuada, like the baby of a tiger, whether the tiger is alive or dead).

In summary, in all social functions, including marital rites, title taking and funeral ceremonies, ***Umuada*** play very important roles. They are always pampered and treated right and with cautious respect, or they will raise storm and hell which no one in his right senses would want to contend with. No one would want to tango with them. In marital rites, the intending bridegroom would give them special treats to win their favor and cooperation.

At this juncture, it will be pertinent to underscore some very vital points vis-à-vis Igbo culture and identity and the place of women in Igbo traditional society.

The role and status of women in the Igbo world are quite unknown to the outside world. Some Igbo culture and traditions that are not exportable.

In the past, some European and other western writers had given the western world the obnoxious impression that in the Igbo world women are to be seen and not heard. In other words, Igbo women had no rights, no voice, no power, no privileges, they were mere domestic objects and instruments of sensual pleasure and procreation. The simplest way to explain out this erroneous idea is that the writers did not do any in-depth research and investigation. They had no ideas whatsoever of the underlining structures of the elements of governance and social control mechanisms in the traditional Igbo society. Otherwise they should have seen or heard that the institution of ***Umuada/Umuokpu*** is as ancient as time, and that it was a formidable instrument of social control, more relevant and more effective than the western concept and practice of family and marriage laws. However, although ***Umuada/Umuokpu*** cannot operate with any effectiveness outside the Igbo homeland, their judicial vitality still remains potent and valid in the home front.

If a man living abroad ignores or shacks his cultural and moral obligations and responsibilities to his parents, or other such relations, at the appropriate time and place, ***Umuada/Umuokpu*** will catch up with him. As the Igbo always say: ***agaracha must come back,*** and because—***nmiri do n'eju doro nwankita,*** the water in the dog's vessel will remain their for the dog.

Secondly, there are some traditions and cultural practices in the Igbo society that are exportable. The institution of ***Umuada/Umuokpu*** cannot function with any effectiveness outside the homeland. The kola-nut institution is exportable, and has survived with amazing and admirable vivaciousness in the diasporas as a vital component of Igbo identity, although some of the luster and pungency of ***njakiri oji*** in the dispora cannot be compared with the home-bred version. This is because ***anaghi eji ura atunyere onwu***—(sleep cannot be equated to death); and of course ***egbe na egbe awughi otu:*** egbe (hawk) and egbe (gun) are not the same.

Chapter Seven

Child Factor and Gender divide in Igbo name Expression

For the Igbo, the cardinal and primary purpose for marriage is procreation, that is to bear children. This is why when conception does not occur soon after marriage, the couple, their parents and their immediate relations worry. It is a state of serious anxiety.The couple and their parents would go to any length to finding a solution to the problem. The importance of child factor is very well articulated in many Igbo traditional names, a few examples cited here effectively underscore this point.

1. ***Nwadinmkpa***: a child is a top priority and a priceless assect. For the Igbo, the child factor is the reason for marriage. The idea of a childless marriage is a very painful disaster and a very nagging social stigma. The birth of a child (children) establishes and consummates marriage. It is also perceived as a divine blessing and adornment. According to the Holy Scripture, after God had created man and woman as husband and wife in the Garden of Eden, he blessed them with a divine pronouncement: "***God blessed them, and said to them, Be fruitful and multiply, fill the earth and subdue it***" (Gen.1:28). Again the Holy Bible says in Psalm 127: 3-5: ***"Behold, children are a heritage of the Lord, and the fruit of the womb is his reward. As arrows are in the hand of a***

man; so are children of the youth; Happy is the man that hath his quiver full of them: he shall not be ashmed, but he shall speak with the enemy in the gate." The Igbo knew all this and believed in it long before the Christian Bible found its way on the shores of the Africa continent. This concept of child factor is expressed in many Igbo traditional names:

2. ***Nwakaaku***: a child is much more precious than any material wealth. A child cannot be quantified in terms of material wealth.
3. ***Nwakaego*****:** a child is greater than riches.
4. ***Nwabuoku***: a child is a very precious asset.
5. ***Nwabuulu:*** a child is a profitable investment.
6. ***Nwabueze***: a child is a kingly prize.
7. ***Nwakaeze***: a child is much more pricely than being a king.
8. ***Nwakanma***: a child is greater than any worldly possession.
9. ***Nwabuafa***: a child gives name and identity to parents.
10. ***Nwabundo***: a child provides shelter and insurance in marriage.
11. ***Nwabuife***: a child is a very precious possession.
12. ***Nwabuona***: a child is a precious jewel.
13. ***Nwabuokpu***: a child is a crown of life.
14. ***Nwagbo (Nwagboluogu*****)**: a child will solve the problem.
15. ***Ulunwa***: the child confers respect and privileges.
16. ***Nwakaude***: a child is better than fame.
17. ***Ukonwa***: a child is a source of pride and glory.
18. ***Utonwa***: a child is a delightful pleasure.
19. ***Nwajekwu***: a child will plead my cause.
20. ***Nwazunafia***: children are not sold in the market, they are gifts from God.
21. ***Nwabuwa:*** a child is a whole world of treasure.
22. ***Uzuakpunwa***: children are not fabricated by smiths, children come from God.
23. ***Nwabugo***: a child is an eagle feather (honor) on the cap of parents.
24. ***Nwabugwu/*** **Ugwunwa:** a child is a thing of pride and hono.
25. ***Nwabiawa:*** let more children to come.

From all the expressions of value, emotion, sentiment and desire, it becomes very clear and evident why a childless marriage is considered a disaster or a terrible misfortune. A childless couple feels unfulfilled. The woman agonizes day and night. Her "enemies" taunt her with painful sarcasms. The man is taunted with bitter sarcasms and innuendoes. More often than not, he is under great pressure to commit bigamy or yield to the ungodly temptation of divorce, or even to seek to have a child from another source. This is the very ugly face of a childless marriage in Igbo culture.

Convention and concept of Gender dichotomy in Igbo name expression

A critical study of Igbo name culture reveals a significant cultural gender divide. In other words, there are certain concepts, ideas, characteristics, values, and natural phenomena that are attributable to a particular gender and not to the opposite gender, and vice visa. Most Igbo names are gender sensitive. In fact, there are very few names in Igbo culture that can be regarded as unisex, or common gender names. A list of this will be provided hereafter.

In the Igbo world view, some attributes and characteristics of what a man should be or possess include the following: power, authority, physical and mental prowess, energy, fearlessness, adventurousness, fierceness, invincibility, bravado, machismo, aggressiveness, super resilience, assertiveness, ability and capacity to confront and subdue, indomitable endurance, formidable dynamism, defiance, supremacy, etc.

Below are examples of male gender expectations, characteristics and attributes expressed in Igbo personal names and titles:

Atuegwu	**Idebuno**	**Egwuonye**
Eguwatu	**Egwudike**	**Aghaogu**
Ochiagha	**Ebubedike**	**Ndianeze**
Akpamgbo	**Obidike**	**Odumodu**
Ikenga	**Asoegwu**	**Amadike**
Ikemba	**Egbeigwe**	**Ginigeme**
Okegbe	**Ananti**	**Onyilidike**

Okikadigbo	**Ikeagu**	**Aguolu**
Oguegbe	**Ogudike**	**Omenuko**
Onyiliofo	**Udedike**	**Ogbataonua**
Asogu	**Aguiyi**	**Ogueri**
Ugwudike	**Ikeanumba**	**Ugodike**
Mgbodile	**Ojukwu**	**Onyiliofo**
Njoku	**Amadi**	**Orji**
Mgbada	**Anucha**	**Kalu**
Kamalu	**Nwodo**	**Osuagwu**
Ugwu	**Igwe**	**Igirigi**

On the other hand, traditional Igbo female names give expressions of the following concepts, values and characteristics: **feminism, beauty, gentleness, virtue, fecundity, grace, piety, humility, love, good character, submissiveness, conduit or source of wealth, precious treasure, asset, diligence, honesty, patience, docility, domestic acumen, etc.** The following are a few examples of traditional Igbo female names which express these values, concepts and characteristics:

Obiageli
Oriaku
Obianuju
Agwawunma
Ndidiamaka
Onachukwu
Adaaku
Nwakaego
Akuchukwu
Ifeyinwa
Nkiruka
Nneka
Amarachi
Nwabundo
Nwabuaku
Ulunwa
Utonwa
Nwaamaka

Urenwa
Ugonma
Ugochi
Ugoeze
Ogbenyeanu
Nwakaku
Nkolika
Chinwenwa
Adanma
Unoaku
Ugboaku
Ugbobuaku
Akueze
Ozuola

It will be a very unspeakable misfit and a cultural misnomer for a female to bear such names as: **Atuegwu, Asoanya, Udedike, Ochiagha, Egwuonye, Ginigeme, Onyilidike, Oguegbe, Ananti, Egwuatu, Amadike, Osuofia, Nwakaibeya, Aghaogu, Ugwudike, Odumodu, Egwudike, and Agudile.** No Igbo man will ever want to propose marriage to such fearsome amazon of a woman.

By the same token, it will be a very incomprehensible absurdity for an Igbo male to bear such names as: **Obiageli, Nkolika, Ifeyinwa, Adaaku, Adaobi, Adanma, Unoaku, Chikwenma, Ifeoma, Urenma, and Ndidiamaka.**

Just as in the western culture it will be very absurd for a male to bear such name as: Agnes, Maria, Josephine, Michelle, and Philomina.

The essence of this focus on the dichotomy in Igbo name culture is to underscore Igbo cultural values as a component of Igbo identity.

Moral and socio—cultural values in Igbo name expression:

Prof. Kalu in his seminar paper ***Under the eyes of the Gods: Sacralization and Social Order in Igboland*** (1988) wrote: "an Igbo moral universe is thoroughly suffused with sacred symbolisms and ritual in a socio-religious system that was deliberately designed to legitimize power, achievement and wealth such as to ensure their acquisition in morally satisfactory ways."

Some traditional Igbo names are statements and expressions of vital and basic moral and ethical values. Invariably, most Igbo moral and ethical values are also universal values. In other words, Igbo value names are names of moral and cultural identity, and acclaimed symbols of code of conduct.

Here are some select examples:

1. ***Eziokwubundu:*** Truth and honesty preserve life (honesty is the best policy).
2. ***Eziafakaego:*** a good name is better than riches.
3. ***Oguejiofo:*** let your efforts and struggles be based on moral justice and principles.
4. ***Ndidiamaka:*** Patience is a great virtue.
5. ***Izukanma:*** wisdom is a great virtue.
6. ***Egwutosi:*** do not indulge in blackmail, character assassination.
7. ***Echezona:*** do not forget a benefactor.
8. ***Ilodinjo:*** enmity is evil and destructive, (it should be avoided).
9. ***Egbuho:*** *(Egbuho ohia o wuru uzo.)* when a bush or forest is cleared, a road or path appears, meaning every good thing is the result of hard work and perseverance, in other words no sweat no sweet.
10. ***Onyeaghana (Onyeaghana nwanne ya)*** no one should abandon or forsake his brother/sister, (you should be your brother's keeper; unity is strength).
11. ***Nmutaka:*** knowledge and wisdom are great assets.
12. ***Udoka (Udokanma)*** peace is better than war.
13. ***Agwawunma:*** good character is beauty; character is strength.
14. ***Ohawuile:*** there is power and strength in number/ unity.
15. ***Ofokaja:*** the power of innocence and honesty is greater than devilish sacrifice.
16. ***Eziokwu (Eziokwu bu ndu)*** truth is life, honesty is the golden rule of life.
17. ***Jideofor (Ome ife jide ofor)*** let every action be guided by moral justice and equity.

18. ***Egbebulu (egbe belu ugo be lu)*** live and let live, (do not block the progress of any one).

As has been said earlier, the naming of a child is a solemn ritual, a kind of cultural initiation and "baptism". It is a statement of prophecy on a child's life. In Igbo belief system, a person lives or reflects his/her name—***afa onye n'edu ya.*** It argues therefore that the life of the carrier or bearer of the prophetic statement, is expected to portray the desirable moral and ethical values, virtues and principles. For the Igbo, a name is not just a mere identity tag, it is a cultural and linguistic expression of a whole world-view of a people, a statement of relationships, history, spiritual, moral and social values, etc. In the Igbo worldview, a name is pregnant with meanings.

Egotism and pride in Igbo name expression:

Sometimes, for some reason, the Igbo parent is obsessed with self pride, egotism, and is driven by a kind of compulsive desire to compel public attention of his achievememt, accomplishment, power or authority, or to express a very strong sense of defiance regarding an issue. The following are a few examples of Igbo traditional names of pride and egotism:

***Ginigeme**:* I don't care the consequence, (I am equal to any eventuality)
Egwuonye: I am not afraid of any one.
Okadigbo (Okikadigbo): Our supremacy is inherent, traditional and unquestionable.
***Nwakibie, Nwakaibeya*:** I am supreme, the first and greatest among my peers.
Omenuko (Omenukoaku): One who can boast of wealth and prosperity all season round, one who can celebrate even in times of depression or scarcity.
Agam (Agamadotuigwe): Should I pull down the sky to prove my worth and power?

Oleforo**:* What else is left for me to do? I have achieved all, and nothing else is left. (Macbeth: *I have done all that becomes a man, who dares more is none:* **Shakespeare).*

Anyika: We are the greatest and the most powerful, we are more than conquerors.

Ogbenyeanu: This (girl) is not designed for poor/ low class suitors, (only the rich can marry this one)

Obianuju: Born into great fortune**,** this one has arrived at a time of plenty.

Ejelinma: This one (girl) is beautiful beyond expression.

Ndeanaeze: We are the ones to be feared, we are fearsome.

Ogbuagu: Killer of tigers and lions.

Ezeugbonyamba: The boat (hero) that carries the nation/ tribe/ clan, an icon of power.

Ikemba (Ikenechemba): The power that protects the people, an icon of power. ***Omeokachie***: One that never runs out of resources, a person of inexhaustible wealth.

Ekwueme: One who has the ability and capacity to do what he says, a man of action.

Oshimiri: Ocean, an expression of great affluence, unlimited resources.

Okuagba (Okuagbamiri): Water is never comsumed by fire, this one is beyond human destruction, (an expression of extraordinary confidence and capacity).

***Ochiagha:* A** war general, brave and fearless warrior

***Osuofia*:** One who clears forests, a frontline warrior.

***Amadike**:* A lineage of brave worriors.

Asika (Asikebili): Ready for any eventuality, war and peace.

Asoegwu: Never afraid of terror.

Oluoha: Defender of the people.

Ejiamatu, Ihejiamatu: The icon/symbol of excellence.

Ihekwuaba: The fortress of the people's pride/ strength.

Ideh: The pillar of power and strength.

***Okwute**:* the unshakeable rock.

Ikeagu: A powerful tiger.

A few examples of some popular abbreviated forms are:

Chichi: for Chinazom, Chizoba, Chimdinma, Chiamaka, Chidiebere, Chidubem.
Ego: for Nwakaego, Nwabuego, Egochukwu, Egobunwoke.
Ije: for Ijeoma, Uzoije, Chimaije, Ijenu, Onyeije, Chukwumerije.
Egwu: for Egwudike, Egwuonwu, Egwuchukwu, Asoegwu.
Onwu: for Onwuegbuchulam, Onwuatuegwu, Onwuasoanya, Onwuamaegbu.
Anya: for Anyadike, Anyafulu, Anyanaso, Obiasoanya, Anyaneche, Anyachukwu.
Ofor: Onyiliofo, Jideofo, Ofodilie, Ofodike, Ofokaja, and Oguejiofo.
Agu: for Ogbuagu, Aguolu, Agudile, Egwuagu, Atueyiagu.
Asi: for Asiloegbunam, Asikebili, Agbasielo.
Ilo: for Iloajoka, Iloagbaeke, Agwubilo, Iloegbunam, Akubuilo, Iloabachie.
Ama: for Amadike, Amaeze, Amaaku, Nwamadi, Amanna, Amachukwu.
Ulo: for Uloma, Ulochukwu, Ulojiofo.
Onyi: for Onyinyechi, Onyekachukwu, Chienyem, Onyido.
Ozo: for Ugwuozo, Chibuozo, Akuozo, Ozochukwu, Chinechiozo.
Ibe: for Ibejide, Ibezimako, Ibejiofo, Ibegbulam, Ibebuogu, Ibeamaka.
Igwe: for Igwebuike, Igweilo, Nwaigwe.
Agwu: for Agwubilo, Agwuna, Agwudike.
Madu: for Madubugwu, Maduemezia, Maduakolam, Madueke, Maduabum.
Okwu: for Okwuchukwu, Okwuoma, Okwudili, Okwuolisa, Okwukaogu.
Aka: for Akachukwu, Akabuogu, Akamelu, Akadike, Akajiaku, Akajiofo.
Agha: for Aghaegbuna, Aghamelu, Aghadinuno, Ochiagha, Obianagha.
Uzu: for Uzuegbunam, Uzudike, Uzuchukwu, Uzuakpunwa.
Azu: for Azubike, Azuakolam, Azubugwu, Azudialo, Azubuogu.
Ogu: for Ogoejiofo, Dikeogu, Oguagha, Obiasogu, Oguebego.
Metu: for Metumaribe, let all actions show compassion and consideration for others.

Chapter Eight

Igbo Name and Cultural Identity.

For the Igbo a name means and speaks a lot. As the saying goes a name is "pregnant with meaning". It is not just an identity label or tag that distinguishes one luggage from another. Primarily, a traditional Igbo name is a linguistic identity and a cultural costume. A traditional Igbo name could be an expression of some cosmological, spiritual, moral, ethical, historical event or experience. A name could be a comment on some social values, or a response to some incident or situation. Above all, the Igbo believe that a name has a potential supernatural dynamic force which would propel the innate essence (the ***chi)*** of the carrier of the name: ***aha/ afa onye n'edu ya.,*** a person lives his/her name, which by extension means that a name is the linguistic embodiment of personality and character. This is why in the traditional society the naming of a child is treated with a lot of ritual solemnity and serious concern. The naming of a child is a sacred prophetic pronouncement over the life of the child. Thereafter, the child will live and die with it.

More often than not, a child's name is a reflection of the family history, experience, expectation, relationships, all encapsulated into one word axiom, idiom, proverb, sarcasm or a subtle innuendo. In essence, the real meaning of a traditional Igbo name is not only culture bound, but is also a linguistically codified expression. This is why if and when a name is taken out of the cultural context, it is bound to lose its vital meaning and signification. A classic case in point: long ago, in the 40s at the Dennis Memorial Grammar School (DMGS) Onitsha, the then Vice-Principal, Rev. P.J. Ross, (an Englishman), the Math and Physics teacher was in very enthusiastic hurry to master Igbo language and the names of his students. Once he bragged to his students that he knew the meaning of their Igbo names. He had a bunch of students in his Physics class with names depicting the traditional Igbo market days. To sunstantiate his claim to this knowledge, he said: **"Nwafor means the son of Afor; Nweke is the son of Eke, Nwankwo is the son of Nkwo; Nwosu is the son of osu".** Unfortunately one of the student's surname was Nwosu and he called the student the son of osu. A big laughter erupted, but it was not anything funny. The teacher had unwittingly stepped on a very sensitive toe. The student whose surname was Nwosu hailed from Ozubulu in the Igbo heartland where the osu cast system was then a very "distasteful" social stigma and taboo. The student quickly rose up in angry protest and demanded a retraction and an apology. The 'expensive joke' did not end in the Physis class. The case eventually got to the Principal who understood the osu cast system himself and he handled the matter with wisdom and great diligence. Behind closed doors the teacher got a cold reprimand. Thereafter, the teacher learned his lesson that there is a world of difference between a hawk and a gun: (the difference between ***egbe a hawk, and egbe a gun),*** and also that ***anaghi eji ihe eji agba nti agba n,anya*** (you don't use the solid object for poking the ear for poking the eye). That student in question eventually became the first Nigerian nuclear physicist and was a prominent team player in the famous Biafran **Ogbunigwe technology concept.**

In the traditional society, every Igbo child is endowed with four names. The system was that as soon as a child was born, the grandparents on both sides are notified and requested to propose names for the child. So there was a name from the paternal grand-parents, another name from the maternal grandparents, a name by the child's father, and a name by the child's mother. Every person involved in the naming exercise takes it as a very solemn cultural obligation, and tries to give very meaningful name that the child will live by, grow with and be proud of. The child will grow to understand and appreciate the circumstances of his birth, some event that has impacted on the family remotely or recently, and what are the expectations of his/her life.

A critical study of the structure and content of Igbo names shows that traditional Igbo names could be classified into ten concept categories:—

1. **Axiomatic or maxim name genre**: a statement expressing a self evident or universally recognized truth, or a rule of conduct or behavior.
2. **Didactic name genre**: a name intended to be instructional for a successful life.
3. **Prophetic name genre**: a pronouncement or statement intended to be inspirational for the fulfillment of a future greatness, fortune, or blessing.
4. **Empirical name genre:** a statement or expression borne out of personal experience.
5. **Assertive / Declarative genre**: statement or expression of power, pride of heritage or achievement.
6. **Ethical/Moralistic name genre**: statement, expression or affirmation of ethical or moral values.
7. **Celestial name genre:** name reflexive of religious or spiritual concepts or attributes of God or deities.
8. **Commemorative name genre:** reflexive of some important event or experience especially in the family or circumstances of the birth of the child.
9. **Lamentation name genre:** a statement reflexive of sorrow, misfortune, or death.
10. **Humanity name genre:** a statement or expression of the mortality or ephemeral nature of mankind, the temporariness of human life.

Below are some examples of each category:
Axiomatic or maxim expression in Igbo traditional names:

- ***Udokanma***: Peace and harmony are vital for survival and progress.
- ***Nwakaego***: A child is more precious than material wealth.

- ***Onwuzuruwa***: Death is a universal phenomenon, common disaster.
- ***Onwuzurigbo***: same as above, death has no boundry in Igboland.
- ***Onwuatuegwu***: Death is fearless, it is not afraid of anybody.
- ***Igwebuike***: Number is strength, there is power and safety in mumber.
- ***Osondu***: (Osondu agwuike) the race for life cannot give up to surrender.

Didactic expression in Igbo traditional names: names that are intended to instruct, teach and under score vital ethical principles of life and conduct.

- ***Ndudinanti:*** wisdom for surviaval comes from listening and hearing and learning
- ***Izubundu***: Wisdom and knowledge sustain life, wisdom is life.
- ***Egbuho*** (Egbuho ohia, o wuru uzo): if you clear the forest, you create a road, the idiomatic expression for "no sweat, no sweet".
- ***Ndidiamaka***: Patience is a high moral virtue.
- **Agharandu_(**Agharandu kpa aku, onye iro erie): if one does not take good care of one's life or health, his wealth and assets will be inherited by his enemies.

Prophetic: name intended to inspire a fulfillment of some expectation, invocation of blessing or virtue upon the life of the child.

- ***Ositadinma***: Hope that henceforth the future will be much better.
- ***Ogadinma:*** It will be well with this child, this child will be blessed.
- ***Ezenwata***: baby king; this child will grow into a king, will be famous.
- ***Nwamauno*** (some times corrupted as Nwamono): This child will be a blessing to his home, family.

- ***Nwando*** (Nwabundo): This child will be a great refuge, shelter and a fortress.
- ***Nwadike***: This child will be great and famous.

Empirical: expression in Igbo tradional name that reflects some personal human experience that impacts on the circumstances of the family

- ***Ogobugwu***: My in-laws have been a source of blessing and success for me.
- ***Ogoma:*** I am blessed to have wonderful in-laws
- ***Aghadinuno***: There is strife, bitterness, feud in the family.
- ***Akubilo***: Wealth creates enmity, jealousy, envy.
- ***Nkolika***: I have a history of memorable experience
- ***Ibeazom:*** My family has been my savior and my strength.
- ***Ibezimako***: My relations have taught me some unforgetable lesson.
- ***Azukego***: My relations are more precious to me than material wealth.

Assertiveness/ declarative: expression in Igbo traditional name that boasts of personal and lineage power, achievement, proud heritage.

- ***Ginigeme***: I don't care what happens, I am equal to any eventuality.
- ***Egwuonye***: I am not afraid of any one.
- ***Oramadike***: People know and respect the brave.
- ***Okadigbo***: Our lineage, reputation and superiority is ancient and incontrovertible.
- ***Anyika***: We are superior, we are a force to reckon with.
- ***Nwakaibeya***: This child will be first and above his peers.
- ***Anajemba***: I have come to stay and survive here, I'm not quitting to anywhere
- ***Ihekweaba:*** This is the cornerstone, pillar of our power, pride.
- ***Ikemba,*** Ikenechemba: The power house and fortress of the clan.

Ethical/moral values: expression in Igbo traditional name.

- ***Agwawunma***: Character is beauty.
- ***Eziaha***, Eziafakaego: A good name is better than riches.
- ***Ofobike***: Moral justice is power, strength.
- ***Ekwutosi:*** Avoid gossip and character assassiunation, don't slander people.
- ***Ejimofo:*** I am innocent, my cause is just my hands are clean.
- ***Onyeaghana***: Be your brother's keeper, do not neglect or forsake your family, relations.
- ***Egbebelu***: Live and let live an expression of and appeal for justice and equity.
- ***Eziokwubundu***: Honesty is the best policy, honesty sustains life.
- ***Zelunjo***: Eschew or avoid evil, wickedness, immorality.

Historical or commemorative names: Igbo names that speak of events, historical landmarks in the life of the family:

- ***Aghamelu***: This misfortune/disaster is a result or consequence of the war.
- ***Obianagha***: Child born during the war.
- ***Obianuju:*** This child has arrived at a time of fortune and plenty.
- ***Amanna:*** Born after the father's death—a posthumus child.
- ***Uzoafia:*** Child was born on the way to the market.
- ***Eluemuno:*** I have returned home, a child born after a family sojourn.

Lamentation or sorrow name: Igbo traditional names that express sorrow, misfortune and death:

- ***Onwumelu***: death has caused this misfortune.
- ***Alilionwu:*** The bitterness and agony of death.
- ***Amuchie***: The source of hope for another child is gone; or this is a replacement.
- ***Emeremole***: What have I done to deserve this misfortune?

- ***Ebegbulem***: May my goodness not turn against me, not be rewarded with evil.
- ***Ogoegbunam:*** May my goodness/kindness not be rewarded with evil.

The frailty of human nature: Name expression of the mortality of mankind:

- ***Onwuzurigbo:*** Death is a universal phenomenon.
- ***Ndupuechi:*** Life is one day at a time.
- ***Efoagui:*** One is lucky if one sees the next morning.
- ***Ndubuaja:*** Life is dust; an empty shadow.
- ***Azotandu*** (Azotandu edebere onwu): We preserve life for ultimate death.
- ***Abadodike*** (Abadodike aja ike ya agwu): The grave terminates the power of a hero, the grave is the end point of the rich and famous.

Pet names, fun names and meaningless sobriquets:

Quite often, some very meaningful and sober Igbo names become so distorted and mutilated in the process to achieve abbreviation and simplification. Quite often the end product loses all originality and meaning, and becomes a meaningless nonsensical jargon, or a linguistic absurdity. Regretably also, the new coinage/fun name, although may sound "sweet", "romantic" and "musical" to the ears, could become a ridiculous contradiction of the full original because all the vital linguistic and cultural signification are lost.

A random example will suffice to illustrate the vanity of it all.

- ***Chichi:*** Out of every context, or root
- ***Ego:*** Money, unless it is put in context, money here makes no sense.
- ***Ije:*** Journey, walk, trip.
- ***Egwu***: Fear, terror.
- ***Onwu***: Death, it is an absurdity for a person to be a symbol or representative of death.
- ***Anya:*** Eye.

- ***Agu:*** Tiger, leopard.
- ***Ilo:*** Enemy, enmity, hatred.
- ***Ulo:*** House.
- ***Ofia:*** Bush, forest.
- ***Agwu***: Deity of insanity, mischief, madness.
- ***Ogu***: Fight, war, battle.
- ***Agha:*** Same as above.
- ***Okwu***: Talk, speech, dialogue, trouble, controversy.
- ***Aka***: Hand.
- ***Atu:*** Buffalo.
- ***Nmuo***: Masquerade, devil, spirit, ghost.
- ***Uzo***: Road, way, street, path.
- ***Azu***: Behind, back.
- ***Ukwu***: Foot.

It is very obvious that no normal Igbo person will like to be called or referred to as Mr. Death, Mr. Enemy, Mr. Hatred, Mr. Fire, or Mr. Insanity, (the translations of the pet names). It is therefore important to be very careful and thoughtful how we coin the simplification of some names in order not to make a mockery of oneself. In other words, one should not cut one's nose to spite one's face. The meaninglessness of a name strips the bearer of a vital cultural identity.

A scenario of total loss of identity:

This was a real and true incident that happened at the annual Summer Camp for **Igbo** Children in Los Angeles California in July 1999.

The campers ranged between 6 and 20 years of age. The senior group consisted of about 35 teenagers aged between 14 and 18. My schedule and assignment was to help these "senior" teenagers understand and appreciate their cultural heritage—**Igbo Cultural Heritage:** We started with name game, an exercise to break the ice: individual self introduction so that everyone would know who's who in the group. The format was: personal names, parents names, name of home state, name of home village, etc. In the process one 14 year old girl introduced herself as Uk—as her personal first name. Of course I stopped the name game and requested her to tell the group her real full name. She doggedly insisted that her name was Uk and that she had no other personal name. To compound the matter all her friends and peers strongly affirmed that her real name was Uk. Of course I knew that it must be a kind of abbreviated fun or pet name. But she insisted that Uk was her registered name in her school and in all her documents. I asked her to find out the full name from her parents. But some how she took offence and asserted that she was old enough to know what her name was, (American freedom of speech style). During the process of the six day camp I made effort to locate the parents of the girl. Both were Igbo. They told me that her full name was Ukonwa, but because Americans could not pronounce the Igbo name properly they decided to shorten it to Uk., the first two letters of the name to make it easier for all and sundry. So right from infancy everybody called her Uk. Unfortunately she grew up as Uk. without ever knowing the meaning of that beautiful name. **Ukonwa** means the glory, honor, respect and dignity which the birth of a child brings to the parents.

From this scenario one can see very clearly how meaningless an abbreviated name could be. Uk sounds quite romantic and easy to say, but does not tell anything about the background or identity of the girl?. Parents owe it a moral and cultural obligation to give their children an identity they can understand and appreciate and be proud of.

Chapter Nine

The concept, nature and character of God in Igbo name expression.

Traditionally the Igbo are very religious people. For them religion has always been a way of life. In the Igbo world view, the sacred and the circular have very faint line of divide. The sacred and the spiritual pervade morality and social code of conduct. In other words, in Igbo cosmology there is no clear dichotomy or demarcation between the spiritual, moral and cultural values. They are very tightly interwoven, and they reinforce one another. For instance, every act of wickedness, or "simple" misdemeanor is attributed to ***oru ekwensu, aka olu ekwensu, nmuo ojoo, agbara, agwu,*** work or act of the devil/satan, evil spirit, some kind of malevolent divinity or demon. When a person's private and public actions manifest a pattern of deviance, rebellion, defiance, mischief, kleptomania, violent temper or uncontrollable anger, the person is considered to be possessed by some kind of evil spirit. In the old dispensation the parents or immediate relations of a victim of such behavior pattern would consult an oracle ***(afa, dibia)*** for some spiritual diagnosis and possible remedy for the malady. In Igbo traditional religious belief system, every human act or life pattern is propelled, directed and shaped by some supernatural forces.

Even some character traits such as: laziness and lack of motivation, bedwetting after early childhood, delay or lack of interest in marriage are cause of concern and anxiety, and were attributed to acts of one kind of evil spirit or another. That superstition extended to delay in some basic stages in human maturation and development: delay in menstruation in girls, prosmiscuity, frequent incidents of accidents, habitual drunkenness, etc. In the Igbo world-view, every kind of these acts or problems could be resolved if and when the appropriate supernatural forces are adequately placated or propitiated. This is why the Igbo take their religion and their gods very seriously. In other words, for the traditional Igbo, religion was a basic socio-cultural phenomenon.

According to Dr. Iwe: "*Viewed in this way, religion becomes both the aspiration to and the reality of individual and collective communion with the deity, with the universal principle of existence, the means of ensuring conformance with this principle as interpreted and conceptualized in the particular setting. That is to say, it becomes a mechanism of social control of enculturation into a way of life.*" (Dr. S. S. Iwe, 1988).

As has been said earlier, the Igbo worshipped and celebrated their gods, and that it was remarkably a system of polytheism, a myriad of local deities and divinities. These nature gods had different names, diverse functions and powers and attributes.

Some were personal gods. Some were family gods. The bigger and more powerful ones were village and clan gods. Some were seasonal gods, some were agricultural gods. Some of the gods resided or were housed in shrines or in sheltered altars. Some dwelled on the hills and in valleys, some in caves and rivers (**mamiwota**). All the four market days were names of the deity associated with the market—Afo, Eke, Nkwo and Orie. The traditional Igbo took their gods seriously and reflected their names and functions in some of the popular traditional names. Thus they have such names as:

Nwafor, Nwaeke, Nwankwo, Nwokorie, Ngbafor, Mbaeke, (to commemorate and invoke the blessings of the particular market deity on the child born on that particular market day).

Other popular traditional names that testify to the religious character of the Igbo include: Nwabara, Nwanjoku, Iwuanyanwu,

Nwigwe, Nwagwu, Nwogwugwu, Udo, Ojukwu, Agwubilo, Edoka, Osuagwu, Osuala, Osunmuo, Nwamadi, Anakwenze, Nwayanwu, Ogwugwueloka, Nwaobodo, Iwuala, Ugwueke, Udeagbala, Nwarusi, Ikenga, Nwangwu, Nwodo, Ugwuedo, Iwuagwu, Ugwuegede, etc.

But in spite of the Igbo religious system of polytheism, the Igbo belief in the existence, nature and power of a supreme Almighty God was never in doubt, even long before the arrival of Christianity in Igbo land. According to Dr. Iwe: "*Even in the center of their polytheism, the Igbo had a strong and unequivocal cosmic consciousness of a supreme being who was bigger, stronger and omnipresent, the great creator and sustainer of heaven and earth.*" However, the false claim or idea that it was the European Christian missionaries that first introduced the concept and knowledge of the Supreme Being still persists in the minds of the uninformed.

The falasy that it was the European Christian missionaries who introduced the concept of the Supreme God to the Igbo can be very easily debunked by the meaning of the traditional names of some of the first Christian 'heathen' converts, the heathens who received and worked with the first CMS missionaries on the Niger Diocese Such names include:

- Mazi. Chudi (short for Chukwudi) meaning God is alive, ominipresent. Ominipotent, ominiscient.
- Mazi. Arinzechukwu: the grace of the Almighty One.
- Mazi. Olisaemeka: the grace or gift of the Almighty One.
- Mazi. Ezechukwu: the supreme God of gods.
- Mazi. Akachukwu: the hand/power of the great God.
- Mazi. Ilechukwu: the power/ strength of the great God.
- Mazi. Chukwuma: only the Supreme Omnicient God knows the future.
- Mazi. Chukwuka: the supremacy and soveignty of the Almighty Deity.
- Mazi Ugochukwu: the supreme nature of God (King of the gods

  (See Niger Ibos, G.T. Basden, 1966)

Those names very clearly articulate the Igbo concept and attributes of the Supreme God. But as soon as those 'heathen' native people were recruited into the services of the missionaries, they were baptized and given the biblical names of: Philip, Jeremiah, Moses, Aaron, Joshua, and Israel. For the missionaries the traditional names were heathen and ungodly names. What an pathological ungodly joke.

Although the Igbo had no formal system or structure for the worship of this Supreme Being, as they had systems and abundant physical structures for the worship and celebration of the minor deities and divinities, the Igbo had a very clear concept of His existence, character, and attributes. For instance long before the arrival of Christianity in Igboland, the Igbo manifested their knowledge and nature of the supreme God in many popular traditional names and titles. What the Christian missionaries introduced was a formal system and practice of **monotheism.** In other words, the physical translation of a mental theory of a consciousness into a physical and material reality, and the systematic eradication of the old traditional system of polytheism.

In his 1988 Ahiajioku Lecture, Dr. Iwe distinguishes clearly the Igbo concept of the *Supreme Being, Chukwu "the creator", and the host of lesser divinities, beneficent or malign, who are properly seen as particular manifestations in time and place of His omnipresence and omnipotence as shaped and fleshed out by the cosmic forces acting on human perception. Dr. Iwe asserts that, "for the Igbo, the Supreme Being is neither uncertain nor remote but an integral aspect of their communal being; such that the refinement of public morality in the light of contemporary belief cannot be achieved without a fruitful dialogue between the Igbo theological heritage and the Christian belief structure which has been superimposed on it by recent history.*"

The primary focus of the present book is not an attempt to engage in a theological or historical argument, but to demonstrate in very convincing terms that the traditional Igbo had a very clear and well articulated knowledge of the existence, nature and attributes of a supreme God who is the creator and sustainer of mankind, and the entire universe, and this is very evident in many traditional Igbo names and in the expression of Igbo moral and ethical values.

The concept of the Supreme God in Igbo name expression

1. God is great and the creator and sustainer of the world:
   Chineke:
   Chukwukere
   Chikere
   Olisabuluwa
   Chiokike
   Chinweuwa

2. God is all powerful and almighty:
   Chukwuka
   Chika
   Chiebuka
   Ifeanyichukwu
   Iheanyi
   Chukwukadibia
   Oliasebuka
   Chukwuebuka
   Ikechukwu
   Chikaeze
   Onyekachukwu

3. God is holy, righteous, awesome:
   Chidiaso
   Ebubechukwu
   Egwuchukwu
   Chidiegwu

4. God owns everything: power, life, wealth children:
   Chinwendu
   Chinweaku
   Chinweoku
   Chinweike
   Chinenyenwa
   Chinweuba
   Chinwe

Chinweze
Chimere
Chinweuwa
Chinweikpe
Chinweude
Uzunakpunwa—the smith that crafts children

5. God is real, alive, active, omnipresent, omniscient:
Chukwudi
Chidi
Chudi
Chimdi
Chukwunofu
Chukwunonso
Chukwuma

6. God is merciful, benevolent, gracious:
Chidiebere
Eberechukwu
Eberechi
Onyinyechi
Ogochukwu
Chiazagom
Chinenye
Olisaemeka
Amarachi
Chime
Chimelogo
Chukwueloka

7. God is Alfa and Omega final arbiter:
Chidera
Odera
Chinweokwu
Chinweusa
Chinweizu
Chinweikpe

Chikwado
Chigbo
Chikodili
Odinakachukwu

8. <u>God is the source and giver of wisdom</u>
Chinweizu
Chimaizu
Izuchukwu
Chikereizu
Chimaobi
Chinweako
Chibuizu

Chapter Ten

Concept of Phenomena and Values in Igbo name expression:

A. Concept of Death in Igbo name expression

The Igbo concept of death as a natural phenomenon is well articulated in many Igbo trditional names. More than any other Nigerian linguistic group, the Igbo have very vivid concept of the nature, character and the agony of death. Below is a brief summary of the concept of death in some Igbo traditional names:

1. **Death as a universal phenomenon:**
   Onwuzuruigbo: *death is a natural and universal phenomenon in Igbo world.*
   Onwuzuruwa: *death is a universal phenomenon, all over the world.*
   Onwuepe: *death spares no body.*

2. **Death is fearless:**
   Onwuatuegwu: *Death is not afraid of any body or situation.*
   Onwuasoanya: *Death has no respect for personage or status.*
   Onwuamadike: *Death has no regard for the high and mighty.*
   Onwuamaeze: *Death has no regard for kings and celebrities*
   Onwuasoigwe: *Death has no fear of or regard for crowd or multitude.*

3. **<u>Death is no respecter of person, status, age, or condition:</u>**
   Onwuakpaoke: *Death is not disceminatory or partial.*
   Onwuamaibe: *Death has no favotites of relations.*
   Onwuamaizu: *Death is senceless and insensitive.*
   Onwuepe: *Death does not spare any one.*

4. **<u>The agony and bitterness of death:</u>**
   Onwudiwe: *Death is painful.*
   Aririonwu: *The agony or bitterness of death.*
   Onwudiufu: *Death inflicts terrible pain and sorrow.*
   Onwubuariri: *Death is a very painful disaster.*
   Onwubuya: *Death is a terrible misfortune.*

5. **<u>Death is merciless and insensitive:</u>**
   Onwuamaegbu: *Death is very insensitive.*
   Onwuatuelo: *Death is very unreasonable and irrational.*
   Ebeleemeonwu: *Death is never sympathetic.*

6. **<u>The tragedy/ agony of death:</u>**
   Onwumelu: *Death caused this tragedy.*
   Onwuemelie: *Death is a terrible conqueror.*
   Onwutaluobi: *Death is the cause of the leanness/misfortune of the family.*
   Onwudinjo: *Death is very painful.*

7. **<u>Death cannot be bribed:</u>**
   Onwuelingo: Death cannot be influence of bribed.
   Onwuanngo: *Death does not accept fee or ransome.*
   Onwuagbaugwo: *Death is a heartless and an unreasonable debth collector.*
   Onwuegenti: Death has no ears, does not listen.

8. **<u>Appeal (cry) to death to take a break/ be merciful:</u>**
   Onwubiko: *Death please take a break.*
   Onwunzo: *Same as above.*
   Onwuegbuzia: *Death please stop killing us.*
   Onwuchekwa: *Death please take it easy.*

***Onwuguzo**: Death please cease for a while.*
***Onwuteaka**: Death please allow a longer interval.*
***Onwuegbuchulam**: Death please don't take me prematurily.*
***Onwughalu**: Death please spare this one.*
***Onwurah**: Death please leave this one for me.*
***Anazonwu**: God please save me from death.*
***Onwuzurike**:* Death please stop and take a break.

B. **The concept of the future in Igbo name expression:**

Here we will attempt to demonstrate how the Igbo conceive and relate to the future, and how they give it expression in their name culture. In the Igbo belief system the future is conceived as:

- Unknown.
- Uncertain.
- Unpredictable.
- Beyond human knowledge and control.
- Only God has knowledge and control of the future.

In Igbo linguistic structure there are two formal terms or nomenclature reference words for the future. These are: ***echi***—tomorrow, and ***iru, ihu*** (front), e.g. Nkiru, Nkiruka; Ihuka, meaning that which is in the front/future will be better. Here are few examples of traditional names which express the concept of the future:

1. ***Onyemaechi**: N*o one knows tomorrow, (no one knows what the future holds).
2. ***Echidime**:* Tomorrow is pregnant, (no one can predict what it will bring forth).
3. ***Ndupu**:* (Ndupuechi) If one can live/ survive till tomorrow.
4. ***Ndulue**:* If we can live to see tomorrow.
5. ***Anene*** (Kaanenechi): Let's watch and hope, (keep looking up to God).
6. ***Sochima**: (So chukwu ma echi)* o Only God knows tomorrow.

7. ***Efoagui**:* We live one day at a time, (we don't know what tomorrow may bring).
8. ***Beluodachi**:* If God permits, (it is only by the grace of God that we can see tomorrow).
9. ***Echieteka**:* Tomorrow is too distant to predict.

C. **The concept of wealth and riches in Igbo name expression:**

The concept of wealth is well articulated in some traditional Igbo names: principally that God is the source, owner, and giver of wealth; that wealth is accessible to all, but that not all persons can achieve wealth; it is only by the grace of God that a person can achieve wealth. Wealth brings fame, wealth is power, wealth can engender and breed hatred, enmity and jealousy. Only the wise and industrious can achieve wealth. And above all, children constitute a man's most precious assets and investment

1. **God is the source and giver of wealth:**
   Chinweuba
   Chikeluba
   Chinweaku
   Chinenyeaku
   Akuchukwu

2. **Wealth is power:**
   Akuwuike
   Udeaku
   Akuwuozo
   Akunazaoku
   Egowunwoke

3. **Wisdom is wealth:**
   Izuwuike
   Izudike
   Akojiaku

4. **Human resources as power and wealth:Children and relations are assets:**
   Nwabuoku
   Nwabulu
   Nwabundo
   Nwanegbo
   Nwabude
   Azubugwu
   Azubike
   Nnabike
   Ikwubike
   Ibebuaku
   Nwawuaku

Concept of wisdom in Igbo name expression:

The value which the Igbo place on knowledge and wisdom is very eloquently expressed in Igbo name culture. For the Igbo excellence, prosperity, power and fame are all by-products of wisdom.

Ndi-Igbo have great value for wisdom, and will do all it takes to acquire it. This is why illiterate and poor parents would mortgage their life substances: their land, their cash crops, even sell their inheritance in order to send their children to school. For the Igbo ignorance and foolishness are serious social and intellectual handicaps. Foolish and ignorant people are the dregs of society. No one reckons with them. In the days of slavery they were the first and easy victims to be disposed of as "good riddance of bad rubbish".

Traditional Igbo name expression of wisdom:

1. **God is the source and giver of wisdom and knowledge**
   Chinweizu
   Chimaizu
   Izuchukwu
   Chinenyeizu
   Chikeluizu

2. **Life and wealth depend on wisdom**
   Ndubizu
   Nduwuizu
   Izujindu
   Ndudinanti
   Izuwuba
   Nzejiako
   Uchejiaku
   Izuamaka
   Izukanma
   Nmutaka
   Izuwunze

3. **Wisdom creates and sustains wealth**
   Izujiaku:
   Izuwuaku
   Uchewuaku
   Izunweaku
   Nzenweaku

4. **Wisdom boosts strength, courage and confidence**
   Akokadike: Wisdom is stronger than might
   Akowuike: Wisdom/knowledge is power
   Akojiobi: Knowledge gives courage
   Akunesiobiike: Wisdom makes the heart brave
   Izuwudike: Knowledge is power
   Izubike: (same as above)
   Akokaegbe: wisdom is more powerful than gun
   Akowuozo: Wisdom is the source of wealth

5. **Wisdom is a very precious asset/treasure**
   Izukanma: Wisdom is the greatest asset
   Izuamaka: Wisdom is better than riches
   Nmutaka: Knowledge is power
   Akowundu: wisdom is life
   Izuagbanafia: Wisdom is not sold in the market. It is acquired by learning and diligence

Izuakolam: May I never lack knowledge
Nzenweaku: Age and wisdom I are the custodians of wealth

Concept of beauty in Igbo name expression:

The Igbo have excelled in the realms of visual and performance arts. Their concept of beauty also transcends the visual and the physical. The Igbo have the concept of moral, spiritual and intellectual beauty, and they give expression of these in their name culture.

1. ***Agwawunma*:** Character is beauty, moral character is beauty beyond the physical.
2. ***Nmaobi*:** Beauty of the mind or soul is better than the beauty of the face.
3. ***Nmawugo***: Beauty is eagle (beauty is power and strength.
4. ***Chikwenma***: Beauty is God's gift, (it is God that makes one beautiful, in other words, God is the source and giver of beauty).
5. ***Nmachukwu / Nmachi***: God is beautiful, This child is the expression of the beauty of God.).
6. ***Chikerenma***: God is the creator of beauty.
7. ***Nmawuko***: A thing of beauty is a thing of pride, (beauty is glorious).
8. ***Nmanwanyi (Nmanyanyi wu be di ya)***: The beauty of a woman is in the house of a husband, (marriage gives beauty and honor to a woman, marriage beautifies a woman).

Human relationships in Igbo name expression:

A name could be an expression of a historical event or experience, a reflection of some family vicissitude or memorial bench mark, an assertion of right, authority, or innocence; expression of traditional values or aspiration, or a lamentation of some catastrophy. In this section we shall attempt to exemplify some Igbo names as idioms, innuendoes and sacarsims of personal human relationships. A name could also be the expression of an outright condemnation or denunciation of some practice or act of impropriety. Some are positives and some are negative portrayal:

The positives

Amuchie: Another one has been born to replace a dead one, God has sent another replacement.

Anochie: Nwanochie: This one has come to replace**.**

Azukaego: My brethren/ family are more valuable than riches.

Ikwukananna: Love and security are best and strongest among siblings.

Ikwuamaka: Family and relations are good human assets.

Ikwuazom: My brethren/relations are my savior and refuge.

Ikwuamaehi: My relations and family are very loving and caring.

Umunnaka: My family is strong and powerful, you can't mess with them.

Nwannediuto: It is very delightful to have a good and loving family.

Nwanneamaka: Siblings are wonderful assets.

Azubugwu: Family guarantees security and refuge.

Ogoamaka: A good in-law is a source of joy.

Ogobuchi: A good in-law is a gift and blessing from God.

Uzogo (Uzuogoechina): May the way to my in-laws remain safe and open, may the goodness and blessings of my in-laws remain permanent for me.

The Negatives

Aghadiuno(Aghadinuno): There is war in the family. (an expression of family feud

Amuchie/Amushie: *There will be no more child,* (this could be an expression of lamentation; that the source or the potential for another offspring is gone, or no longer exists due to some tragedy or misfortune).

Iloegbunam: Let my enemies not kill me.

Ilokaonwu: This enemity/ hatred is more dangerous than death.

Ilodinuno: There is deep seated enmity in the family (the same as Aghadinuno above)

Aghauno: (Agha-uno-ajoka) family feud is very dangerous.

Anyaegbunam: (Anya ilom egbunam) may the hatred of my enemy not consume me.

***Ebegbulem**: M*ay my goodness/kindness not kill/ hurt me (an expression of regret of goodness rewarded with evil.

Ibegbunam: May my relations not kill me.

Umunnakwe: If my kindred allows or supports me (an expression of fear and jealousy of one's kindred.).

***Amandiaeze (*Amaeze)**: I don't know whom to fear or avoid.

Ejimnkeonye (Nkeonye): My hands are clean, I have not offended any one.

Emerole/Emeremole: What wrong have I done to deserve this?

Onyekamjiugwo: Whom have I offended? (I have not defrauded/ wronged any one, expression of innocence, a person being unjustly persecuted).

Onyeuno (Onye uno egbughi onye, isi acha ya awo): If one's relation does not kill one, one will live long and have gray hairs.

Ibebuogu: My brethren are my worst enemies.

Igbo Visual and Performing Arts:

Igbo people love and cherish beauty and aesthetics. For them beauty and the beautiful exist in many different dimensions—material, physical, moral, spiritual, and intellectual. In the fine arts dimension Ndi-Igbo have produced some of the greatest African artists, musicians, dancers, potters, sculptors, and weavers in textile technology.

The late Dr. Ben Enweonwu: his record as Africa's greatest sculptor still stands, (see Ben. Enweonwu Chapter Three).

The Nkpokiti and Etilogwu acrobatic dancers, and the Abam war dancers are world famous. They have performed in most world capital cities and in many national and international festivals.

The selected few art forms below are of great importance in the realms of Igbo cultural identity.

The **Igbo-Ukwu pottery**
The **Awka carving**
The **Akwuete textile industry**
The **Ijele king masquerade**

Igbo-Ukwu Pottery and ceramics: The remarkable archeological discoveries at Igbo-Ukwu are highly significant not only for the history and art of the Igbo but for all of Nigeria and the West African sub-region. "A series of radiocarbon dates from these excavations cover the tenth century A.D. which places them well before the fine and better known metal and terracotta arts of Ife, Owo, and Benin. Among the Igbo-Ukwu finds are the earliest known African bronze castings, the earliest complicated 'shrine' assemblage, the earliest elaborated regalia for a leadership and royalty, and the finest Nigerian textiles. Even by contemporary standards Igbo-Ugwu art remains the most technically advanced, virtuosic and delicate art styles south of the Sahara. Thus its intrinsic importance and its implications are enormous for all Africa, and, of course, it is central to Igbo culture-history and identity." (Herbert Cole and Chike Aniakor, Museum of Cultural History, 1984) (see historical time line Chapter One above).

Chapter Eleven

Igbo Food Culture As Identity

In this presentation the focus will be narrowed down to the two principal traditional Igbo snacks and delicacies, and Igbo basic traditional soup culture, rather than on the total spectrum of food culture which the present writer has neither the qualification nor expertise to delve into. Although the basic food items are the same all over the Igboland such as: yam, cassava, beans, and maize, the traditional snacks, delicacies and soup culture vary almost along the dialectical zones. This chapter will focus on the most popular and most cherished traditional snacks and Igbo soup culture:

Snacks and delicacies:

- **Ngwongwo isi ewu**
- **Ugba**

Ngwongwo isi ewu:

Ngwongwo isi ewu is a healthy meaty spicy treat, exuding appetizing flavor and aroma. It is the king of snacks, just as Ijele is the king of masquerades. ***Ngwongwo*** is exclusively an adult privilege. It is not an every day treat, it is not a snack for all and sundry. In Igbo social parlance ***ngwongwo bu ogbenye anu***—it is not a snack for the poor, because ***ngwongwo*** is quite expensive. It is a high class delicacy. Another popular Igbo expression is: ***ngwongwo bu akaji aku***, it is a favorite delicacy for the privileged class.

Ngwongwo isi ewu, also simply known as ***ngwongwo*** is meaty spicy concoction of goat head and its "***particulars***", the particulars include the entrils, the kidney, heart, and sometimes the trotters. It is the "particulars" that quantify and classify the grade of isi ewu.

There are two grades of isi ewu, the ordinary or half bowl, and the full package or ***ikenga isi ewu.*** The content of the half bowl is basically only the meat from the head of a goat, without the particulars. The ikenga class is enriched with the meat from the particulars. Generally the price of the ikenga class doubles that of the other. Among some elite class the grades are referred to as "A Level" (the ***ikenga*** package), and "O Level" (the half bowl).

Recipe:

Process Stage 1

- goat head and trotters sienged over the fire to burn off the hairs, the hooves and horns are knocked out or peeled off.
- the stomach and intestines very well cleaned and washed.
- the intestines packed into the stomach and tied up.
- the heart and kidney.
- all the above cooked together to tender.
- all the flesh of the goat head is carefully flayed from the skull, the jaw bones are stripped and discarded.
- the skull is cut open to extract the brain, then the empty shell is discarded.
- all the meat of the head and the stomach and the intestines are sliced into small pieces.

Stage 2: Ingredients (spices)

- Some ground red pepper
- Uzuza
- Uda
- Red palm oil
- Akanwu (potash)

- Very small amount of utazi for flavor
- Some salt to taste

Stage 3: the mixing or final preparation stage
A wooden bowl (okwa) and a wooden ladle (eku).

- Crack the goat skull and extracxt brain
- Put the brain in the bowl and blend into a paste.
- Add red palm oil and akanwu and blend. The akanwu (potash) has the chemical element (alkaline potassium hydroxide) which changes the red palm oil into a bright yellowish brown color.
- Add the rest of the meat and ingredients and mix until everything is well blended.
- Add pepper and salt to taste.

A delicious and spicy bowl of ngwongwo is ready for consumption. Ngwongwo goes well with fresh palm wine or cold beer for those who like alcohol. Among the Igbo nothing excites the appitite like ngwongwo. It is very nutritious and proteinous. Ngwongwo is expensive because the preparation is very pains-taking and the spices are not very easy to come by especially outside the homeland.

Ngwongwo is one Igbo snack that has gone commercial and international. It is also very popular with all African people, Black Americans, and young white people with liberal appetite for the African stuff. No other indigenous snack draws the Igbo elite and business men together like a good ngwongwo spot.

Note: Ngwongwo must not be confused or equated with pepper soup. Pepper soup is essencially a watery stuff, eaten with spoon. In fact no one can eat pepper soup without a spoon. Pepper soup is not Igbo identity snack. Ngwongwo ise ewu is typically Igbo identity snack. And whereas any body can cook pepper soup, only indigenous Igbo specialists know the secret and technology' of ngwongwo ise ewu.

Ugba:

Like its "big brother" ngwongwo, ugba is the second most popular Igbo snack. Ugba delicacy snach is more popular in Imo, Abia and

Anambra States. Ugba the basic ingredient is the seed of the oil bean tree. In Anambra State it is called *ukpaka*. The ugba seed is embedded in a long hard pod in the structure of a legume. A pod could contain between three and six bean seeds. The seed is embedded in a dark pink/brown pericarp.

Process stage 1:

There are various ways in which the ugba seed is extracted from the pod among the various Igbo groups. There are also various ways ugba is prepared. It differs from state to state. But basically the general process can be summarized as follows:

- The kernel is extracted from the hard pericarp and boiled for about many hours, or over night.
- The ccooked bean seeds are then sliced into strands and pieces width-wise or length-wise.
- The slices are spread out and allowed to dry in the sun or wrapped in plantain leaves to ferment for two or three days. In Imo and Abia States the sliced ugba is usually put in an earthen bowl and covered with plantain leaves for two or three days. The crispiness of the ugba decrease very rapidly. Most people like it crispy especially in Imo and Abia States. Whereas in Anambra state they prefer it slightly more tender.

Recipe for preparing the ugba snack:

Ingredients:

- red palm oil
- some ground hot pepper
- crayfish
- pieces of dry fish or stock fish (okporoko)
- uzuza
- afufa (nkpuru anara) cut into halves or quadrants
- Pour the sliced seeds and all the ingredients into a large bowl and mix

- add salt to taste
- warm the mixture over some heat for a couple of minutes
- serve warm or cold

Ugba could always be enriched with ***abacha/ mbesimbe akpu*** (processed sliced cassava).

Contrasts

Both *ugba and ngwongwo* are typical Igbo identity delicacies.

But whereas ***Ugba*** is usually eaten with a spoon, ***ngwongwo*** is not generally eaten with a spoon, it is a five finger business.

Whereas ugba could be prepared and served to all and sundary at important social ceremonies and gatherings, ngwongwo is never served at meetings and social gatherings because of the high cost and processes. Ngwongwo is "aristocratic" and not an all-comers privilege. In the American parlance ***Ngwongwo*** is not minimum wage stuff.

Ugba as identity in Owerri Clan:

Ugba is the most popular snack in Imo and Abia States. In the old Owerri Province ***ugba*** was as primary as kola-nut. In fact among the people of Abia and Imo States ugba is the choice kola-nut. In Owerri clan ugba is a sine-qua-non (Latin—without which, nothing). Except in very serious ritual matters and occasions, where kola-nut must be served, ugba comes first as the most important item on the program. Among Owerri people ugba must be either the prologue or the epilogue, the first or the last, either the appetizer or the dessert. Which ever way, it must happen. It is also noteworthy that only Owerri people enrich their ***ugba*** with fresh ***okazi*** vegetable and ***sungu*** (smoked sardine). ***Okazi*** adds very special taste and flavor to ***ugba.***

Among the Owerri both at home and in the diaspora, ugba is a better and more welcome substitute for kola-nut. The popular saying in Owerri: ***Ntaala ugba nuo nmii, ndi ogaranya bara ma*** (Once I can have ugba to eat and palm-wine, I careless how others get rich and build mansions).

Note of observation: This expression which smacks of lack of ambition, laziness, and laissez-faire was attributed to an old illiterate village peasant over a century ago. Although ugba still holds the pride of place as a cultural identity in Owerri clan, the meaning of the saying is absolutely not true of the nature and character and disposition in modern day Owerri. It is not controversial that Owerri has produced some of the greatest politicians, famous university professors, doctors, distinguished sciencitists, engineers, business tycoons, honorable ststesmen and women.

A case in point: In 1990, I had the opportunity to attend an international conference in Copenhagen (capital of Denmark) from Nigeria. During a weekend off from the conference, we visited the famous Tivoli (the Disneyland in Denmark). There I stumbled on a Nigerian couple, natives of Owerri who were residents in Denmark. They were the only blacks I saw in that very huge entertainment center. It is very rare to find Nigerians in that part of Europe. We fell into a most exciting and heart warming conversation. They took me to their house. The man was an auto Engineer in the Volvo Motor Industry in Copenhagen, the wife was a pharmacist (Ph.D Pharm) in a Teaching Hospital. To my greatest surprise, the wife quickly prepared a large bowl of ugba steaming with aroma and flavor, heavily stuffed with ***oporo*** (dry shrimps) and **okporo** (stock fish) and ***okazi***. She said in a strong and typical Owerri accent, ***"ka m chere gi oji ndi be ka anyii"*** (let me serve you our traditional kola). When I inquired how on earth they came about ugba in that very far away land, the wife showed me parcles of processed ugba seed and bags of dried green ***okazi*** in a huge deep freezer. "Our stock of ugba is always replenished every time we visit home, or whenever any of our parents come to visit", she said. When I was commenting on the richness of the delicious ***ugba,*** the man said in humor, ***bitee m m'lee,*** (you can't beat this one) meaning although we are out here, my wife's ***ugba*** is as good as what you can expect back home. So the truth of the matter is that Owerri people are all over the world, and that they carry their favorite traditional ***ugba*** with them. It is very obvious that whenever Owerri scientists will perfect their science of space technology, their astronauts will take ***ugba*** up there with them.

Igbo soup culture.

The Igbo have very rich soup culture with varieties. The soup culture varies along dialectical zones. Each soup kind derives its name from the main vegetable or ingredient used in the preparation. Generally, the Igbo use a lot of spices and a variety of ingredients; this is why traditional Igbo soups are very tasty and spicy. Igbo women are very creative and resourceful in their culinary arts. There is an Igbo adage about a bad cook (woman): ***nwanyi ajo ite wu udara dabara n'nsi*** (a woman who is a bad cook is like an apple that fell into human excrement). Because every woman is expected to be very efficient and exceedingly professional at cookery and food crafts, a bad cook is considered a tragedy, ***nwanyi ajo ite wu nta afo: (***a woman who is a bad cook is as distastable as belly ache). This is the reason responsible mothers always take pains to teach and train their daughters in proper domestic science especially in the very intricate art of soup craft. In the good old days, a bad cook was a recipe for polygamy because the Igbo man has strong addiction for delicious soup. Parents always warn their grown up daughters that good cooking is the key/secret to the heart of a husband: ***uto ofe na eru n'obi di,*** (a delicious soup reaches the heart of a husband). There is also the popular saying "na good soup make husband lick bottom pot". A very good cook (wife) is always referred to as: ***nwanyi na esi obi diya:*** (a woman whose cooking touches the husband's heart). Igbo men are always very proud of their wivies delicious soup and dishes, and always like to invite friends over to dine with them. In the converse, when a man always takes his friends to eat out instead of inviting them to dine in his house, it is not complimentary about his wife's food quality.

In this section only the most popular traditional soup kinds from across the Igbo States will be discussed.

- **ofe onugbu (olugbu)**
- **ofe egwusi**
- **ofe ogbono (agbolo)**
- **ofe nsala (nsara)**
- **ofe ugu**
- **ofe achara**

- **ofe okazi (ukazi)**
- **ofe okwuru (okro)**
- **ofe oha (uha)**
- **ofe akwu**
- **ofe uzuza**

Ofe onugbu /olugbu (bitter leaf soup)

"In recent times western pharmacology has come up with a pharmaceutical opinion that bitter leaf is medicinal for diabetis". (American Institute of Pharmaceuticle Research)

Bitter leaf soup is the most popular favorite of the Anambra State people. The onugbu vegetable is washed of its bitterness, and turned into a tasty eadible stuff and used as vegetable soup ingredient. The soup is usually a thick paste. Igbo women use various stuffs to thicken the soup, the thickening ingredients include egwusi, pounded cocoa yam, or pounded yam and ukpor. Out here in the diaspora Igbo women improvise with other stuffs such as quaker oats, oat meal, farina, and bisquick for thickening, because the traditional thickner stuffs are not easy to come by.

Ofe onugbu is usually very heavily stuffed with meat, dry fish and ***okporoko***. The basic spice that makes ***ofe onugbu*** real and authentic is ***ogiri***, a strong type of seasoning. In fact in Anambra State ***ofe onugbu*** without ***ogir***i is not real and authentic. Ogiri is a peculiar seasoning made from processed seeds of melon—egwusi, or from the seeds of ogiri ugba—castor oil seed. The seeds are shelled and cooked soft, then fermented and blended and packed in small packets. The fermentation makes it very odoriferous, and gives the soup a peculiar flavor. The flavor makes the soup very palatable and delicious. Not all Igbo people like the odor of the ogiri, but for the Anambra people ***ogiri*** is the magic that excites the appetite. ***'ogiri bu ogwu ofe'.*** Among the Igbo of Anambra State, in any party or celebration ***ofe onugbu*** is a pretigious treat. Guests always rush it more than any other soup kind. Any woman or house wife that knows the secret of ofe onugbu, is very highly respected in cultural gathering, such a woman is a proud eagle feather on her husband's cap (ugo di ya)

Ofe egwusi: (egwusi is the seed of African melon)

The basic ingredient is egwusi—ground into a powdery stuff. Some vegetable of choice could be added. The quantity of the egwusi determines the thickness of the soup. Ofe egwusi, like ofe onugbu, is usually heavily suffed with meat, dry fish, and quite often with okporoko. Other ingredients include: ground cray-fish, red palm-oil, pepper and salt. Across Igboland and internationally, ofe egwusi is more popular than ofe onugbu beause it is easier to prepare, and more importantly because of the ogiri spice element which Igbo people outside the Anambra State do not easily tolorate. Of course one man's meat could be another's aversion. Moreover, the washing of the bitter leaves is a very arduous task which most people always want to avoid. Onugbu and ugu are the most popular vegetables for ofe egwusi.

Ofe ogbono: (ogbolo)

This is another very popular traditional Igbo soup. Ogbono is the main ingredient which makes it thick, and draws as an elastic paste. Usually with the exception of okwuru, plain ofe ogbono does not take any leafy vegetable. It takes quite a lot of spices, a lot of fish and meat, cray-fish, pepper, and palm oil. Ofe ogbono is not very popular among the Imo and Abia people.

Ofe nsala:

The main ingredient in ofe nsala is fresh fish. Ofe nsala is very nutritious and very easy to prepare. This is why it is sometimes referred to as emergency soup. Because of the main ingredient—fresh fish, it is very popular among the riverine people of Onitsha, Asaba, Aguleri, Oguta, Ogbaru and the Rivers State. In fact for the hinterland people, this soup kind is not in their popular culinary vocabulary.

Ofe ugu:

As the name implies, the main vegetable is the ugu leaves. Ofe ugu is very popular among the Igbo of Imo, Abia, and Rivers States. It is their own version of the onugbu soup in Anambra State. The common popular traditional ingredients that go very well with ofe ugu include: snail (eju), dry fish, cray-fish, prewinkle, pepper, salt and palm-oil. Ofe ugu is very rich in vitamins. However, it is not a social or party soup.

Ofe achara:

This is a very local stuff and very traditional among the Umuahia ***(ndi ota achara)*** and parts of Ngwa people of Abia State. Achara is the tender leaves of "domesticated" elephant grass. It is very rich in vitamin and iron. It is a very rich source of fiber which facilitates digestion and prevents constipation. Ofe achara is watery and usually heavily stuffed with ***eju*** (snail), dry meat, dry fish and ***esem*** (periwinkle), and oporo (dried shrimps). Nothing excites the appetite of the Umuahia folks as ofe achara. There is a popular saying that: ***if an Umuahia man comes back from ala bekee and does not eat ofe achra, it is possible that his father was not a real son of the soil).***

Ofe okazi:-

Okazi is a very popular vegetable in Imo, Abia and the Rivers. Like achara it is very rich in fiber which is very good for the digestive process. When fresh and green it adds very delicious taste to the soup especially if the okazi is cooked to tender. Ofe okazi takes a lot of eju, dry meat, ***sungu, okporo***, pepper and other spices. Ofe okazi is usually darkish green and watery.

Ofe okwuru:—(okra)

As the name implies okwuru (okra) is the main vegetable, but quite often other vegetables such as inine (green), ugu and ***ahihara*** could be added to complement the okra. ***Ofe okwuru*** is very popular across the length and breadth of Igboland. With plenty of meat, fish, and okporoko okwuru soup excites the appetite. Children love it more than any kind of soup because it makes fufuu, eba, farina and other stuff slide down smoothly and quickly. If adults don't watch it children are prone to over feed with okwuru soup and cry about their painful stomach. A note of caution, ofe okwuru always has the tendency to leave some evidence on the clothes.

Ofe akwu:—(banga soup)

Ofe akwu could be prepared in two different ways for two different purposes—as a medicinal stimulant or as regular emergency soup for eating food.

As a therapeutic stimulant ***ofe akwu*** is efficacious in the relief of common cold, flu, constipation, minor diarrhea, food poisoning, and some degree of delirium. I recall that in my boyhood days ***ofe akwu*** used to be my mother's first aid for most ailments, and it worked. At least we were made to believe it did.

Ofe akwu is more medicinal as a stimulant than just ordinary soups. In the traditional form, the fresh palm fruit is boiled and squeezed to yield the fresh oil. The fiber and nuts are washed and the oily pulp is sifted to remove the roughage. Then the oil is cooked with the relevant ingredients. The red palm oil is very rich in vitamins A and D minerals.

As a curative potion, ***ofe akwu*** is not very delicious (like most medicines), requires no vegetables, no fresh meat, only little pieces of dry fish or dry shrimps, are added, and a lot of hot spices like pepper, uzuza, and some salt to taste. As a curative it is drank hot to stimulate immediate release of stomach and intestinal enzymes for quick absorption.

Ofe akwu as soup: is quite different from ofe akwu as a therapeutic stimulant. The process of extracting the oil is basically the same, but the soup is designed as a sauce for eating foods such as boiled rice, boiled yam and fufu. It is not an every day or regular kind of soup. It is an occasional treat, a once in a while kind of stuff.

Ofe uzuza:-

Also known as ***ofe omugwo*** or ***nmiri oku ngwo*** is a therapeutic stimulant. It is unlike any other kind of Igbo soup. In a way it is very peculiar because it is specifically a therapeutic concoction, prepared exclusively for post natal mothers, never for men and children. ***Ofe uzuza*** appears only after the delivery of a baby, and it is exclusively for the post—natal mother. This is the reason for the aliases ***ofe omugwo, ofe ngwo, nmiri oku ngwo.*** In the traditional setting, the new mother has to enjoy or endure this hot and very spicy stuff every day for eight days ***izu abuo*** after delivery.

Ofe uzuza as therapeutic stimulant has the medicinal potency:

- For cleaning up and healing the birth canal.
- To prevent or minimize infection.
- To stimulate the mammary glands to release breast milk.
- To sharpen the appetite of the new mother so that she can feed well and recuperate faster. Ofe uzuza is very efficacious in fighting and removing the thrush (an oral infection that covers the taste buds in the tongue and palates, a common post natal infection) that kills the appetite. The aroma and flavor of ***ofe uzuza*** is appetizingly strong and very stimulating.

Ofe uzuza is a watery, very pungent, hot and spicy and is meant to be administered or taken hot. This is the reason for the linquistic euphemism ***nmiri oku*** (hot water). The Igbo slang ***A nam anu nmiri oku*** is an idiomatic expression meaning my wife has just had a baby.

As the the name implies, the most important ingredient in this soup is ***uzuza***—a hot spicy tiny grain. Other very important ingredients include: dry utazi vegetable leaves, uda, red hot pepper, a lot of dry fish and meat, crayfish, and salt to taste. In the traditional setting, it is the mother of the woman or her mother in-law that prepares the ***ofe uzuza***. Usually all the essential ingredients for ***ofe uzuza*** are procured by whosoever will perform the responsibility and function of ***omugwo*** (post natal care). Also in the traditional setting the quantity and quality of the fish and meat (especially bush meat ***anu nchi, anu mgbada,*** and goat meat) and stockfish for the ***ofe omugwo*** are more often than not a reflection of the degree of love and affection the new mother enjoys, and also the gender of the baby the husband desired. ***Ofe uzuza*** is a typical Igbo identity soup. It is not found in any restaurant or hotel. It is also exclusively a female gender "privilege".

CHAPTER TWELVE

DOWN MEMORY LANE: THE GOOD, THE BAD, AND THE UGLY

GLOSSARY OF TERMS, PERSONAGES, AND LANDMARKS.

Terms: Terminologies, expressions and slangs that have become ingrafted into Igbo contemporary etymology, and have become so typically Igbonised as an identity because no one outside the Igbo linguistic horizon can perfectly appreciate or decode them. Some of them are expressions of the aftermath of the Nigeria/Biafra war and have since become commonplace vocabulary of every day usage. Some of them are as ancient as the people and have the linguistic sataus of an icon.

1. ***Igbo kwenu:*** This is an Igbo clarion call, a strong expression of demand for action. It arrests and compels attention for silence, or action for solidarity. In another context, it is a very powerful cry of salutation and compliment. Strictly speaking the expression **Igbo kwenu** has a format and convention which many contemporary Igbo may not be fully aware of: the definite number of times it should be said in a particular context, the body language and tone of the speaker, and the appropriate audience response. In informal or ordinary situations or gatherings, people usually use the expression

just any how, to call attention, to make a point, or to offer a salutation.

But not so in very serious or very formal occasions or meetings. At such formal occasions, the expression ***Igbo Kwenu*** not only has a definite format, but also very cosmic connotations and import. In Igbo cosmology the number 'Four' has very mystic connotation. There are four market days in the Igbo week ***izu,*** namely, ***Eke, Afor, Nkwo, Orie.*** In Igbo cosmic relationships there are: ***elu na ala***, ***ezi na uzo,*** (four cosmic elements)***, nmuo na madu, ikwu na ibe*** the living and the dead, (past and present, family and relations). In Igbo kola-nut culture, the kola-nut that has four lobes is a symbol of fraternity and harmony. In the days when the cowrie was the physical cash and form of currency, cowries were counted in units of four, four cowries was ***otu isi ego,*** that was the basic or lowest unit, (the American cent, the Nigerian kobo, the British penny).

In conformity with the mystic concept of Four in Igbo cosmology, the number Four becomes the traditional/formal number of times for the expression of ***Igbo Kwenu*** at serious social and cultural gatherings. The essence is to invoke and summon the cosmic and ancestral forces to unleash and impose their powers to compel attention on the occasion.

Perhaps the most effective way to demonstrate the import of ***Igbo Kwenu*** as a linguistic identity is graphically illustrated by Chnua Achebe in his famous classic: ***Things Fall Apart:***

> ***"In the morning the market place was full. There must have been about ten thousand men there, all talking in low voices. At last Ogbuefi Ezeugo stood up in the mist of them and bellowed four times, 'Umuofia kwenu', and on each occasion he faced different direction and seemed to push the air with a clenched fist. And ten thousand men answered 'Yaa!' each time. Then there was perfect silence. 'Umuofia kwenu', he bellowed a fifth time (the five villages in Umuofia clan), and the crowd yeiled in answer".***

This excerpt from **Things_Fall_Apart,**_says it all: about the use and format of the Igbo expression—***Igbo Kwenu!*** In fact ***Igbo Kwenu*** is the most powerful magic expression for attention and silence or unity of action. It is the most powerful literary expression of Igbo identity.

2. ***'Okongwu':*** Igbo cultural slang for elderly and old folks, sometimes also used as a deriogratory term for the ignorant or foolish, or out of fashion folk.
3. ***'Megee':*** very new fresh looking coin or currency.
4. ***'419':*** Igbo slang for criminal fraud, deception, swindling, dupping, racketeering.
5. ***'Sabo':*** slang for a saboteur, a military or civilian sell-out, traitor, or spy, and any one considered unpatriotic during the war.
6. ***'Air raid':*** nickname for Col. Joe Achuzie during the Nigerian-Biafra war, he was dreaded for his zero tolerance for indiscipline and any form of unsodierly behavior, mediocrity or cowardice.
7. ***'Ogbunigwe.:*** Biafran high power and very deadly multipurpose land mine produced by the RAP (Research and Production) Unit during the war, also called '***ajukwu boket'*** by the Nigerian soldiers. Ogbunigwe killed and maimed by wave effect percussion and dispersal of shrapnel. It was shaped either as a cone or cylinder and could be used as a land mine, a ground to ground projectile against troop concentrations or ground to air anti-personnel "air burst" cluster bomb.
8. ***'Biafran mine':*** code name **"mamiwoter"** Birfran home-made weapon system. It was a combination of many different weapon components including the dangerous ***ogbunigwe,*** convectional bombs, rockets, etc. set up together for mass action effect, electronically connected in series along coastlines and detonated in predetermined sequences. The idea was to make casualty evacuation, retreat and tactical dispersal extremely hazardous from secondary detonations.
9. ***RAP:*** Acronym for Biafran Research and Production Organization. This organization brought together and coordinated the efforts of different science groups focusing on Airports, roads, chemicals, heavy equipment and industrial materials, weapons production, biological processes, fuel

refining, rocketry, explosives, electronics and essential foods.

10. ***'Abagana Armada':*** On March 31, 1968, Biafran army won their biggest battle on the Onitsha–Awka sector of the war, by ambushing and destroying a 98 vehicle column of Nigerian soldiers and armament, supplies and reinforcement from Makurdi to Onitsha. It was a great disaster that was very expertly executed by an ambush. The bombs and explosives in the convoy continued to erupt and explode like an angry volcano for over one week. The humiliating Abagana defeat prompted Yakobu Gowan to remove Col. Muritula Mohammed as the General Commanding Officer of the Onitsha sector.
11. ***'Asaba Massacre':*** October 7 1967: This was a very wickedly contrived genocide by the Nigerian army against innocent unarmed civilians. Nigerian soldiers entered Asaba, rounded up as many as 600 Igbo men—all civilians and shot them in cold blood. The victims were all buried in mass graves. This is a cultural sacrilege, especially since the men burried included titled chiefs and traditional rulers**, *ndi nze na ozo.***
12. ***'Biafran Babies': B*iafran** Air Force Mig jets.
13. ***VOB:*** Voice of Biafra Broadcasting Service.
14. ***'Corporal Nwafor':*** code name for a Nigerian Saladin armoured vehicle captured by the Biafran forces and reconditioned for service.
15. ***'Red Devil':*** Biafran home made armoured vehicle adapted from trucks, or other earth moving equipment re-fashioned and equipped by the Heavy Equipment and Industrial Materials Group. It was a very crude but very effective military armament.
16. ***'BOFF':*** Acronym for Biafran Organization of Freedom Fighters.
17. ***'Annabelle':*** operational name for Biafra's Uli-Ihiala air strip.
18. ***'Land Army':*** a sub-group of the Biafran Science Group, devoted to food production under the economic blockade.
19. "**Attack**": Biafran code word for secret trade and business across or behind the enemy line. During the war, because of

the vicious total military blockade of Biafra, some essential food items and some very vital commodities became very scarce and very difficult to come by. But because man must survive, and man "***must wack",*** Ndi-Igbo had to use and apply "Number 6", to penetrate enemy lines and territories by foot tracks and hidden vehicle roads, to purchase those essential commodities and make them available in Biafran markets. It was a very risky and hazardous venture. **Attack** was principally a women's field because able-body Biafran men were expected to be engagged very actively in the war effort. Women and girls were free to move around, but men became ***"afia iwu"*** human contrabands because of the conscription. The **Attack** era was a spell of "woman power" and it brought out the best and the worst in women. It was a terrible phenomenon that will not be dicussed in this presentation. The most essential and basic **attack** commodities were: salt, rice, beans, flour, baby foods, basic health drugs, flashlight batteries, soaps, cigarettes, stockfish, and motor fluids. Many men and women lost their lives in the attack business.

20. **'Ati Mgbo':** Biafran slang for victims of shell shock and bomb blast deafness. Soldiers at the war fronts were dangerously exposed to the terribe deafening blasts of bomb and rocket explosions. The blasts affected or damaged the ear drums and the sense of hearing and equilibrium, causing partial or total deafness and the loss of coordination in related nervous system. It also resulted in the malfunction of the sense of reason and speech, and proper social coordinates. The victims always yell to speak, and if you don't talk very loud or shout they could not hear you. So if a person demonstrates inability to understand or articulate properly, he was daubed "***onye ati ngbo".***
21. ***'Ironside':*** British nickname for Major Gen. J.U.T. Aguiyi—Ironsi, first military Head of State of Nigeria, killed by the Nigerian soldiers in Ibadan in July 1966.
22. **Nigerian air raids**: During the war Nigerian war planes which were flown by mercenary Egyptian and Russian pilots, and were instructed that every piece of land and feature in Biafra

was a legitimate target. But this is against the international rules of engagement. The first and early raids of these planes suffered heavy losses and damage from Biafran anti aircraft defence system. Subsequently, those mercenary pilots learned their lessons to avoid areas they suspected would have Biafran air cover. So they chose to attack defenceless areas such as open markets, church and school buildings, hospitals, and busy road junctions. A few of those civilian and non-combatant targets which they attacked included:

- **The_raid_on_a_church_in_Umuahia**: It happened at about 8:30 am on that fateful Sunday morning. Worshippers were exiting the church after the early morning mass when two Nigerian fighter-bombers descended on the church and masscered innocent and defenseless Christians.
- **The_Otu_Ocha_open_maket_in_Aguleri**: This was one of the worst dastardly and most despicable act of the Nigerian air force. It was an open relief market in full swing. Two Nigerian fighter planes descended on the market people with bombs, rockets and machine gun fire. The jets hovered and soared lazily around for several minutes discharging their lethal ammunition. At the end of that massacre, shattered pieces of human and cattle littered the whole place. More than a hundred market people and dozens of livestock—cows and goats were slaughhtered in cold blood.
- **The_massacre_at_the_Aba_Railway_crossing**: This was another dastardly act of the Nigerian war planes. It happened on a Friday morning rush hour, a long freight train with over 20 goods wagons was passing along a very busy commercial part of the town. The railway level crossing gate was lowered and motor traffic was held up for over twenty minutes, hundreds of cars and trucks lined up on both sides of the level crossing. Along the busy roads were three gas stations in operation. Two Nigerian fighters zoomed down and raided bombs and rockets all over the place. The gas stations and dozens

of cars and trucks were set ablaze. The jets left a trail of charged vehicles and human remains.

- **The_Orifite_Grammar_School_air_raid**: That institution was bombed several times during the war. It would appear the the jet pilots had the wrong map, they thought that their target was a military camp. The school was completely destroyed.
- **The_attack_on_Ogbate_Market_in_Enugu**: was another deliberate and vicious massacre of unarmed innocent civilians. The Nigerian jets rained rockets, machine gun fire and granades on the open relief market on two different occasions. One of the most gruesome and repulsive spectacle after the raid was that of a headless young mother, a rocket had blown off her head, and there she laid in a pool of her blood, with her four month old baby strongly straped on her back.
- **Hospitals_and_refugee_camps**: Those were very easy targets and thousands of unarmed civilians, miles away from any Biafran military installations, were massacred and hundreds maimed.

The most comprehensive reports of deliberate air strikes on the civilian population in Biadra came from Mr.Churchill, grandson of Sir Winston Churchill. They were published in the **Times_of_London** during the first week of March, 1969. "It is clear", said Mr. Churchill, "that the Egyptian pilots hired by the Federal Government regarded all of Biafra as free bomb targets or were so instructed."

In a raid on Ozu-Abam market in full session, Mr. Churchill and Mr. Llyod Garrison of the **New_York_Times** reported an area of more than 10,000 sq. yards was completely devastated. In the "Times of London" report of February 26, 1969, these journalists said that the bombs were "high expolsive incendiary or possibly phosphorus with high capacity to incinerate human body so that most of the victims were so severely burned to survive and died not long after."

Personages:

1. **Omenuko:**
   (by Pita Nwana) published in 1933, was an award winning novel in the All—African Literary contest in indigenous African languages, organized by the International Institute of African Languages and Culture. Pita Nwana was the first Igbo to publish fiction in Igbo language. It was a classic and a monumental achievement in the age.

2. **Israel Njemanze Nwoba:**
   Israel was the first Igbo highlife musician and celebrated vocalist, born in Owerri Eastern Region. Business took him to Lagos in the late 1940s, where he established a very popular musical band known as "*The Three Night **Wizards**"*. By the early '50s Israel Nwoba was a household name throughout Nigeria. His lyrics were phenomenal, and he waxed hundreds of records. One of his most popular piece which immortalized him was about himself, his minature stature, and it was very prophetic about his tragic end. Here it goes:

   The title: *I AM VERY SHORT:*
   You know why I am very short
   My mother was very short
   My father was very short
   My sisters, all are very short-eth
   And my children
   I suppose they will be very short
   Measure me with the guitar I play
   I am short
   Guitar is short
   I am short
   I am only four feet
   Eleven inches
   All around me, very short-eth
   Even my life too, I suppose will be very short
   Low and behold his life was cut short on Thursday April 17, 1955, he was brutally assassinated after a night show by his colleages. We Salute You!

3. **Col. Tim. Onwuatuegwu:** (of Nnewi) The "Terror Firebrand" of Biafran Army, the most dreaded name in the Nigerian army during the Nigerian-Biafran war. Nigerian soldiers and commanders branded him **"the invincible Devil of Biafran Army."** Unfortunately he was killed on the eve of the end of the war. You deserve a twelve gun salute!. We Salute You!
4. **Boniface Ofokaja:** Veteran Broadcaster—The Golden Voice of "Voice of Biafra International" We Salute You!
5. Okonkwo Onwuruigbo Umezurike: Voice of Biafra, Akuko Uwa (World **News)** in Igbo: His translation of some military terms and language were phenomenal and rib-cracking. His descriptive translation of a bomb was '***ngwa agha nakpagbuonwe ya ike aruruala'.; ogbonigwe***—the formidable Biafran mine '***oku nagba ozara dina ngwagha.*** His translation for political diplomacy was—***'aruruala bekee'.*** We Salute You!
6. **Oko Okon Ndem: 'Voice of Biafra War Report':** We Salute You!
7. **Bishop Onyeabo**: (of Onitsha) The first Anglican Bishop on the Niger. He championed the translation of the Bible into Igbo language.
8. **Virginia Ngozi Etiaba**: The first woman governor in the history of Nigerian politics. She was governor of Anambara State from November 2006 to February 2007. Her instalement came as the previous governor, Peter Obi, was impeached by the state legislature for alleged gross misconduct. She relinquished office and transferred back power to Obi when an appeal court nullified the impeachment. Etiaba is a native of Nnewi, in Nnewi North Local Council of Anambra State.

Landmarks: Old and famous educational institutions in Igboland

1. **1 DMGS: Onitsha founded 1925**
2. **CKC, Onitsha founded 1933**
3. **Methodist Boys High School, Uzuakoli, founded 1922**
4. **St. Marks Teacher Training, Awka,**

5. **St. Paul's Teachers College, Awka**
6. **QRC, (Queen of the Rosary) Onitsha**
7. **St. Charle's Teachers College, Onitsha founded 1928**
8. **All Hallows Seminary, Onitsha**
9. **St. Monica's Women Teachers College, Ogbunike**
10. **Merchants of Light Grammar School, Oba, founded 1949**
11. **Okongwu Memorial Grammar School, Nnewi**
12. **St. Thomas' Teachers College, Ibusa**
13. **T.T.C. (Teacher Training College) Nsukka**
14. **Aggrey Memorial College, Arochukwu**
15. **Bishop Lasberry, Teacher Training College, Irete, Owerri**
16. **St. Patrick's Asaba**
17. **Bishop Shanaham, Orlu**
18. **Enitonia High School, Port Harcourt, founded 1932**
19. **Holy Ghost College, Owerri**
20. **Government College, Owerri**
21. **Government College, Umuahia, founded 1929**
22. **Stella Maris, Port Hacourt**
23. **Queen's School, Enugu**
24. **Zixton Grammar School, Ozubulu**
25. **St. Augustine Grammar School, Nkwere**
26. **Elelenwa Girls College, Umukoroshe, Port Harcourt**
27. **Biggard Seminary, Enugu.**

Comment: In those days if anyone did go to any of those institutions, it was jokingly said the person did not go to college "***O jere commercial typing and short hand.***"

A Historic Landmark:

Aba Women Riot, 1929 (*Ogu Nwanyi*): The historical and political import of this event had very far-reaching consequences. First, it established very convincingly that Igbo women were much more politically sensitive and articulate than their Nigerian counterparts in the rest of the country. Secondly, it also established the fact that Igbo Women had a very active and well-organized social structure which the colonial masters never understood nor cared to recognize. And the lesson was: ***elelia nwa ite, o gbonyuo oku,***—a small pot could boil over and spill over and quench the fire.

That historical event which lasted for about two weeks started on 24 November, 1929. The rioting women numbered more than 30, 000, rose in angry protest against what they regarded as:

1. Over taxation of their husbands and sons, which they felt was pauperizing them and causing economic hardship for the entire community.
2. The women resented the British imposition on the community of hand-picked warrant chiefs and local court judges. Most of those British agents were puppets and Whiteman's stooges who were not men of any traditional consequence nor had any traditional qualifications of leadership or respectability. The abuses of the British appointed native court judges and the tax enumerators impelled the women to stage a protest march to the District Offices. The white District officer, ***(nwa deecee)*** called out the police on the rioters. The violent protest hit-and-run battle lasted for several days, but was finally quelled with excessive police gun power at the cost of about 50 lives. But the lesson was clearly demonstrative of the fact that "***umu nwayi Igbo awughi ihe nwa bekee ga eji gba futubol***".

   (Igbo women folk are not made of the weak stuff which the Whiteman can play around like a football). (Mazi Gov. Mbakwe).

Chapter Thirteen

The Ikemba Saga

William Shakespeare said: "Some are born great; some achieve greatness; some have greatness thrust upon them." (Twelfth Night, Act 2; Sc. V)

Chinua Achebe said of Okonkwo the hero of ***Things Fall Apart:*** "Onye chi ya muanya, ikenga ya di ike, di ire"

Chukwuemeka Odumegwu Ojukwu aka Ikemba was a typical embodiment of all the above.

Ikemba was born great with gold and diamond spoons in his mouth. His father Sir Louis Philip Odumegwu Ojukwu, best known as Sir LP, was the richest African in his generation. He was the wealthiest and greatest landlord, real estate and transport magnet in Nigeria. He was the first African millionaire to trade in London Stock Exchange. Sir LP. was the first African who rode a Rolls Royce limousine. This fantastic affluent and aristocratic background enabled the young Emeka to attend the best schools both in Nigeria and in Britain: Kings' College Lagos, Epson and Oxford. In 1944 at age 12, Emeka was briefly arrested for assaulting a white British colonial teacher who was humiliating a black woman at King's College, an event which generated widespread headline news in the local newspapers.

Lesson: From this very significant incident, even the blind and the deaf can perceive a very distinct and powerful trait of character of innate revulsion against and natural abhorrence of oppression and injustice in this young pre-teen. Secondly, that the propensity to identify with and fight the cause of the common man at the risk of everything was inherent in him, rather than a selfish circumstantial political opportunism or a radical jingoism which his detractors and 'enemies' always ascribed to him. Thirdly, that the aversion for and abhorrence of domination by race or class in whatever guise, whether colonial or by domestic power advantage, was very strong in his blood. He did not learn it as an adult, neither did he inhale it in military uniform.

At age 13, his father sent him to England, at first to Epson College and later to Lincoln Oxford University. At age 19 in Oxford the young Emeka was cruising in a Rolls Royce the second Rolls Royce limousine at Oxford, the other was owned by an old British Professor. Although his father wanted him to study law, he ended up with a Masters degree in History at Oxford.

He achieved greatness: On his return to Nigeria (1956), Emeka had a brief stint in the Eastern Region Civil Service as an Administrative Officer at Udi. Extremely boring and very distasteful to him he left and enlisted in the Nigerian Army (1957) as a junior officer. He was the second Nigerian soldier with a university degree, the first was O. Olutoye (1956). The other university graduates in the Nigeria Army were: Emmanuel Ifeajuna, (1957); C.O.Rotimi (1960), and A. Ademoyega (1962). At that time, the Nigerian Military Forces had 250 officers and only 15 were Nigerians. There were 6,400 other ranks, of which 336 were British.

Because of his educational background and experience, he moved fast to the rank of a Lt. Col. He recorded a brilliant military career and served under the command of Major General Aguiyi-Ironsi in the United Nations Peace Keeping Operations in the Congo. On his return to Nigeria he was posted to Kano as the Commander of the 5th Battalion, 1964.

Greatness was thrust upon him:

The political crises and military coups of 1966 caused the military to seize power and Gen. Aguiyi-Ironsi as the Military Head of State. On Monday 17 January 1966, the Military Head of State appointed Military Governors for the four regions. Lt. Col. Emeka Odumegwu

Ojukwu was appointed Military Governor of Eastern Region (he did not usurp or manipulate himself into power). Others were Lt. Col. Hassan Usman Katsina (North), Francis Adekunle Fajiyi (West), and Lt. Col. David Akpode Ejoor (Mid West), Unfortunately the Nigerian crises escalated beyond the control of the Federal administration. By 29 June 1966, there was a pogrom in Northern Nigeria in which thousands of Nigerians of southeastern origin were targeted and brutally massacred. The coup of July 29, 1966 was followed by further massacres of Ndi-Igbo throughout northern Nigeria. The continued killings of August and September 1966, coupled with failure of the Gowon junta to faithfully implement the Aburi Accord placed the East in the situation where on May 30, 1967 the people were forced to take the radical decision to opt out of Nigeria.

Daily lorry and truck loads of badly mutilated and headless bodies were streaming from the North to the East. The International Red Cross gave a very conservative estimate of the casualties: 60,000 killed, and over 600,000 shattered and devastated refugees. This presented heart breaking problems to Governor Ojukwu. But he did everything in his power to prevent reprisals and even encouraged people to return, as assurances for their safety had been given by his supposed colleagues up North and out West. But the crises and genocide continued to escalate unabated.

The Aburi Accord: At Aburi Ghana the Supreme Military Council unanimously adopted a Declaration proposed by Lt. Col. Ojukwu to:

- Renounce the use of force as a means of settling the Nigerian crises;
- Reaffirm their faith in discussions and negotiation as the only peaceful way of resolving the Nigerian crises;
- Agree to exchange information on the quantity of arms and ammunition available in each unit of the Army in each Region and in the allocated stores, and to share out such arms equitably to various commands;
- Agree that there should be no more importation of arms and ammunition until normalcy was restored; and above all,
- The Federal Military government should quickly and effectively address the agonizing stress of the refugee problem created by the crises.

The full text of the Declaration was signed by all members.

To add insult to injury, the Aburi Accord which was brokered in Accra Ghana that could have effectively eased tension and defused temper, was dishonored and reneged by the Gowon junta. While Odumegwu Ojukwu and the Easterners were crying and shouting "On Aburi We Stand", Gowon was busy amassing troops, armament and war machines of genocidal proportions around the Biafran borders. When the Easterners saw that they have been driven to the wall and that the only way open for their survival was to opt out of that situation, from a country where they were no longer wanted and which could not guarantee their safety. "It is only a tree that will stand even if you are approaching to kill and uproot it with knives, diggers, axe and chain-saw." So on May 27, 1967 the Joint Assembly of the Council of Elders and the Eastern Region Consultative Assembly unanimously mandated Governor Emeka Odumegwu Ojukwu to assume Headship and proclaim the historic Ahiara declaration:

> ***"Having mandated me to proclaim on your behalf, and in my name, that Eastern Nigeria be a sovereign independent Republic, now, therefore I, Lieutenant Colonel Chukwuemeka Odumegwu Ojukwu, Military Governor of Eastern Nigeria, by virtue of the authority, and pursuant to the principles recited above, do hereby solemnly proclaim that the territory and region known and called Eastern Nigeria with her continental shelf and territorial waters, shall, henceforth, be an independent sovereign state of the name and title of The Republic of Biafra,"***

That was the birth of the Republic of Biafra. In other words, the Eastern Region seceded as an act of survival and self preservation.

Gen. Emeka Odumegwu Ojukwu was stigmatized with various negative names and adjectives: war monger, rebel, ambitious secessionist, greedy, revolutionary, etc. But those who knew him and who followed the events of history very closely and without preconceived prejudice, will agree that the Ikemba was none of the above.

- The Ikemba was not a war monger as some of his detractors and political 'enemies' always portrayed him. He refused to join and cooperate with the operators of the first military coup of January 1966, a decision that almost cost him his life. He refused to cooperate with the coup plotters not out of cowardice, but out of his personal conviction and belief in the unity and survival of a one united Nigeria.
- From the day of the first coup to the day of the Ahiara Declaration, Ojukwu was always advocating for peace, suing for peace, and pursuing peace. Even at the height of provocation, when lorry loads of dead and mutilated bodies of Easterners were being brought back to the East, and temper was over boiling for action and revenge. He kept his cool and refused to yield to violence. Rather he used the army and the police to ensure that no Northerners and Westerners in the East was harassed or attacked. He used the army and the police to ensure their safe passage back to their respective states of origin.
- At Aburi he talked peace, reconciliation and unity more than any other member of the delegation.
- According to Professor Sylvanus Cookey in his interview with Henry Chukwurah (Sunnews February 27 2012), the late Ikemba worked hard to preserve the unity and corporate existence of Nigeria. "All he wanted was a restructured Nigerian nation that guarantees security, equality and equal development of its component parts. Had the federal structure canvassed at the aborted Lagos Conference and the Aburi Accord been faithfully adhered to, Ojukwu would not have proclaimed Biafra and the civil war could have been averted." (Professor Cookey is an eminent and one of the most internationally respected African historian of River State origin)
- On Friday February 17, 2012 at the same venue where the historic Ahiara Declaration was made, and at exactly the same time 12.00 am on June 1, 1969, Ndi-Igbo of Timber and Caliber of Southeast and South-souh geo-political zones of Nigeria assembled at Ahiara Ahiazu LGA of Imo State on the

platform of the Conference of Democratic Scholars (CODES) to pay homage and honor Ikemba. The participants at that august colloquium included: President General of Ohaneze Ambassador Ralf Uwachie, Senator Chris Anyanwu, Senator Chris Ngige, Senator Sylvester Anyanwu, Col. "Air Raid" Achuzie, Capt. Iheanacho, Mrs. Josephine Effiong (wife of Gen. Philip Effiong), Dr. Dozie Ikedife (former President General Ohaneze), Eze Desmond Ogugua, Dr. Anthony Victor Obinna-Catholic Bishop of Owerri, Chief Miik Ahamba (SAN), Chief Rojas Okorocha, and a host of traditional chieftains from Abia, Anambra, Enugu, Imo, Bayesa, Rivers, and Anioma States.
Prof. Uzodinma Nwala the Colloquium chairman and National President CODES

"In his keynote address the chairman stated very clearly that: "The Ahiara Declaration made by Gen. Ojukwu during the Biafra-Nigeria war embodies: "The vision of a new society, and that it was not a declaration of war (as Gowon and his foreign cohorts proclaimed it was). It was a Declaration of a vision of a nation state with shared common aspirations and shared values."

- Gen. Emeka Ojukwu from the day he was appointed the Military Governor of Eastern Region in January 1966 to the day he left the country on self imposed exile to the Ivory Coast in 1970, Ojukwu refused to take any salary from any government. He served in all capacities without charge or fee. I don't know of any other Nigerian dead or alive, white or black, who has been so selflessly magnanimous, charitable and down right so patriotic. Name the one.
- The Ikemba spent a great proportion of his father's immense wealth and his own personal fortune in the prosecution of the Biafran course.
- The Ikemba was not a tribalist. In fact his best friends and confidants included Professor Sam Aluko, Professor Wole Soyinka, the Emire of Kano. The Ikemba went beyond tribal bigotry and made friends. That was why he spoke Hausa and

Yoruba with mastery and fluency, in vernacular accent and native finesse.

- The Ikemba was not power-drunk, although every where he went, and every time he spoke people always hailed him in salutation and admiration: Power! Power!. In his own words: ***"The Biafran Revolution is the People's Revolution. Who are the people? You ask. The Farmer, the Trader, the Clerk, the Businessman, the housewife, the student, the civil servant, the soldier, you and me are the People. Is there anyone here who is not of the People? Such a man has no place in our Revolution. If he is a leader, he has no right to leadership because all power, all sovereignty, belongs to the People. In Biafra the People are supreme; the People are master; the leader is servant. You see, you make a mistake when you greet me with shouts of "Power, Power" I am not power.—you are. My name is Emeka. I am your servant, that is all".*** (The Ahiara Declaration, The Principles of the Biafran Revolution, 1st. June 1969)

Biafra: Postmortem

By nature Ojukwu was a visionary and a revolutionary, not a militant reactionary. Like Martin Luther Jr., like Jomo Kenyatta, like Kwame Nkuruma, like Nelson Mandella, like Dr. Nnamdi Azikwe, he envisioned the future and prophesied it. A few believed, some doubted. Some did all they could by action or inaction to frustrate every positive move to sustain the Biafran dream. Christians will remember that Joseph was hated and sold off by his own brothers because he dreamt dreams. But did his dreams not come to pass several years after?

If the truth must be told, it was not the superior armament and fire power of the Nigerian army and their foreign allies that won the war. Biafra lost the war due to: 70% internal sabotage, and 30% external treachery/ betrayal.

Internal sabotage.

- Igbophobia
- Tribalism/ jealousy
- Greed and gluttony
- Betrayal/treachery

Inside the Brifran enclave there were agents of fear, cowardice, tribalism, greed, gluttony, jealousy. Some elements in the East preferred to go back and remain in bondage in 'Egypt' rather than weather the storm and rough it out across the wilderness to the 'Promised Land.'

Saboteurs: in different cloaks and shapes as typified in the Holy Bible.

1. **Cowards** and spineless fellows who preferred to remain emasculated stooges for mere bread and butter:

   Exodus Chapter 14: 10-12 "***As Pharaoh and his chariots drew near, some sons of Israel looked and behold, the Egyptians were marching after them, and they became frightened and said to Moses: Why have you dealt with us in this way, bringing us out of Egypt? Is this not the word we spoke to you in Egypt saying, "Leave us alone that we may serve the Egyptians? For it would be better for us to serve the Egyptians than to die here in this wilderness."*** (New American Standard Version)

2. **Sensualists**: Gluttons and Epicureans: People whose appetite and craving for physical pleasures, frivolous and ostentatious life style (addicts of Cuban cigarette, Scottish whiskey, Russian Vodka, Parisian cousin, and Caribbean massage) could not endure the temporary hardships and discomfort of the reality of the conflict,

   Numbers chapter 11: v.4: ***The rabble who were among them had greedy desires; and also the sons of Israel wept again and said, "Who will give us meat to eat?***

v. ***5: We remember the fish which we used to eat free in Egypt, the cucumbers and the melons and the leeks and the onions and the garlic,***

v. 6***: But now our appetite is gone. There is nothing at all except this manna.”*** (New American Standard Version)

Those were the victims of the demon of addiction and gluttony.

Some were **sellouts (sabo)** the children of Esau who were always ready to sell their heritage and birth right for a plate of porridge, (Gen 25: 26-34). These kinds, for personal and monetary gains, secretly colluded with the enemies of Biafra, leaked security and confidential information, putting Biafran troops, military locations and vital social structures in great harm and jeopardy.

Some were **alarmists** and **false prophets of doom**. Like the ones who brought bad and false news to Moses—the spies he sent out to spy Canaan. These agents of sabotage saw the Nigerian soldiers as Anaks—invincible giants and the Biafran forces as grasshoppers, no match at all against the Nigeria soldiers. (Numbers Chapt.13: 31: ***We are not able to go up against the people, for they are stronger than we. V.*** **32.** ***And they spread among the Israelites a bad report about the land they went to spy. They said:***

“The land we spied devours those living in it. All the people we saw there are giants, . . . We seem like grasshoppers in our own eyes, we look the same to them.”

Those ones were busy spreading fearful and discouraging rumors and false propaganda potentially demoralizing the populace and every war effort.

Tribalism and Igbophobia:

Some other ethnic groups in the East saw the Biafran struggle as purely an Igbo problem, and Igbophobia—the fear of Igbo domination had always been an economic and social nightmare to them. In their selfish and myopic minds, if in the event Biafra succeeded and survived, it would be an Igbo empire and they would be completely swelled up. In their bigoted tribalistic political lens Ojukwu was the Hitler for Igbo expansionism and hegemony, and the concept of Biafra was a dreadful hydra-headed monster that must not be allowed any chance to hatch or incubate. So for those kinds frame of mind, every thing must be done to ensure that Biafra must die. This stance was very prevalent and apparent in the riverine and Delta areas. For such ones the conflict was a golden opportunity to settle scores with the Igbo "who had for long usurped, dominated and monopolized their economic and social birthrights." They colluded with and welcomed the enemy soldiers, gladly and positively aided and abated. The obnoxious "**Abandoned Property"** is a case in point.

Greed and pessimism among the Igbo: Some wealthy Igbo elite misconstrued the Ahiara Declaration as a "socialist cum-communist political philosophy, making some Igbo elite feel frightened, disenchanted or 'betrayed' by the same Biafran government that was crusading for their survival," This class of the Ndi-Igbo did nothing positive to aid, sustain or cooperate in the struggle. Some just sat in abject disgust and aloofness and watched in silence and despair. Some engaged in negative psychological propaganda against the war effort, thus demoralizing the hope and courage of the populace. Those were more mindful of their riches and moaning the loss of business due to the war than the freedom and liberty which victory would ultimately bring. Some used their power and influence to exploit and capitalized on the suffering and hardship of the common people by hoarding and over pricing 'essential commodities'.

External factors: Treachery and betrayal. When the Gowon junta blatantly and defiantly reneged on the Aburi Accord, and when the Easterners threatened to secede, some top and highly respected leaders of thought in the West mooted a solidarity with the East: Chief Awolowo was quoted as saying: "if the East left the federation, the Yoruba would have to leave the federation." (Prof. Sam Aluko; "***What Ojukwu told me before, during and after the war",*** Interview by Duro Adeseko, Saturday Dec. 03, 2011)

The Interviewer noted: "That was March 1967. Awolowo was very frank with him: "Look, Governor (referring to Ojukwu), you cannot secede. You cannot go it alone. Just as you fear the North, the West also fears the North. The soldiers from the North are occupying the West. So we have the same common interest,"

The Big Question!

What happened thereafter? How and why did the Chief's proposition vanish into thin air?

Was Chief Awolowo's, (the most highly respected and most nationally revered elder statesman) proposition a hoax? Was it a brain wave? Was it a deception? Was it an out right treachery? Was it a betrayal of the Judas Iscariot political version? (Judas betrayed his friend with a kiss) Or was it a political demonstration of the popular Yoruba proverb which says, "It is not where the face is that the cap faces"? One thing is very certain, he was not under any duress.

The Bigger Question!!

Why did the Chief play such prominent role in the prosecution of the war against Biafra? These two Big Questions will linger sour for time and eternity. It will not go away.

Back to the private and confidential conversation of the big three: The scene of that very confidential dialogue was Enugu. The dialogue was between Ojukwu, Prof. Sam Aluko and Chief Awolowo. Prof. Aluko later confessed (after the death of Ojukwu) that he disclosed all the details of the top private meeting to Gowon. Also very worthy of note: Prof. Aluko confessed he also cautioned Gowon about the Aburi conference that he (Gowon) must ensure that he went with very intelligent legal experts because "Ojukwu is a very brilliant and smart guy and could easily bamboozle and outwit him with his powerful eloquence."

Professor Sam Aluko made all these startling revelations at the interview he gave two weeks after the death of Ikemba. That is why some Igbo writers and journalists of conscience are bold to ask: "**Aluko: saint or sinner?, friend or traitor?", "friend in life, traitor at death?".** Unfortunately, however, Prof. Aluko also died in a London hospital on February 7, 2012 barely 6 weeks after Ikemba. One must always be very careful what one says or does about the dead. Shakespeare said, "The evil that men do lives after them." (Julius Ceasar Act 111, Sc. 11). So let it be with Sam Aluko. May his soul rest in peace.

POSTMORTEM: THE DREAM.

Now that Ikemba is gone physically and the spirit of Biafra still lies dormant in the cooler, (but not in the mortuary), it is time for all and sundry to take stock and do some postmortem reflections. Rewind to the pre-war era, the Igbo were stigmatized and singled out for extermination and frequently subjected to acts of vicious brutality and the agony of ethnic cleansing throughout the moslem north. Then all other ethnic groups of southern origin saw it as a purely an Igbo problem. They all sat aside and watched from the ring side. But when the ethnic cleansing gathered momentum and exploded in the pogrom of 1966, other southerners were not spared. Now long after the 'unification' of the country after the civil war, the jihad and the ethnic cleansing have assumed a much more dangerous and wider dimensions. It is now an all out Islamic jihad against all southerners and all Christians resident not only in the northern states, but also in the free federal capital of Abuja. And let no one be fooled or blindfolded with the smoke screen of this Islamic masquerade in the guise of Boko Haram. Boko Haram is not an independent isolated radical phenomenon. He is the manifestation of the mind and spirit of the cattle Hausa Fulani oligarchy. Boko Haram's mission and philosophy boldly and vehemently declares: "Nigeria belongs to the moslems, Islam must be the religion in and across all Nigeria, and Shari law must be the Nigerian constitution". This is the reason this Islamic blood thirsty monster by the name and cloak of Boko Haram is massacring Christians and southerners, rampaging, destroying and burning down Christian churches and institutions with audacious impunity and nonchalant demonic bravado. Because he is an instrument and expression of the ruling class, he is a very sacred cow and enjoys absolute immunity of arrest and prosecution.

In a January 25 video posting on YouTube, Boko Haram proudly took responsibility for the attacks and arsons in which over 200 people were killed and said: "I am not against anyone, but if Allah asks me to kill someone, I will kill him and I will enjoy killing him like I am killing a chicken."

Western Observers and the foreign media are appalled by this Islamic jihadism. The following are excerpts from foreign correspondents and from the internet:

1. "Meanwhile, the Muslim elite is brooding and grumbling over the ascendancy of President Goodluck Jonathan–a southern Christian. A former university lecturer, Jonathan was dubbed the Accidental President by the local press after he succeeded Umaru Yar'Adua, a Muslim who died in 2010."
2. "Boko Haram wants to impose Sharia law across Nigeria and oust the current president, a Christian, named Goodluck Jonathan. "to Islam he (the president) is Mr. Badluck"
3. "In Hausa, the dominant language in northern Nigeria, Boko Haram means "Western Education is sinful., it is a sacrilege to Islam" Its official name, Jama'atu Ahlis Sunna Lidda'awati-Jihad, is Arabic for "Group Committed to Propagating the Prophet's Teachings and Jihad."
4. If according to Boko Haram and his sponsors that western education and civilization are evil and sinful, why have they not started destroying and burning down universities and institutions in the north with departments and faculties of Medicine, Engineering, Agriculture, Architecture, Pharmacy, Science and Technology, etc? Why have they not attacked and beheaded all the lecturers and professors in those institutions as agents of western education? Why only Christians, Christian institutions and people of southern origin? Why have they not attacked and destroyed Teaching Hospitals, Radio and Television studios, Airports, Railway stations and systems in the moslem north?. These folks ride in cars and vehicles on macadamized roads and streets; they have and watch televisions in their homes; they have and use cell phones with the latest technology. All these and more are products of western education and technology. In their homes they use electricity, electric and gas cookers, air conditioners, refrigerators. They wear expensive Swiss wrist watches. They drive their children to schools and hospitals in foreign made

luxury limousines and SUVs. Yet western education and technology are sinful. Even the very guns and automatic riffles they use in shooting and killing Christians and southerners are products of western education and technology.

5. "With fighters and suicide bombers trained in Sudan, Libya and Somalia, the Boko Haram Islamic militants have embarked on a serious campaign to turn Nigeria into an Islamic republic like Iran."
6. "With this intension to Islamize Nigeria by all means came suicide bombing of the UN headquarters in Abuja, Nigeria's capital last August killing 18 people;
7. "On Christmas Day Sunday December 2011, a string of bombings struck churches in five Nigerian cities in and around Abuja, killing dozens of worshippers;
8. "On Monday December 26, 2011 Boko Haram issued a THREE DAY ultimatum to ALL CHRISTIANS AND ALL SOUTHERNERS TO LEAVE ABUJA AND ALL NORTHERN STATES." In broad day light the Boko Haram bloody thirsty gangsters drove round the streets of Abuja and suburbs in open pickup vehicles and mini buses, brandishing their flags and cult banners, using very powerful megaphones to blast intimidation and terror on Christians and "foreigners" to vacate Abuja or face decapitation. Where else on earth can this type of stone age barbarism happen with impunity?"
9. "Since 2010 more than 1000 churches, Christian schools and Christian religious institutions including hospitals and private clinics have been burnt and destroyed, more than four thousand innocent Christians—men, women and children have been brutally massacred in Nigeria by this Islamic militants with the silent connivance and acquiesce of the northern states and local governments. Otherwise why has he or the members of his nefarious gang never been arrested and brought to justice?

"(Winnipeg Free Press) Update 2: "Get this ! The UN headquarters car bombing suspects were previously arrested in 2007 and quickly released by the Nigerian Muslim president A'Umaru Yar' Adua to "placate Muslim groups"

10. "ABUJA NIGERIA—Nigeria detained several radical muslims suspected of being terrorists in 2007—including a man who officials now say helped organize last week's deadly car bombing at the UN headquarters in the nation's capital, a top high-ranking official told The Associated Press."

    This catalogue of brazen atrocious acts of barbarism and the horrific pictures of massacre and arson litter the pages of papers and abound in the internet, and it tells the rest of the world what kind of country Nigeria is, and what Islamic jihad is all about. It also tells the world why Eastern Nigeria (Biafra) cannot call Nigeria home any more. Nigeria is a country whose leadership sponsors and condones barbarism of the worst order. This is the relevance of Biafra. If Biafra had survived and 'Oduduwa conceived and birthed, this blood thirsty demonic madness in the name of Boko Haram would never have seen the light of day. There are some Igbo proverbs which explain this type of unfortunate situation: ***"Orji da chie uzo, umu nyanyi aria ya elu.*** When an iroko tree falls across the road, women climb over it. ***Ukwu jie nwagu, ewu na mgbada abia raya ugwo,*** when both legs of a tiger are crippled, goats and antelopes provoke it with impunity.

But let nobody be deceived, this devil incarnate Boko Haram is a mere messenger, a megaphone on two legs, amplifying his masters voice. The killing and massacre of Ndi-Igbo in northern Nigeria had been a regular phenomenon long before Boko Haram was born. He did not orchestrate nor participated in the 1966 pogrom. It was only recently that the Hausa-Fulani oligarchy found this daredevil, hired, equipped and commissioned him to accelerate the process of complete Islamization of the whole Nigerian nation.

The Relevance of Ikemba.

The immortal Shakespeare said:

> ***"There is a tide in the affairs of men,***
> ***Which, taken at the flood, leads on to fortune;***
> ***Omitted, all the voyage of their life***
> ***Is bound in shallows and miseries.***
> ***On such a full sea are we now afloat,***
> ***And we must take the current when it serves,***
> ***Or for ever lose our ventures."***
>
> **(Julius Caesar Act 4, scene 3.)**

Prophets, poets, great thinkers, and philosophers quite often make very prophetic pronouncements that impact on the present and the future, of time and eternity because they are visionaries. They see and perceive with their spiritual eyes what the ordinary naked eyes and minds cannot see or perceive. They Igbo adage says: ***Ihe agadi nwoke noduru ala na ime obi ya hu, nwatakiri rigoro elu orji, o'gaghi ahu ya***." (What an old man sitting on the floor of his hut sees, a youth will not see it from the top of an iroko tree). This was typical and apt in the context of Ikemba and Biafra. Some elements of of Ndi-Igbo people contributed to the demise of dream. Even other non-Igbo ethnic groups have also learnt the hard truth from experience that an ill wind blows nobody good.

In a very broad sense the entire South on both sides of the River Niger are now coming to grasp with the relevance of Ikemba and the Biafran concept. The present historical realities of the Boko Haram phenomenon that southerners and Christians cannot live and work in the country's federal capital; the prospect of enforcing Sharia on the Nigerian constitution; the absurdity that the whole of the northern states are out of bounds to Christians and all southerners. These constant threats and daily massacres are making bolder and louder the relevance of Ikemba.

The Bible says: ***"the stone which the builder rejected, has come to be the head cornerstone."*** (Psalm 118 v. 22; and Matt. 21 v. 42)

If Biafra had survived, most probably soon after, through systematic humane democratic processes she would have evolved or developed into a proud and powerful political entity in the nature of The United States of Biafra. Among other things the Republic would ensure:

- **Safe haven for Religious freedom**: All Christians will have full and unrestricted freedom of worship. In other words, this current menace of the Boko Haram madness could never be of any anxiety in the United States of Biafra.
- **Education and manpower development**: The peoples of the former Eastern Region were known for their insatiable appetite for education and knowledge as the primary bases for development and happiness. The United States of Biafra would ensure the development of Higer Education and technological training, encourage intellectuals, scientists, researchers, inventors, and entrepreneurs to perform and achieve their optimum so that they can contribute significantly to knowledge and world culture. As against the Islamic posture and belief that "western education is sinful." In other words, enthroning ignorance and decadence.
- **Natural resources and Revenue allocation**: The exploitation of the natural resources very abundant in Biafra would be used in the development of: first and foremost for the healthy development of the source of derivation; and secondly, for the economic and social development of the entire Republic.
- **Equity and justice**: In the Educational system for instance, Biafran youths will no longer be subjected to any kind of discrimination regarding admission to institutions of learning, as against the Nigerian policy which favors students from the northern states against students of southeastern origin. In Biafra all students will be recognized and rewarded on merit and performance.
- **Equal opportunity employment**: In a United States of Biafra employment and reward would be based purely on individual merit and achievement. For instance: "in one area in of Nigeria, they preferred to turn a nurse who had worked for five years into a doctor rather than employ a qualified doctor from another part of Nigeria; barely literate clerks were

made Permanent Secretaries; a university Vice-Chancellor was sacked because he belonged to the wrong tribe."

- **Sharia Law and Arab-Muslim Expasionism: The United States of the Republic of Biafra being very dominantly a Christian society, would strongly resist any incursion of Islamic terrorism and the imposition of Sharia law on the Christian people. The contagion of moslem jihad has menaced and ravaged the African continent for twelve centuries. But our Biafran ancestors remained immune from the Isalamic contagion, and modern Biafra will remain committed to keep that heritage.**
- **An Egalitarian Society: According to Gen. Ojukwu Head of State of The Republic of Biafra, in the historic Ahiara Declaration stated as follows:**

  "Biafran society is traditionally egalitarian. The possibility of social mobility is always present in our society. The New Biafran Social Order will reject all rigid classification of society. Anyone with integrity, anyone with imagination, anyone who works hard, can rise to any height. . . . . "Our New Society is open and progressive. We believe that human effort and will are necessary to bring about changes and improvements in the light of rapid developments in the our contemporary world. Biafra will always cherish the best elements of our culture, drawing substsnce as well as moral and psychological stability from them. But Biafra will never be afraid to adapt what needs to be adapted or change what has to be changed."

  From his vast knowledge of world history, political systems, his personal practical experience of world governments, and his forthright sense of justice and leadership, his relevance in the concept of Biafra remains very unquestionable and very significant.

The Aftermath Quotable Quotes and Reflections:

- "Your Majesty, I no longer wish to wear the garb of British Knighthood. British fairplay, British justice, and the Englishman's word of honour which Biafra loved so much and

cherished have become meaningless to Biafrans in general and to me in particular."
(Dr. Akanu Ibiam)

- "Biafra had to happen somehow, Somewhere, Anywhere but in Igboland. . . . . And so we fought our war, our way."
- "The Revolution is indestructible and eternal."
- "The bloody massacre of Igbos in the North is a shameful act which will abide with the Nigerian state for as long as there are humanbeings on this earth. It happened—there is no debating it. Gowon knew it would happen; he did nothing to stop it when it did."
- "The Biafran Revolution believes in the sanctity of the human person. The Biafran sees the willful and wanton destruction of human life not only as a grave crime, but as an abominable sin." (Gen. Ojukwu)
- "The Biafran Resolution upholds the dignity of man. The Biafran Revolution stands firmly against genocide, against any attempt to destroy a people, its security, its right to life, property and progress. Any attempt to deprive a community of its identity is abhorrent to the Biafran people. Having ourselves suffered genocide, we are all the more determined to take a clear stand now and at all times against this crime."
- "The pogrom is a sad chapter in Nigeria's turbulent history. No one is ever going to sweep it under the carpet. It is an indelible stain of shame on Yakubu Gowon' junta."
- "The Igbo were being slaughtered . . . Anyone who had any sense or conscience would oppose the Pogrom that was taking place . . ." (Bola Ige, ex-governor of Oyo State)
- " . . . I believe that it is better even from the point of survival to fight and be conquered than to surrender without fighting." (George Orwell, ***Animal Farm)***
- "The political equation in Nigeria was re-ordered by the Civil War, with political and military powers now resting with the Hausa-Fulani in the North, economic power with the Yoruba West, and the Igbo of the East left with mere crumbs from the masters' table."

- "The lessons of Biafra are numerous. We the Igbo, will do well to learn from that experience, and use it to shape the future that lies before us. We must tap into the inventive genius of our people that was unleashed during that conflict, as exemplified by the myriad inventions and innovations that were occasioned by the war. The mistakes that were made during the war must serve as guide posts as we march into the future. The war also has a lot of lessons to teach the outside world, including those who fought against us." (Uzo Okoroanyanwu, Igbo-net)
- "The Igboland will rise again and take its position on the world stage. . . . . I recommend for us to move slightly apart rather to burn ourselves with the friction of closeness." (Gen. Ojukwu)
- The Igbo story must be told by us—the Igbo, otherwise others will tell our story to suit their agenda." (Oyibo Achebe)
- "The Biafran story must be told to our children and generation yet unborn because it is the truth. Never, never, never again. Together we must ensure genocide against the Igbo never happens again." (Zeribe Ezeanuna)
- "Why Biafra lives"
  . . . . Biafra still lives;
  It is a living testimony of political wickedness
  which time will not heal
  because it is physical and psychological.
  And the power of Biafra remains that,
  As an idea against political oppression,
  It can never die." (Lewis Obi)

Epilogue:

THE GIANT AND THE GENERAL !

Chukwuemeka, Odumegwu Ojukwu
Ike neche mba !
Born great
lived great
died great

Born before his age
lived before his age
died before the dream came true

Saw
what others did not see
what others refused to see
what others did not want to see
Said
What others
Did not want to hear
What others did not like to hear
What others hated to hear
Called
They did not answer
Sang
They did not dance

Prophesied
Eagle and vulture
Don't nest together
Hyena and sheep
Cannot tango
What the gods
Did not join together
Should remain asunder

Born in aristocratic affluence
Swam in superfluity
Yet cringed to the populace
To dine
And walk
With kit and kin
Than cocoon in Olympian splendor
"Because I am Involved"

When the scales
Fell off their eyes
They saw what he had been saying
But it was too late
To shut the chicken pen
When the fox had fled
With the loot

EPITAPH

John Brown's body
Is lying in the grave
But his soul
Goes marching on!

Ikemba
Your soul restless
Restless will lay
Until the Deed is done
And the RisingSun shines

Though it may delay
It will not tarry
It shall come to pass
In the fullness of time

Ikemba!
You are not like us
You are not like them
You are a different kind of animal

Ikemba!
Epitome of hero spirit
Your name shrined in
Granite and gold
In eternity Hall of fame
Ikemba!
We salute your Execllency
We salute your spirit
We salute your bravery
We salute your Sacrifice
We salute you
Capless, on bended knees
Hero of the Biafran Sun
We Salute You!
Another you
Will never be.

Biafra National Anthem.

(Land Of The Rising Sun)

Land of the rising sun, we love and cherish,
Beloved homeland of our brave heroes;
We must defend our lives or we shall perish,
We shall protect our hearts from all our foes;
But if the price is death for all we hold dear,
Then let us die without a shred of fear.

Hail to Biafra, consecrated nation,
Oh fatherland, this be our solemn pledge:
Defending thee shall be a dedication,
Spilling our blood we'll count a privilege;
The waving standard which emboldens the free
Shall always be our flag of liberty.

We shall emerge triumphant from this ordeal,
And through the crucible unscathed we'll pass;
When we are poised the wounds of battle to heal,
We shall remember those who died in mass;
Then shall our trumpets peal the glorious song
Of victory we scored o'er might and wrong.

Oh God, protect us from the hidden pitfall,
Guide all our movements lest we go astray;
Give us the strength to heed the humanist call:
"To give and not to count the cost" each day;
Bless those who rule to serve with resoluteness,
To make this clime a land of righteousness.[1]

Chapter Fourteen

The Role Call

The catalogue of Igbo traditional names contained in this presentation although substantially much more elaborate than any previous record, does not claim to be exhaustive. It will be very presumptuous and unscholarly to state otherwise. No one individual can claim the monopoly or the infinitude of knowledge. But a very serious effort has been made to reflect and present the richness of Igbo name culture. In this effort we have just added to what many Igbo scholars and writers have already done with great success. This presentation is designed to provoke thought and controversy, to engender comment and dialogue, and to add one more volume to the library of Igbo language and literature.

The author will be very grateful and delighted to welcome positive and constructive criticisms, comments and ideas. And be rest assured that your views, comments and criticisms will be taken very seriously and in good faith, and could be used to enrich a subsequent edition that is already on the drawing board.

It is the humble submission of the author that if your name, or no name of your entire family or kindred is not reflected in this volume, that calls for very sober and serious concern about your cultural identity, ***Onye ahu were ire ya guo eze ya onu.*** The reason is that a lot of diligence, research and collection of physical material from across the length and breadth of the Igbo literature have gone into the compilation of the more than four thousand names in this catalogue.

It was not the primary objective of the present volume to interprete or assign meanings to each individual name in the catalogue. A subsequent work that is already on the drawing board—(Volunme Two), will address that aspect. Meanwhile let us appreciate the creativity of the Igbo in their name culture, the vast spectrum and range of Igbo names, and the dialectical variations and variants in Igbo name expression. That is who we are.

Igbo kwenu !
Igbo kwenu !!
Igbo kwenu !!!
Igbo kwezue nu !!!!
Anyi ga di.

Now the Roll Call

1. Abachie
2. Abachielam
3. Abachina
4. Abachiro
5. Abachide
6. Abachukwu
7. Abado
8. Abadodike
9. Abadom
10. Abaekobe
11. Abaeze
12. Abagom
13. Abaikwu
14. Abakwuru
15. Abalihu
16. Abalogu
17. Abalogu
18. Abalue
19. Abangwu
20. Abanishe
21. Abanobi
22. Abara
23. Abarikwu
24. Abase
25. Abatam
26. Abaukwu
27. Abazie
28. Abaziem
29. Abazina
30. Abazu
31. Abgogwu
32. Abi
33. Abiadike
34. Abiakam
35. Abiazirim
36. Abumchi
37. Abunmere
38. Achalonu
39. Achara
40. Achebe
41. Achife
42. Achike
43. Achilefu
44. Achilihu
45. Achilike
46. Achim
47. Achima
48. Achinike
49. Achinivu
50. Acholonu
51. Achoma
52. Achomuba
53. Achomuonye
54. Achonam
55. Achonu
56. Achowafu
57. Achuba
58. Achufusi
59. Achukaonye
60. Achukonye
61. Achunike
62. Achunnwa
63. Achusim
64. Achuzia
65. Achuzie
66. Adaaku
67. Adachi
68. Adachukwu
69. Adaego
70. Adaenyi
71. Adaeze
72. Adaigwe
73. Adanma
74. Adanna
75. Adanne
76. Adaobi
77. Adaogaranya
78. Adaogu
79. Adaora
80. Adaozo
81. Adaugo
82. Adaukwu
83. Adauwa
84. Adawai
85. Adele
86. Adeobi
87. Adibe
88. Adibua
89. Adichie
90. Adiekwe
91. Adiele
92. Adigwe
93. Adike
94. Adikwue
95. Adili
96. Adilue
97. Adimora
98. Adindu
99. Adiole
100. Adirika
101. Adiukwu
102. Aduba
103. Adugba
104. Afamaka
105. Afamefule
106. Afamefuna
107. Afanedu
108. Afigbo
109. Afoka
110. Afoma
111. Afonne
112. Afooma
113. Afuekwe
114. Afulueke
115. Afuluenu
116. Afulueze
117. Afulukwe
118. Afumogo
119. Afunanya
120. Afunugo
121. Afuzue
122. Ạgabiga
123. Agadaga
124. Agadobi
125. Agaezuba
126. Agam
127. Agamadotuigwe
128. Agamagbakwuchi
129. Agamagwa

130. Agamebi
131. Agamebi
132. Agamefelu
133. Agamekwuole
134. Agamekwuruchi
135. Agamesobi
136. Agametochukwu
137. Agaranna
138. Agazue
139. Agbachie
140. Agbaduba
141. Agbaekobe:
142. Agbafor
143. Agbafor
144. Agbaghara
145. Agbagwa
146. Agbaim
147. Agbakaa
148. Agbakala
149. Agbakoba
150. Agbakoba
151. Agbakuru
152. Agbakwa
153. Agbakwuru
154. Agbamoro
155. Agbamuche
156. Agbanari
157. Agbaraji
158. Agbarakwe
159. Agbarakwe
160. Agbarandu
161. Agbaraukwu
162. Agbasi
163. Agbasia
164. Agbasiere
165. Agbasimelo
166. Agbata
167. Agbataku
168. Agbazue
169. Agbazue
170. Agbbiga
171. Agbim
172. Agbo
173. Agbo
174. Agbochukwu
175. Agbochukwu
176. Agbodike
177. Agbodike
178. Agboeze
179. Agboeze
180. Agbogu
181. Agbogu
182. Agboh
183. Agboma
184. Agboma
185. Agbonma
186. Agbonna
187. Aghabie
188. Aghadi
189. Aghadi
190. Aghadiegwu
191. Aghadinuno
192. Aghaedo
193. Aghaegbe
194. Aghaegbuna
195. Aghaeli
196. Aghaezi
197. Aghagbue
198. Aghaghibe
199. Aghaghotu
200. Aghaji
201. Aghajiuba
202. Aghamelu
203. Aghanam
204. Aghanihu
205. Aghaogu
206. Agharandu
207. Aghaugo
208. Aghauno
209. Aghauno
210. Aghazu
211. Aghazu
212. Aghedo
213. Agim
214. Agina
215. Agina
216. Agodi
217. Agodichukwu
218. Agogbuam
219. Agomuo
220. Agomuoh
221. Agubalu
222. Agucha
223. Agudanma
224. Agude
225. Agudile
226. Agudire
227. Agugua
228. Agugua
229. Aguh
230. Aguiyi
231. Agulefo
232. Agulefo
233. Agunechemba
234. Agunmo
235. Agunnaya
236. Agunobi
237. Agunobi
238. Agunwa
239. Aguocha
240. Aguocha
241. Aguocha
242. Aguolu
243. Aguolu
244. Agusiobi
245. Agusionu
246. Aguwa
247. Aguzie
248. Agwaeyiagu
249. Agwagu
250. Agwakanma
251. Agwamba
252. Agwamife
253. Agwawunma
254. Agwo
255. Agwubilo
256. Agwudile
257. Agwudire
258. Agwuegbu
259. Agwuna
260. Agwuncha
261. Agwunobi
262. Ahaeijgamba
263. Ahamba
264. Ahana

265. Ahanotu
266. Ahanotu
267. Ahanyi
268. Ahaoma
269. Ahaoma
270. Ahaukwu
271. Ahiaoma
272. Ahiwe
273. Ahumibe
274. Ahunna
275. Ahunwanne
276. Ahuoma
277. Ahuuzo
278. Ahuzo
279. Ahuzue
280. Ajachukwu
281. Ajagu
282. Ajagwu
283. Ajah
284. Ajala
285. Ajamekwu
286. Ajamuo
287. Ajaonu
288. Ajaraogu
289. Ajawara
290. Ajei
291. Ajene
292. Ajero
293. Ajidua
294. Ajomiwe
295. Ajuba
296. Ajubiga
297. Ajude
298. Ajudua
299. Ajufo
300. Ajuluchukwu
301. Ajumobi
302. Ajumobi
303. Ajuzie
304. Aka
305. Akaagu
306. Akabedo
307. Akabie
308. Akabiem
309. Akabieokwu
310. Akabuego
311. Akabuogu
312. Akachebe
313. Akachi
314. Akachie
315. Akachukwu
316. Akadialo
317. Akadike
318. Akadinma
319. Akadire
320. Akadiugwu
321. Akaegbe
322. Akaegbonwu
323. Akaegbuna
324. Akaelu
325. Akaenyi
326. Akaeze
327. Akaezu
328. Akaezue
329. Akagebi
330. Akagha
331. Akaghadike
332. Akahaiwe
333. Akaigwe
334. Akajiaku
335. Akajide
336. Akajigha
337. Akajimba
338. Akajindu
339. Akajiobi
340. Akajiofo
341. Akajioha
342. Akajiokwu
343. Akajiuba
344. Akajiugo
345. Akaku
346. Akakwauzo
347. Akalaka
348. Akalia
349. Akalonu
350. Akalua
351. Akalue
352. Akaluo
353. Akamdiocha
354. Akamelu
355. Akametalu
356. Akamnonu
357. Akandu
358. Akanechemba
359. Akanechendo
360. Akaneme
361. Akaniru
362. Akanmuo
363. Akanu
364. Akanweze
365. Akanyelugo
366. Akaocha
367. Akaolisa
368. Akaosa
369. Akaraka
370. Akariwe
371. Akasia
372. Akasiba
373. Akataobi
374. Akatosia
375. Akaugo
376. Akibe
377. Akoakolam
378. Akoazunafia
379. Akobuche
380. Akobude
381. Akobudike
382. Akobueze
383. Akobundu
384. Akobuokwu
385. Akobuozo
386. Akodinobi
387. Akolisa
388. Akomas
389. Akomasi
390. Akonechendu
391. Akonobi
392. Akonze
393. Akorodike
394. Akosa
395. Akosia
396. Akosoba
397. Akowam
398. Akpaka
399. Akpamgbo

400. Akparanta
401. Akpom
402. Akpomonye
403. Akponye
404. Akpugo
405. Akpulonu
406. Akpunonu
407. Akuabia
408. Akuagbazie
409. Akuagwu
410. Akuagwusia
411. Akuakolam
412. Akuakonam
413. Akuamaka
414. Akuanyo
415. Akuasoma
416. Akuba
417. Akubasi
418. Akube
419. Akubeze
420. Akubiawa
421. Akubilo
422. Akubizu
423. Akubude
424. Akubude
425. Akubudu
426. Akubue
427. Akubuenyi
428. Akubueze
429. Akubugo
430. Akubugwu
431. Akubuike
432. Akubuno
433. Akubuokwu
434. Akubuozo
435. Akuchukwu
436. Akudigwe
437. Akudinobi
438. Akudolu
439. Akudozie
440. Akuegbulem
441. Akueju
442. Akueke
443. Akuemelie
444. Akuezu
445. Akuezue
446. Akuezuoke
447. Akujieze
448. Akujiobi
449. Akujobi
450. Akujuba
451. Akujuobi
452. Akulueuno
453. Akuluno
454. Akuma
455. Akumasi
456. Akumjeli
457. Akunazaoku
458. Akunazaoku
459. Akunazo
460. Akunazondu
461. Akunechendo
462. Akunesiobi
463. Akunkwo
464. Akunnaya
465. Akunne
466. Akunuba
467. Akunwafo
468. Akunwafo
469. Akunwafo
470. Akunwanne
471. Akunwata
472. Akunyere
473. Akuobi
474. Akuozo
475. Akuozo
476. Akusiuba
477. Akusoba
478. Akuwuba
479. Akuwude
480. Akuwuenyi
481. Akuwugwu
482. Akuwuike
483. Akuwundu
484. Akuwuokwu
485. Akuwuozo
486. Akwaeke
487. Akwarandu
488. Akwari
489. Akwaugo
490. Akwaugo
491. Akwuba
492. Akwudolu
493. Akwuozo
494. Aladinma
495. Aladiume
496. Alaoma
497. Alaka
498. Alarazu
499. Alaribe
500. Aleke
501. Alele
502. Aligwe
503. Aligwo
504. Alilionwu
505. Alozie
506. Alufuo
507. Alutu
508. Amabiri
509. Amachara
510. Amachukwu
511. Amadi
512. Amadieze
513. Amadike
514. Amadinwa
515. Amaechi
516. Amaechina
517. Amaechina
518. Amaefula
519. Amaefule
520. Amaefuna
521. Amaenu
522. Amaeze
523. Amah
524. Amaizu
525. Amaji
526. Amajioyi
527. Amakam
528. Amakeze
529. Amakohia
530. Amakom
531. Amaku
532. Amakwaizu
533. Amalachukwu
534. Amali

535. Amalike
536. Amalime
537. Amalinze
538. Amalinze
539. Amalonye
540. Amalu
541. Amalukwo
542. Amamchim
543. Amamchukwu
544. Amamefule
545. Amamonye
546. Amamuche
547. Amamuzo
548. Amanambu
549. Amangwu
550. Amangwu
551. Amankolor
552. Amanna
553. Amanolu
554. Amanze
555. Amaobi
556. Amapuga
557. Amara
558. Amarachi
559. Amarachukwu
560. Amaradike
561. Amaraikwu
562. Amaraizu
563. Amaralam
564. Amaribe
565. Amarizu
566. Amasionwu
567. Amatam
568. Amaucheazi
569. Amauchechukwu
570. Amaudo
571. Amaugo
572. Amaukwu
573. Amaukwu
574. Amazi
575. Amazie
576. Amazigo
577. Amazinwa
578. Amaziuwa
579. Amazu
580. Amene
581. Amobi
582. Amogechukwu
583. Amonye
584. Amuchie
585. Amugo
586. Amuma
587. Amunadi
588. Amuno
589. Amuzie
590. Anabaluchi
591. Anabaludike
592. Anabaluolisa
593. Anabogu
594. Anabude
595. Anabuike
596. Anachebe
597. Anachebe
598. Anadi
599. Anadinma
600. Anadu
601. Anaebere
602. Anaechechi
603. Anaedu
604. Anaele
605. Anaelechi
606. Anaeme
607. Anaemeka
608. Anaemelu
609. Anaemelu
610. Anaeto
611. Anagbaluchi
612. Anagbaluokwu
613. Anagbaluonwu
614. Anagbaoso
615. Anagboka
616. Anagha
617. Anagha
618. Anago
619. Anagu
620. Anagudo
621. Anajekwu
622. Anajemba
623. Anaka
624. Anakonwa
625. Anakpandu
626. Anakwe
627. Anakwenze
628. Anakwenze
629. Anamasoro
630. Anamelechi
631. Anamsochi
632. Ananedu
633. Ananedu
634. Anara
635. Anasaoibe
636. Anatogu
637. Anayo
638. Anayochukwu
639. Anayolisa
640. Anazo
641. Anazoba
642. Anazodo
643. Anazogini
644. Anebosa
645. Anebuo
646. Anechebe
647. Anedi
648. Anedu
649. Aneke
650. Aneke
651. Anekwe
652. Anekwu
653. Anelechi
654. Aneli
655. Aneliaku
656. Anemelu
657. Anene
658. Anenechi
659. Aneneolisa
660. Aneriaku
661. Aneriaku
662. Anerika
663. Anerobi
664. Aneze
665. Anezube
666. Aniago
667. Aniagolu
668. Aniakor
669. Aniamalu

670. Aniche
671. Anichebe
672. Anichie
673. Anidi
674. Anidi
675. Anidiaso
676. Aniebonam
677. Aniegboka
678. Aniegbonam
679. Aniejielo
680. Aniemeka
681. Aniemeka
682. Aniezue
683. Anigbo
684. Anigezu
685. Anigha
686. Anigo
687. Anijielo
688. Anikwe
689. Animalu
690. Aninyei
691. Anizoba
692. Anochie
693. Anochiem
694. Anochirionye
695. Anoka
696. Anoliefo
697. Anolika
698. Anopueme
699. Anoruo
700. Anoruwe
701. Anosa
702. Anozie
703. Anuakpando
704. Anubena
705. Anuchaa
706. Anuchie
707. Anuebunwa
708. Anuforo
709. Anugom
710. Anukam
711. Anuliefo
712. Anuliefo
713. Anuligo ^
714. Anulika ^
715. Anulika ^
716. Anuluoha
717. Anuluoha
718. Anumba
719. Anumudu
720. Anumudu
721. Anunobi ^
722. Anunwa
723. Anunwa
724. Anupue
725. Anusiem
726. Anusiobi
727. Anusonwu
728. Anuzuo
729. Anwagom
730. Anwasia
731. Anwatu
732. Anwunah
733. Anya
734. Anyaaso
735. Anyabike
736. Anyachebe
737. Anyachebelu
738. Anyachi
739. Anyachiaso
740. Anyachie
741. Anyachukwu
742. Anyachukwu
743. Anyadiegwu
744. Anyadike
745. Anyaduba
746. Anyaduba
747. Anyaeche
748. Anyaeche
749. Anyaegbunam
750. Anyaelue
751. Anyaezu
752. Anyaezu
753. Anyafuaku
754. Anyafugo
755. Anyafulu
756. Anyafuluaku
757. Anyafulukwe
758. Anyafuogu
759. Anyagafu
760. Anyaike
761. Anyailo
762. Anyairo
763. Anyaji
764. Anyaji
765. Anyakamji
766. Anyakaogu
767. Anyakaora
768. Anyaku
769. Anyaku
770. Anyakudo
771. Anyakwo
772. Anyakwo
773. Anyalechie
774. Anyalewechi
775. Anyalewem
776. Anyalue
777. Anyamele
778. Anyanahu
779. Anyanaso
780. Anyaneche
781. Anyaneie
782. Anyaneje
783. Anyaneto
784. Anyankwo
785. Anyanwu
786. Anyanyo
787. Anyaogu
788. Anyaoha
789. Anyaoku
790. Anyaora
791. Anyara
792. Anyasie
793. Anyaugo
794. Anyazulu
795. Anyazuluoha
796. Anyiam
797. Anyibuofu
798. Anyichie
799. Anyika
800. Anyikwa
801. Anyim
802. Anyinya
803. Araka
804. Aralu

805. Aranotu
806. Aranya
807. Araonu
808. Arazu
809. Areh
810. Arianna
811. Arimah
812. Arinze
813. Arinzechi
814. Ariotachi
815. Ariotam
816. Ariotandu
817. Ariri
818. Aririegbunam
819. Aririguzo
820. Aririnwa
821. Aririonwu
822. Ariwodo
823. Aroh
824. Arugorunna
825. Arunne
826. Arunsi
827. Asadu
828. Asagwaram
829. Ashiagwa
830. Ashiagwu
831. Ashimole
832. Asiegbu
833. Asika
834. Asike
835. Asimole
836. Asimonye
837. Asinobi
838. Asoanya
839. Asodike
840. Asoegwu
841. Asogwam
842. Asomadike
843. Asomba
844. Asomonu
845. Asomonye
846. Asomugha
847. Asonye
848. Asouzu
849. Atakulu
850. Atamusi
851. Atigwe
852. Atuanya
853. Atuchukwu
854. Atuegbu
855. Atuegwu
856. Atueyichi
857. Atuigwe
858. Atukuba
859. Atulegwu
860. Atulogu
861. Atuloma
862. Atuma
863. Atundu
864. Atusiogu
865. Atusionwu
866. Atusiuba
867. Awa
868. Awaji
869. Awaogu
870. Awele
871. Aweze
872. Awiko
873. Awilunanya
874. Awoh
875. Awugosi
876. Awujo
877. Awujo
878. Ayaezuba
879. Ayanamiru
880. Ayogu
881. Aziagba
882. Azie
883. Aziekwe
884. Aziekwenambu
885. Azike
886. Azikiwe
887. Azikwe
888. Azingi
889. Azotandu
890. Azuakolam
891. Azuamaka
892. Azuamaka
893. Azubike
894. Azubuenyi
895. Azubueze
896. Azubugwu
897. Azubuilo
898. Azubundo
899. Azubundu
900. Azubuogu
901. Azuchebe
902. Azudialor
903. Azudinma
904. Azudiogu
905. Azuebube
906. Azuegbunam
907. Azuenyi
908. Azugbo
909. Azugbodo
910. Azugbomkpa
911. Azugo
912. Azuka
913. Azukeme
914. Azungwu
915. Azunna
916. Azunze
917. Azuobodo
918. Azuobuka
919. Azuogu
920. Azuogu
921. Azuoma
922. Azuonye
923. Bedebe
924. Bekuechi
925. Belonwu
926. Beluchukwu
927. Belueke
928. Beluodachi
929. Bewerechi
930. Bielodachi
931. Biosah
932. Bosah
933. Chalunjo
934. Chaluokwu
935. Chazawom
936. Chdorom
937. Chebechukwu
938. Chebeolisa
939. Chebiri

940. Chedolisa
941. Chegidechi
942. Chegidenna
943. Chekwube
944. Cheluchi
945. Cherem
946. Chetachukwu
947. Chetam
948. Chetanna
949. Chetaolisa
950. Chewaechi
951. Chiabaka
952. Chiadikobi
953. Chiafugo
954. Chiagalam
955. Chiagbalumogu
956. Chiagbaoke
957. Chiaghanam
958. Chiagorom
959. Chiagozie
960. Chiaka
961. Chiakibe
962. Chiakolam
963. Chiakonwa
964. Chiaku
965. Chiakwanam
966. Chiamaka
967. Chianugo
968. Chiasoanya
969. Chiawuotu
970. Chiazalam
971. Chiazam
972. Chiazota
973. Chibiko
974. Chibuike
975. Chibundo
976. Chibundu
977. Chibunze
978. Chibuugo
979. Chichetam
980. Chichorom
981. Chidalu
982. Chidebe
983. Chidebelu
984. Chidebere
985. Chidegha
986. Chidera
987. Chidi
988. Chidiadi
989. Chidiaso
990. Chidiaso
991. Chidibere
992. Chidiegwu
993. Chidielo
994. Chidifu
995. Chidime
996. Chidindu
997. Chidinka
998. Chidinma
999. Chidinma
1000. Chidinso
1001. Chidiogo
1002. Chidiugwu
1003. Chidiukwu
1004. Chidolue
1005. Chidozie
1006. Chidubem
1007. Chidubem
1008. Chidum
1009. Chidumaga
1010. Chidume
1011. Chidume
1012. Chidumeje
1013. Chidunwa
1014. Chiebuka
1015. Chiechetam
1016. Chiedego
1017. Chiedozie
1018. Chiegbu
1019. Chiegbulam
1020. Chiegbulam
1021. Chiegbunam
1022. Chiegeonu
1023. Chiegwu
1024. Chiejina
1025. Chieka
1026. Chiekwena
1027. Chiekwugo
1028. Chieloka
1029. Chielota
1030. Chiemeka
1031. Chiemela
1032. Chiemelie
1033. Chiemenam
1034. Chiemenyem
1035. Chiemenyem
1036. Chiemerem
1037. Chiemetam
1038. Chiemewo
1039. Chiemezie
1040. Chienweatu
1041. Chienweusa
1042. Chienyegom
1043. Chienyekwam
1044. Chienyemobi
1045. Chienyemugo
1046. Chienyenam
1047. Chienyewom
1048. Chierika
1049. Chietolam
1050. Chigalum
1051. Chigbalumogu
1052. Chigbata
1053. Chigbo
1054. Chigbogu
1055. Chigbonwu
1056. Chigekpe
1057. Chigorom
1058. Chigosim
1059. Chigowaram
1060. Chigozie
1061. Chihazie
1062. Chihazie
1063. Chihazie
1064. Chika
1065. Chika
1066. Chikaeze
1067. Chikaku
1068. Chikamma
1069. Chikasi
1070. Chike
1071. Chikeluba
1072. Chikere
1073. Chikere
1074. Chikerenma

1075. Chikereuba
1076. Chikereze
1077. Chikezie
1078. Chikezue
1079. Chikwado
1080. Chikwauzo
1081. Chikwe
1082. Chikwelu
1083. Chikwendu
1084. Chikwenma
1085. Chikwere
1086. Chikwube
1087. Chikwura
1088. Chilaka
1089. Chiledum
1090. Chiletam
1091. Chilotam
1092. Chimaechi
1093. Chimaenu
1094. Chimaenye
1095. Chimaeze
1096. Chimaluke
1097. Chimama
1098. Chimamanda
1099. Chimaobi
1100. Chimaoge
1101. Chimaoke
1102. Chimara
1103. Chimazo
1104. Chimbiko
1105. Chimbueze
1106. Chimdi
1107. Chimdiegwu
1108. Chimdike
1109. Chimdindu
1110. Chime
1111. Chimebuka
1112. Chimegwatam
1113. Chimelogo
1114. Chimeremma
1115. Chimereze
1116. Chimezie
1117. Chimnenye
1118. Chimnonso
1119. Chimnoso
1120. Chimsaraokwu
1121. Chimuanya
1122. Chimuanya
1123. Chimzi
1124. Chinagbaogu
1125. Chinago
1126. Chinagorom
1127. Chinagwa
1128. Chinalum
1129. Chinara
1130. Chinasa
1131. Chinatu
1132. Chinatuokwu
1133. Chinaza
1134. Chinazom
1135. Chinazunwa
1136. Chinedu
1137. Chinegbo
1138. Chinekwu
1139. Chinele
1140. Chineme
1141. Chinemelu
1142. Chinemeze
1143. Chinene
1144. Chinenyeaku
1145. Chinenyenwa
1146. Chinenyeuba
1147. Chineyeanya
1148. Chineze
1149. Chinma
1150. Chinomuso
1151. Chinonso
1152. Chinwa
1153. Chinweaku
1154. Chinweike
1155. Chinweikpe
1156. Chinweizu
1157. Chinwemeli
1158. Chinwendu
1159. Chinwenwa
1160. Chinweoge
1161. Chinweoke
1162. Chinweoku
1163. Chinweokwu
1164. Chinweozo
1165. Chinweuba
1166. Chinweugo
1167. Chinweuko
1168. Chinweusa
1169. Chinweuwa
1170. Chinweuzo
1171. Chinweze
1172. Chinyeaka
1173. Chinyekwam
1174. Chinyere
1175. Chinyerum
1176. Chinyezie
1177. Chinyirionwu
1178. Chioke
1179. Chira
1180. Chisara
1181. Chisarokwu
1182. Chitobe
1183. Chitobem
1184. Chitolonye
1185. Chitoom
1186. Chitubemugo
1187. Chituru
1188. Chiwuagbo
1189. Chizaram
1190. Chizimuzo
1191. Chizitere
1192. Chizoba
1193. Chizoma
1194. Chizube
1195. Chizubelu
1196. Chizue
1197. Chizume
1198. Chude
1199. Chudi
1200. Chukuba
1201. Chukwoma
1202. Chukwuanugo
1203. Chukwude
1204. Chukwudi
1205. Chukwudiaso
1206. Chukwudifu
1207. Chukwudinka
1208. Chukwudiogo
1209. Chukwudum

1210. Chukwuebuka
1211. Chukwueke
1212. Chukwueke
1213. Chukwuelingo
1214. Chukwueloka
1215. Chukwuemeka
1216. Chukwugozie
1217. Chukwuka
1218. Chukwukadibia
1219. Chukwukadum
1220. Chukwukelu
1221. Chukwukere
1222. Chukwulobe
1223. Chukwuma
1224. Chukwumerije
1225. Chukwunakueze
1226. Chukwunedum
1227. Chukwunweike
1228. Chukwunweikpe
1229. Dabeluchukwu
1230. Dala
1231. Dejili
1232. Dike
1233. Dikedinobi
1234. Dikeocha
1235. Dikeukwu
1236. Dilibe
1237. Dilibe
1238. Dimkpa
1239. Diribe
1240. Dubem
1241. Dumbiri
1242. Dumkelechi
1243. Dumkwu
1244. Dumyobachukwu
1245. Dumyochi
1246. Dunu
1247. Dunusie
1248. Duru
1249. Duruesie
1250. Duruhesie
1251. Duruji
1252. Ebegbulem
1253. Ebekwuru
1254. Ebelechukwu
1255. Eberechi
1256. Eberechukwu
1257. Eberendu
1258. Ebereoma
1259. Ebiebichukwu
1260. Ebiem
1261. Ebieogu
1262. Ebierike
1263. Ebieroha
1264. Ebieronwu
1265. Ebigbo
1266. Ebimalu
1267. Ebimara
1268. Ebimngaonye
1269. Ebiriekwe
1270. Ebirim
1271. Ebiringa
1272. Ebizue
1273. Eboka
1274. Eboma
1275. Ebonam
1276. Ebubeagu
1277. Ebubechukwu
1278. Ebubedike
1279. Ebubeke
1280. Ebubenna
1281. Ebunie
1282. Echebiga
1283. Echebiri
1284. Echefu
1285. Echefuna
1286. Echema
1287. Echendu
1288. Echeruo
1289. Echesi
1290. Echetaebe
1291. Echezona
1292. Echezonam
1293. Echezonchukwu
1294. Echiagu
1295. Echidifu
1296. Echidime
1297. Echidinma
1298. Echidiugha
1299. Echieagu
1300. Edike
1301. Edoga
1302. Edoga
1303. Edoka
1304. Edokwe
1305. Edozie
1306. Edoziem
1307. Eduputa
1308. Efoagui
1309. Efobi
1310. Egbebike
1311. Egbechukwu
1312. Egbeigwe
1313. Egbeonu
1314. Egbobiri
1315. Egbochie
1316. Egbochunwa
1317. Egbodike
1318. Egboji
1319. Egboka
1320. Egbosi
1321. Egbosimba
1322. Egbosimba
1323. Egbosinwa
1324. Egbosionu
1325. Egbosionwu
1326. Egbuchulam
1327. Egbughara
1328. Egbuho
1329. Egbuhor
1330. Egbuji
1331. Egbujiobi
1332. Egbuke
1333. Egbuniwe
1334. Egbunkeonye
1335. Egbuonu
1336. Egechi
1337. Egejuru
1338. Egemonye
1339. Egenti
1340. Egeonu
1341. Egeonuigwe
1342. Egere m
1343. Egerue

1344. Egoabunwa
1345. Egoawuchi
1346. Egoawunwa
1347. Egobudike
1348. Egobuilo
1349. Egoegbonwu
1350. Egoliem
1351. Egolum
1352. Egonwa
1353. Egoyibo
1354. Egudu
1355. Egwim
1356. Egwuagu
1357. Egwuatu
1358. Egwuatuogu
1359. Egwuatuonwu
1360. Egwuchukwu
1361. Egwudike
1362. Egwuenu
1363. Egwunwoke
1364. Egwuonwu
1365. Egwuonye
1366. Egwuoyibo
1367. Egwuwa
1368. Ehimudu
1369. Ehimudu
1370. Ehiobu
1371. Ehiokwere
1372. Ehiokwu
1373. Ehirim
1374. Ehuru
1375. Ejeagha
1376. Ejeh
1377. Ejelinma
1378. Ejeluem
1379. Ejemba
1380. Ejere
1381. Ejezie
1382. Ejeziri
1383. Ejezue
1384. Ejiagwu
1385. Ejiamatu
1386. Ejideaku
1387. Ejideaku
1388. Ejidike
1389. Ejigbalu
1390. Ejike
1391. Ejikeme
1392. Ejimbe
1393. Ejimnkeonye
1394. Ejimofor
1395. Ejimogu
1396. Ejimole
1397. Ejimonye
1398. Ejimonyeugwo
1399. Ejindu
1400. Ejiofo
1401. Ejiofobiri
1402. Ejiogu
1403. Ejizu
1404. Ekeada
1405. Ekeamaka
1406. Ekeanyanwu
1407. Ekechi
1408. Ekechi
1409. Ekechi
1410. Ekechukwu
1411. Ekedozie
1412. Ekedum
1413. Ekeh
1414. Ekeibe
1415. Ekejekwu
1416. Ekejeme
1417. Ekejimbe
1418. Ekejindu
1419. Ekejiokwo
1420. Ekejiuba
1421. Ekeke
1422. Ekekwe
1423. Ekekwe
1424. EkEkweanua
1425. Ekelechi
1426. Ekemezie
1427. Ekemezie
1428. Ekemodo
1429. Ekenachi
1430. Ekenma
1431. Ekenma
1432. Ekenna
1433. Ekennia
1434. Ekenwa
1435. Ekeodu
1436. Ekeopara
1437. Ekezia
1438. Ekezinwa
1439. Ekolu
1440. Ekpebie
1441. Ekpebiri
1442. Ekpechi
1443. Ekperejindu
1444. Ekpereka
1445. Ekperekamji
1446. Ekperendu
1447. Ekpereoma
1448. Ekpezina
1449. Ekpunobi
1450. Ekwealor
1451. Ekweani
1452. Ekweanuo
1453. Ekwebelam
1454. Ekwebie
1455. Ekwebiri
1456. Ekwebiri
1457. Ekwegba
1458. Ekwegbalu
1459. Ekwegho
1460. Ekweife
1461. Ekwekwe
1462. Ekwelike
1463. Ekwelike
1464. Ekwelugo
1465. Ekwelum
1466. Ekwema
1467. Ekwemuo
1468. Ekwenachi
1469. Ekwenam
1470. Ekwenchi
1471. Ekwendu
1472. Ekwenike
1473. Ekwenobi
1474. Ekwenonu
1475. Ekwensi
1476. Ekweozo
1477. Ekweozor
1478. Ekwera

1479. Ekweredike
1480. Ekwerem
1481. Ekweremadu
1482. Ekwerendu
1483. Ekweribe
1484. Ekwerike
1485. Ekwesia
1486. Ekweta
1487. Ekweugo
1488. Ekweuno
1489. Ekwezuo
1490. Ekwoanya
1491. Ekwudebe
1492. Ekwudo
1493. Ekwueme
1494. Ekwulugo
1495. Ekwunife
1496. Ekwuno
1497. Ekwuotu
1498. Ekwurah
1499. Ekwusaiaga
1500. Ekwusia
1501. Ekwusigo
1502. Ekwutosi
1503. Ekwuzia
1504. Ekwuzie
1505. Eleagu
1506. Eleanya
1507. Elebechi
1508. Elebie
1509. Elebiri
1510. Elechi
1511. Elechidi
1512. Elechukwu
1513. Eledebe
1514. Elekebe
1515. Elekwachi
1516. Elekwauwa
1517. Elekweizu
1518. Eleleodi
1519. Elelia
1520. Elemchi
1521. Elemdi
1522. Elemonye
1523. Elenmuo
1524. Eleodichi
1525. Eleodichi
1526. Eleodichukwu
1527. Eleodinmo
1528. Eletandu
1529. Elewamchi
1530. Eleweuwa
1531. Elobendu
1532. Elochukwu
1533. Elofue
1534. Eluemuno
1535. Elueze
1536. Elumelu
1537. Eluwa
1538. Emabota
1539. Eme
1540. Emebela
1541. Emebiri
1542. Emebo
1543. Emechebe
1544. Emecheta
1545. Emedom
1546. Emedosi
1547. Emefie
1548. Emefine
1549. Emefo
1550. Emegafu
1551. Emeghali
1552. Emegwali
1553. Emehelu
1554. Emejonam
1555. Emejulu
1556. Emejuru
1557. Emekam
1558. Emekwanam
1559. Emelogu
1560. Emelue
1561. Emembolu
1562. Emenam
1563. Emenanjo
1564. Emenari
1565. Emenife
1566. Emenike
1567. Emeodi
1568. Emerem
1569. Emeremgini
1570. Emeremnini
1571. Emeriaku
1572. Emeribe
1573. Emerigo
1574. Emeriogu
1575. Emerole
1576. Emeruwa
1577. Emesobe
1578. Emetaram
1579. Emetole
1580. Emezie
1581. Emezinwa
1582. Emezue
1583. Emodi
1584. Emodo
1585. Emoka
1586. Eneaji
1587. Eneanya
1588. Enebe
1589. Enebechi
1590. Enebedum
1591. Enebelam
1592. Enebeli
1593. Enechi
1594. Enedo
1595. Eneghara
1596. Eneh
1597. Enejeanya
1598. Enejere
1599. Enekebe
1600. Enekwachi
1601. Enekwe
1602. Enekwizu
1603. Eneli
1604. Enemchukwu
1605. Enemuo
1606. Enendu
1607. Enenia
1608. Enenwali
1609. Enesolu
1610. Enesotu
1611. Enetaizu
1612. Enetandu
1613. Eneweaku

1614. Eneweobi
1615. Eneweonu
1616. Eni
1617. Enijoku
1618. Enuamaka
1619. Enubuwa
1620. Enuchbe
1621. Enudiegwu
1622. Enudike
1623. Enughalu
1624. Enujah
1625. Enujekwu
1626. Enuji
1627. Enujiofo
1628. Enuka
1629. Enukoha
1630. Enukora
1631. Enukwe
1632. Enumah
1633. Enumara
1634. Enunwa
1635. Enunwa
1636. Enuoma
1637. Enuoyibo
1638. Enuwa
1639. Enwedo
1640. Enweonwu
1641. Enwerem
1642. Enwerem
1643. Enweremchi
1644. Enweremchiukwu
1645. Enweuwa
1646. Enyeobi
1647. Enyesiobi
1648. Enyewezo
1649. Enyezu
1650. Enyezue
1651. Enyiamaka
1652. Enyidiegwu
1653. Enyikanwanne
1654. Enyikwom
1655. Enyinnaya
1656. Enyioma
1657. Enyiwuchi
1658. Enyiwuenyi
1659. Enyiwuozo
1660. Enyogai
1661. Eribiri
1662. Erike
1663. Erinne
1664. Eriobu
1665. Eriobuna
1666. Eriuwa
1667. Erokwu
1668. Erondu
1669. Eronini
1670. Eronobi
1671. Eruchalu
1672. Esekokwu
1673. Esimai
1674. Esogbue
1675. Esoluonu
1676. Esomchi
1677. Esomonye
1678. Esotu
1679. Etiaba
1680. Etolue
1681. Etoniru
1682. Etudo
1683. Etukokwu
1684. Ewelukwa
1685. Ewenike
1686. Ewerem
1687. Ewezuga
1688. Ewudo
1689. Ewulo
1690. Ewuzie
1691. Ezeabasi
1692. Ezeabasili
1693. Ezeabata
1694. Ezeadi
1695. Ezeadigo
1696. Ezeagha
1697. Ezeagu
1698. Ezeagwula
1699. Ezeaku
1700. Ezeakwalam
1701. Ezeala
1702. Ezeamaka
1703. Ezeamaukwu
1704. Ezeana
1705. Ezeanakwe
1706. Ezeani
1707. Ezeanioma
1708. Ezeanya
1709. Ezeaso
1710. Ezebilo
1711. Ezebiri
1712. Ezechi
1713. Ezechima
1714. Ezechinwoye
1715. Ezechukwu
1716. Ezedibia
1717. Ezedimbu
1718. Ezedinma
1719. Ezefunamba
1720. Ezegwu
1721. Ezeibe
1722. Ezeife
1723. Ezeigbo
1724. Ezeigbo
1725. Ezeigwe
1726. Ezeigwe
1727. Ezeilo
1728. Ezeimo
1729. Ezeji
1730. Ezejiofo
1731. Ezejioha
1732. Ezekwe
1733. Ezekwelu
1734. Ezekwesili
1735. Ezelagbo
1736. Ezelue
1737. Ezelum
1738. Ezemba
1739. Ezemodo
1740. Ezemonye
1741. Ezenagu
1742. Ezendu
1743. Ezennaya
1744. Ezenolue
1745. Ezenwa
1746. Ezenwafo
1747. Ezenwaka
1748. Ezenwamadu

1749. Ezenwankwo
1750. Ezenwata
1751. Ezenwata
1752. Ezenweaku
1753. Ezenweike
1754. Ezenweilo
1755. Ezenweobi
1756. Ezenweoku
1757. Ezenweora
1758. Ezenweugo
1759. Ezenweuko
1760. Ezenwude
1761. Ezenyeora
1762. Ezeoba
1763. Ezeobi
1764. Ezeobodo
1765. Ezeofia
1766. Ezeofo
1767. Ezeoha
1768. Ezeokafo
1769. Ezeoke
1770. Ezeokeke
1771. Ezeokoli
1772. Ezeokolo
1773. Ezeokwelume
1774. Ezeonu
1775. Ezeonu
1776. Ezeonwa
1777. Ezeonwuka
1778. Ezeonye
1779. Ezeora
1780. EzeriohaEzeude
1781. Ezeudo
1782. Ezeudu
1783. Ezeugbana
1784. Ezeugo
1785. Ezeugwu
1786. Ezeuko
1787. Ezeukwu
1788. Ezeume
1789. Ezewiro
1790. Ezewudo
1791. Ezewulu
1792. Ezewuobi
1793. Ezewuru
1794. Eziabaka
1795. Eziafakego
1796. Eziafamaka
1797. Eziamaka
1798. Ezibe
1799. Eziefula
1800. Ezigbo
1801. Ezika
1802. Ezika
1803. Ezike
1804. Ezim
1805. Ezimako
1806. Ezimora
1807. Ezindu
1808. Ezinma
1809. Ezinma
1810. Ezinmuo
1811. Ezinne
1812. Ezinwa
1813. Ezinwanne
1814. Eziogo
1815. Eziokwubundu
1816. Eziokwudinma
1817. Ezioma
1818. Eziugwu
1819. Eziukwu
1820. Eziuzo
1821. Ezudike
1822. Ezuka
1823. Ezukanmah
1824. Ezukoba
1825. Ezulike
1826. Ezumah
1827. Ezumezu
1828. Ezuo
1829. Ezurike
1830. Ezuruba
1831. Ezurudike
1832. Gbabanachi
1833. Gbakwuchukwu
1834. Gbakwuibe
1835. Gbakwunna
1836. Gbakwuolisa
1837. Gbasochi
1838. Gbasochukwu
1839. Ginigeme
1840. Ginijeme
1841. Ginikamelu
1842. Ginikanwa
1843. Gosim
1844. Guzo
1845. Gwabaolisa
1846. Gwachim
1847. Gwamife
1848. Gwamniru
1849. Gwaolisa
1850. Ibeabuchi
1851. Ibeachum
1852. Ibeagha
1853. Ibeagwa
1854. Ibeagwu
1855. Ibeako
1856. Ibeakonam
1857. Ibeanu
1858. Ibeawuchi
1859. Ibebogu
1860. Ibebuchi
1861. Ibebuilo
1862. Ibebuizu
1863. Ibedialor
1864. Ibedilo
1865. Ibediro
1866. Ibedum
1867. Ibegbu
1868. Ibegbu
1869. Ibegbulam
1870. Ibegbuna
1871. Ibegbunam
1872. Ibegwam
1873. Ibegwam
1874. Ibegwam
1875. Ibejide
1876. Ibejim
1877. Ibejiofor
1878. Ibejiokwu
1879. Ibeka
1880. Ibekailo
1881. Ibekwe
1882. Ibekwere
1883. Ibekwue

1884. Ibeme
1885. Ibemenam
1886. Ibemere
1887. Ibenazo
1888. Ibenegbu
1889. Ibeneme
1890. Ibenne
1891. Ibenweike
1892. Ibenweilo
1893. Ibenweude
1894. Ibenyeaka
1895. Iberika
1896. Ibeto
1897. Ibewuike
1898. Ibewuiro
1899. Ibezam
1900. Ibezim
1901. Ibezimako
1902. Ibezom
1903. Ibiam
1904. Ibuaku
1905. Ibuamaka
1906. Ibuanyiaku
1907. Idebungwu
1908. Idebuno
1909. Ideh
1910. Idengwu
1911. Ideorji
1912. Idigo
1913. Idika
1914. Idimogo
1915. Idoka
1916. Idoko
1917. Idozuka
1918. Ifeacho
1919. Ifeadi
1920. Ifeadigo
1921. Ifeadikachi
1922. Ifeadikanwa
1923. Ifeajuna
1924. Ifeakachukwu
1925. Ifeakaibe
1926. Ifeakandu
1927. Ifeakandu
1928. Ifeakanwa
1929. Ifeakaonwu
1930. Ifeakwanam
1931. Ifeamaluke
1932. Ifeamama
1933. Ifeanacho
1934. Ifeanacho
1935. Ifeanyi
1936. Ifeanyichukwu
1937. Ifeanyimba
1938. Ifeanyinmo
1939. Ifeanyionwu
1940. Ifeatu
1941. Ifebelunoke
1942. Ifebeluoke
1943. Ifebeluoke
1944. Ifebi
1945. Ifebi
1946. Ifebie
1947. Ifeboludike
1948. Ifebonam
1949. Ifebuka
1950. Ifecheludike
1951. Ifecheluobi
1952. Ifechukwu
1953. Ifedelu
1954. Ifedi
1955. Ifediba
1956. Ifediche
1957. Ifedigbo
1958. Ifedigbo
1959. Ifedike
1960. Ifedike
1961. Ifedili
1962. Ifedimbu
1963. Ifedinamba
1964. Ifedinma
1965. Ifedinma
1966. Ifediogo
1967. Ifediora
1968. Ifediugwu
1969. Ifefoku
1970. Ifeghalu
1971. Ifegwu
1972. Ifeikeneme
1973. Ifejiamatu
1974. Ifejiofo
1975. Ifejioha
1976. Ifejiora
1977. Ifekadike
1978. Ifekaibeya
1979. Ifekaizu
1980. Ifekaji
1981. Ifekandu
1982. Ifekweludike
1983. Ifekwelueze
1984. Ifekwelumba
1985. Ifekwunigwe
1986. Ifemadike
1987. Ifemalu
1988. Ifeme
1989. Ifemalume
1990. Ifemedebe
1991. Ifemeludike
1992. Ifemenam
1993. Ifemesi
1994. Ifemezia
1995. Ifenacho
1996. Ifenna
1997. Ifenu
1998. Ifenyilinba
1999. Ifenyiliora
2000. Ifeobu
2001. Ifeobu
2002. Ifeodelu
2003. Ifeoma
2004. Ifeonye
2005. Ifeonyema
2006. Ifeora
2007. Ifeseike
2008. Ifesie
2009. Ifesinachi
2010. Ifesoaku
2011. Ifesodike
2012. Ifesogu
2013. Ifesoilo
2014. Ifesondu
2015. Ifesonwa
2016. Ifesonwu
2017. Ifesora
2018. Ifeudu

2019. Ifeyinwa
2020. Ifeze
2021. Ifezube
2022. Ifezuligbo
2023. Ifezulike
2024. Ifezulora
2025. Ifichukwu
2026. Ifiegbunam
2027. Ifiego
2028. Ifiemenam
2029. Ifienu
2030. Ifinwa
2031. Ifinwanne
2032. Ifiogo
2033. Ifioha
2034. Ifioma
2035. Ifionu
2036. Ifionwu
2037. Ifunanya
2038. Igbeka
2039. Igboakaeze
2040. Igboamaeze
2041. Igboamalu
2042. Igboanugo
2043. Igboanusi
2044. Igboasoanya
2045. Igbodiegwu
2046. Igbodike
2047. Igboeli
2048. Igboemesi
2049. Igboenweze
2050. Igboesika
2051. Igboezue
2052. Igboka
2053. Igbokamba
2054. Igboke
2055. Igbokwe
2056. Igbokwere
2057. Igbokwili
2058. Igbomezie
2059. Igbonekwu
2060. Igirigi
2061. Iguedo
2062. Igweasoanya
2063. Igweasogu
2064. Igwebike
2065. Igwebugwu
2066. Igwedibia
2067. Igwediegwu
2068. Igwedike
2069. Igwedu
2070. Igwegbe
2071. Igweka
2072. Igwekaeze
2073. Igwekanma
2074. Igweke
2075. Igwekezie
2076. Igwemadu
2077. Igwemba
2078. Igwenazo
2079. Igwenyi
2080. Igweonu
2081. Igweuike
2082. Igwewugwu
2083. Igweze
2084. Igwilo
2085. Igwuani
2086. Iheakanna
2087. Iheagwam
2088. Iheagwarachi
2089. Iheahurukwe
2090. Iheakolam
2091. Iheakaoha
2092. Iheaku
2093. Iheama
2094. Iheanaju
2095. Iheanatu
2096. Iheancho
2097. Iheanuri ^
2098. Iheanyahuru
2099. Iheanyanwu
2100. Iheanyichukwu
2101. Iheaso
2102. Iheatu
2103. Ihechidere
2104. Ihechimere
2105. Ihechinyere
2106. Ihechituru
2107. Ihechukwu
2108. Ihedi
2109. Ihediaro
2110. Ihediaso
2111. Ihediche
2112. Ihediegwu
2113. Ihedimbu
2114. Ihedinamba
2115. Ihedinma
2116. Ihediogo
2117. Ihedioha
2118. Ihedioha
2119. Ihediohamma
2120. Ihedire
2121. Ihediri
2122. Ihediugwu
2123. Ihediwa
2124. Iheebube
2125. Iheejiamatu
2126. Ihejieto
2127. Iheforo
2128. Ihegeme
2129. Iheghara
2130. Ihegwesiri
2131. Iheiroemelam
2132. Iheiromere
2133. Iheji
2134. Ihejiaka
2135. Ihejiako
2136. Ihejiaku
2137. Ihejiejemba
2138. Ihejieto
2139. Ihejimba
2140. Ihejindu
2141. Ihejindu
2142. Ihejiofo
2143. Ihejioha
2144. Ihejiokwu
2145. Ihejirika
2146. Ihejirika
2147. Ihejiuba
2148. Ihejiugo
2149. Ihejiuwa
2150. Ihekadike
2151. Ihekaenyi
2152. Ihekaire
2153. Ihekandu

2154. Ihekanze
2155. Ihekaoha
2156. Ihekweazu
2157. Ihekwere
2158. Ihekwoaba
2159. Ihemachi
2160. Ihemadu
2161. Ihemaizu
2162. Ihemara
2163. Ihemba
2164. Ihembajieto
2165. Ihembajieto
2166. Ihemchere
2167. Ihemchoro
2168. Ihemdinma
2169. Ihemdirim
2170. Iheme
2171. Ihemeje
2172. Ihemere
2173. Ihemerechi
2174. Ihemezie
2175. Ihemji
2176. Ihejiako
2177. Ihemjiekwu
2178. Ihemjika
2179. Ihemkweaba
2180. Ihemtuga
2181. Ihenyiaoha
2182. Ihenyirioha
2183. Iheoha
2184. Iheoma
2185. Iheomakolam
2186. Iheonukara
2187. Iheonumere
2188. Iheonwumere
2189. Iheonyeadinjo
2190. Iheonyema
2191. Iheonyemetara
2192. Ihesinachi:
2193. Iheteaka
2194. Iheukwu
2195. Iheukwumere
2196. Ihewuihe
2197. Ihewuike
2198. Ihewuuka
2199. Ihezube
2200. Ihezueoha
2201. Ihezuru
2202. Ihezuruigbo
2203. Ihezuruike
2204. Ihezurumba
2205. Ihezuruoha
2206. Ihezuruoke
2207. Ihichukwu
2208. Ihinmadu
2209. Ihinwa
2210. Ihiogu
2211. Ihioma
2212. Ihionu
2213. Ihuadinjo
2214. Ihuaku
2215. Ihuamara
2216. Ihuanyanwu
2217. Ihuchukwu
2218. Ihueze
2219. Ihuigwe
2220. Ihumara
2221. Ihunna
2222. Ihuoma
2223. Ihuugo
2224. Ijeako
2225. Ijeamaka
2226. Ijeawele
2227. Ijedike
2228. Ijego
2229. Ijelue
2230. Ijendu
2231. Ijenu
2232. Ijenwa
2233. Ijenwanne
2234. Ijeogo
2235. Ijeoma
2236. Ijeomanta
2237. Ijeuwa
2238. Ijewuako
2239. Ijewuizu
2240. Ijewuizu
2241. Ijezie
2242. Ikeagboso
2243. Ikeagu
2244. Ikeagwuani
2245. Ikeahurukwe
2246. Ikeakor
2247. Ikeaku
2248. Ikeala
2249. Ikeanya
2250. Ikeanyichukwu
2251. Ikeanyichukwu
2252. Ikeanyinmo
2253. Ikeanyionwu
2254. Ikeanyionwu
2255. Ikeanyisi
2256. Ikeasoanya
2257. Ikeasoegwu
2258. Ikeasogu
2259. Ikeasomba
2260. Ikeazom
2261. Ikeazor
2262. Ikeazota
2263. Ikebuaku
2264. Ikebudu
2265. Ikebugwu
2266. Ikebundu
2267. Ikebuzo
2268. Ikechebe
2269. Ikechi
2270. Ikechukwu
2271. Ikedi
2272. Ikedife
2273. Ikedigbo
2274. Ikedike
2275. Ikedima
2276. Ikedinobi
2277. Ikedionwo
2278. Ikedire
2279. Ikediugwu
2280. Ikefuaku
2281. Ikefule
2282. Ikegbata
2283. Ikegbe
2284. Ikegbonwu
2285. Ikegbu
2286. Ikegbue
2287. Ikegbuna
2288. Ikegburu

2289. Ikegbusi
2290. Ikegbusi
2291. Ikegwere
2292. Ikegwuonu
2293. Ikeigwe
2294. Ikejiaku
2295. Ikejiani
2296. Ikejimba
2297. Ikejiofor
2298. Ikekesia
2299. Ikeketa
2300. Ikekwe
2301. Ikekwere
2302. Ikeliani
2303. Ikeliani
2304. Ikelie
2305. Ikelimba
2306. Ikelionwu
2307. Ikelionwu
2308. Ikelue
2309. Ikemba
2310. Ikeme
2311. Ikemefule
2312. Ikemefuna
2313. Ikemere
2314. Ikeneche
2315. Ikenechemba
2316. Ikenechendo
2317. Ikenechengwu
2318. Ikenechiora
2319. Ikenegbu
2320. Ikenegbu
2321. Ikenga
2322. Ikengwu
2323. Ikengwu
2324. Ikenna
2325. Ikenwa
2326. Ikenyi
2327. Ikenyiri
2328. Ikenze
2329. Ikeobasi
2330. Ikeobi
2331. Ikeocha
2332. Ikeonu
2333. Ikeonwu
2334. Ikeotuonye
2335. Ikeri
2336. Ikeriaku
2337. Ikerie
2338. Ikerieaku
2339. Ikerimba
2340. Ikerionwu
2341. Ikerionwu
2342. Ikeriugwo
2343. Ikesie
2344. Ikeugo
2345. Ikewelu
2346. Ikewelugo
2347. Ikezoba
2348. Ikezube
2349. Ikezue
2350. Ikoabasi
2351. Ikokwu
2352. Ikonne
2353. Ikpeama
2354. Ikpeamachi
2355. Ikpeamaonwu
2356. Ikpeazu
2357. Ikpeazu
2358. Ikpechi
2359. Ikpechukwu
2360. Ikpediba
2361. Ikpediri
2362. Ikpekaogu
2363. Ikpenna
2364. Ikpenze
2365. Ikpeonu
2366. Ikpeosa
2367. Ikpeze
2368. Ikpezie
2369. Ikpezue
2370. Ikpo
2371. Ikuku
2372. Ikwenne
2373. Ikwuabaka
2374. Ikwuakonam
2375. Ikwuaku
2376. Ikwuama
2377. Ikwuamaehi
2378. Ikwuamaka
2379. Ikwuanusi
2380. Ikwuazam
2381. Ikwuazom
2382. Ikwubueze
2383. Ikwubugwu
2384. Ikwubuike
2385. Ikwubuike
2386. Ikwubundum
2387. Ikwudialor
2388. Ikwuebuka
2389. Ikwuegbulam
2390. Ikwuegbuna
2391. Ikwueme
2392. Ikwueme
2393. Ikwuemeka
2394. Ikwuemoka
2395. Ikwuka
2396. Ikwukara
2397. Ikwukwelu
2398. Ikwuma
2399. Ikwumara
2400. Ikwumere
2401. Ikwumere
2402. Ikwunazo
2403. Ikwunma
2404. Ikwuogu
2405. Ikwuogu
2406. Ikwuoma
2407. Ikwuzalu
2408. Ikwuzoba
2409. Ikwuzube
2410. Ileagu
2411. Ilechukwu
2412. Iledike
2413. Ileka
2414. Ilenwa
2415. Ileonwu
2416. Ilikannu
2417. Iloabachie
2418. Iloabaka
2419. Iloachonam
2420. Iloafunam
2421. Iloaganachi
2422. Iloagbaonwu
2423. Iloagbeke

2424. Iloakpaoke
2425. Iloamoke
2426. Iloanunam
2427. Iloanuobi
2428. Iloanya
2429. Ilobie
2430. Ilochonwu
2431. Ilodelu
2432. Ilodiba
2433. Ilodibe
2434. Ilodiegwu
2435. Ilodimbu
2436. Ilodinjo
2437. Ilodinobi
2438. Iloegbunam
2439. Iloeje
2440. Iloejiofo
2441. Iloejiofo
2442. Iloelunachi
2443. Iloemoka
2444. Iloemoka
2445. Iloenyenam
2446. Iloenyosi
2447. Iloezunam
2448. Ilogbafue
2449. Ilogbaka
2450. Ilogbaluaka
2451. Ilogbulueke
2452. Iloghalu
2453. Ilogu
2454. Ilojiuba
2455. Iloka
2456. Ilokagbusia
2457. Ilokansi
2458. Ilokanulo
2459. Ilokanuno
2460. Ilokaonwu
2461. Ilokaonwu
2462. Ilomelu
2463. Ilomuanya
2464. Ilondu
2465. Ilonna
2466. Ilononso
2467. Ilonwa
2468. Ilonze
2469. Ilonzo
2470. Iloputaife
2471. Ilouno
2472. Ilozube
2473. Ilozulike
2474. Ilozulu
2475. Ilozumba
2476. Iriemenam
2477. Iroaga
2478. Iroanya
2479. Iroazu
2480. Irodinjo
2481. Iroegbu
2482. Iroegbuchulam
2483. Iroegbunam
2484. Iroeje
2485. Iroejiogu
2486. Iroha
2487. Irokansi
2488. Iromuanya
2489. Ironkwe
2490. Ironsi
2491. Irukwu
2492. Iruoma
2493. Ishiagu
2494. Ishiaku
2495. Isiadinso
2496. Isiaku
2497. Isiama
2498. Isichei
2499. Isiguzo
2500. Isiguzo
2501. Isikwe
2502. Isindu
2503. Isingwu
2504. Isiokwu
2505. Isioma
2506. Isiugo
2507. Iweafunam
2508. Iwediba
2509. Iwedinjo
2510. Iwegbu
2511. Iwegbunam
2512. Iweh
2513. Iweilo
2514. Iweka
2515. Iweke
2516. Iwekonwu
2517. Iwenofu
2518. Iweobi
2519. Iweonu
2520. Iweonu
2521. Iwuaku
2522. Iwuala
2523. Iwuamaeze
2524. Iwuanyanwu
2525. Iwuchukwu
2526. Iwueze
2527. Iwunze
2528. Iwuoha
2529. Iwuora
2530. Iyiegbuoha
2531. Izuagba
2532. Izuakolam
2533. Izuakonwa
2534. Izuakonze
2535. Izuakor
2536. Izuamaka
2537. Izuazunafia
2538. Izubike
2539. Izubuako
2540. Izubuaku
2541. Izubudike
2542. Izubundu
2543. Izuchukwu
2544. Izudike
2545. Izudima
2546. Izuegbunam
2547. Izuezuoke
2548. Izukanachi
2549. Izunazo
2550. Izundu
2551. Izunwa
2552. Izunwanne
2553. Izunze
2554. Izuogu
2555. Izuoma
2556. Izuora
2557. Izuozo
2558. Jaachimma

2559. Jamike
2560. Jiagbogu
2561. Jibuaku
2562. Jibueze
2563. Jibuno
2564. Jideofo
2565. Jubachukwu
2566. Kaanene
2567. Kaanyibiri
2568. Kabonye
2569. Kachi
2570. Kachikwuru
2571. Kachimdi
2572. Kachisicho
2573. Kachisike
2574. Kaebirinudo
2575. Kaemena
2576. Kaemeucheya
2577. Kaeneje
2578. Kaenene
2579. Kalu
2580. Kalunta
2581. Kamalu
2582. Kamdi
2583. Kameemena
2584. Kamnolu
2585. Kamnoro
2586. Kamnulue
2587. Kamsicho
2588. Kamsobiri
2589. Kamuche
2590. Kanayo
2591. Kaneje
2592. Kanekperechi
2593. Kanu
2594. Kaodichukwu
2595. Kaodili
2596. Kaodinma
2597. Kaonyedi
2598. Kaonyesicho
2599. Kaosidichukwu
2600. Karachi
2601. Kasarachi
2602. Kasie
2603. Kazie
2604. Kechinyere
2605. Kelechi
2606. Kemjika
2607. Kemnagum
2608. Kenechukwu
2609. Keneolis
2610. Kezie
2611. Kodilinye
2612. Korochi
2613. Kosarachi
2614. Kosicho
2615. Kpaduwa
2616. Kperechi
2617. Kpewerechi
2618. Kpokuechi
2619. Kpowachi
2620. Kpowachukwu
2621. Kpowaolisa
2622. Kubechi
2623. Kuchie
2624. Kurube
2625. Kurudike
2626. Kuruibe
2627. Kurum
2628. Kurunwanne
2629. Kuruuba
2630. Kuruume
2631. kwadike
2632. Kwebiri
2633. Kwelunachukwu
2634. Kwembiri
2635. Kwudebe
2636. Kwueziokwu
2637. Kwupuruchukwu
2638. Kwurunachi
2639. Kwuruneziokwu
2640. Lebechi
2641. Lekwam
2642. Lekwauwa
2643. Lemechi
2644. Lewechi
2645. Lotachukwu
2646. Lotaechi
2647. Lotanna
2648. Lotaolisa
2649. Machie
2650. Maduabaka
2651. Maduabuchi
2652. Maduabuchukwu
2653. Maduabum
2654. Maduafokwa
2655. Maduakolam
2656. Maduakor
2657. Madubike
2658. Madubugwu
2659. Madubuko
2660. Maduchie
2661. Maduebo
2662. Maduegbunam
2663. Madueke
2664. Maduekwe
2665. Maduemezia
2666. Maduforo
2667. Maduka
2668. Madukaejika
2669. Madukaife
2670. Madukaku
2671. Madumere
2672. Maduwuobi
2673. Makachukwu
2674. Makachukwu
2675. Maluoke
2676. Marachi
2677. Maraibe
2678. Maraizu
2679. Mbaama
2680. Mbaaso
2681. Mbachu
2682. Mbadiegwu
2683. Mbadike
2684. Mbadike
2685. Mbadinuju
2686. Mbadiuju
2687. Mbadiwe
2688. Mbadugha
2689. Mbaebi
2690. Mbaeliachi
2691. Mbaelu
2692. Mbaeyi
2693. Mbagwu

2694. Mbah
2695. Mbajito
2696. Mbakaogu
2697. Mbakwe
2698. Mbamalu
2699. Mbanefo
2700. Mbaneko
2701. Mbanu
2702. Mbanugo
2703. Mbaoma
2704. Mbaukwu
2705. Mbazuigwe
2706. Mbazulike
2707. Mbazurike
2708. Mbelede
2709. Mbeledeogu
2710. Mbonu
2711. Megafu
2712. Megwaram
2713. Megwatam
2714. Mekam
2715. Mekaowulu
2716. Mekwunye
2717. Melie
2718. Menakaya
2719. Meniru
2720. Menkiti
2721. Mepuruchi
2722. Meremezie
2723. Mezieobi
2724. Mezue
2725. Mgbada
2726. Mgbanuelunanwa
2727. Mgbata
2728. Mgbeahurike
2729. Mgbeahurukwe
2730. Mgbechikwere
2731. Mgbemena
2732. Mgbenu
2733. Mgbeobatalu
2734. Mgbeojikwe
2735. Mgbeojiriga
2736. Mgbeoma
2737. Mgbodile
2738. Mgbokwere
2739. Mkpadi
2740. Mkparu
2741. Mlemchi
2742. Mmachi
2743. Mmachukwu
2744. Mmako
2745. Mmeje
2746. Modebelu
2747. Modile
2748. Mofunanya
2749. Mogbo
2750. Moghalu
2751. Mojekwu
2752. Mokelu
2753. Mokwugwo
2754. Molokwu
2755. Molokwu
2756. Momah
2757. Moneke
2758. Moneme
2759. Morah
2760. Mozie
2761. Mpi
2762. Mukolu
2763. Mukosolu
2764. Mukosolu
2765. Munachim
2766. Munonye
2767. Munonyedi
2768. Muodozie
2769. Muoemenam
2770. Muofunanya
2771. Muokelo
2772. Muokelu
2773. Muokwe
2774. Muomelu
2775. Muomere
2776. Muoneke
2777. Muoronu
2778. Muoto
2779. Nchedo
2780. Nchekwube
2781. Ncheta
2782. Nchezo
2783. Ndabere
2784. Ndekwu
2785. Ndeokwere
2786. Ndeomaluke
2787. Ndianeze
2788. Ndibe
2789. Ndidiamaka
2790. Ndigwe
2791. Ndiokwere
2792. Ndiomaluke
2793. Ndiwe
2794. Nduaguba
2795. Ndubaku
2796. Ndubeze
2797. Ndubilo
2798. Ndubisi
2799. Ndubizu
2800. Ndudinanti
2801. Nduka
2802. Ndukaego
2803. Ndukaife
2804. Ndukaife
2805. Ndukaihe
2806. Ndukaku
2807. Ndukuba
2808. Ndukwu
2809. Ndulue
2810. Ndumbiri
2811. Ndupuechi
2812. Nebechi
2813. Nebedum
2814. Nebedum
2815. Nebeolisa
2816. Nebo
2817. Nedu
2818. Neghalu
2819. Nesochi
2820. Nesochi
2821. Nezianya
2822. Nezieanya
2823. Ngabala
2824. Ngalaba
2825. Ngalachukwu
2826. Ngaodichukwu
2827. Ngbanuelunanwa
2828. Ngbodile

2829. Ngele
2830. Ngerem
2831. Ngige
2832. Ngobiri
2833. Ngoka
2834. Ngoka
2835. Ngonadi
2836. Ngozichukwuka
2837. Ngozika
2838. Ngozimka
2839. Ngwu
2840. Ngwube
2841. Ngwudile
2842. Ngwudile
2843. Nibo
2844. Nibo
2845. Njaka
2846. Njelita
2847. Njemanze
2848. Njepu
2849. Njeribeako
2850. Njeze
2851. Njideka
2852. Njoku
2853. Njubigbo
2854. Nkanu
2855. Nkanyinmo
2856. Nkasiobi
2857. Nkeafuluanya
2858. Nkeakam
2859. Nkechinyem
2860. Nkechinyere
2861. Nkechukwu
2862. Nkeiruka
2863. Nkejiamatu
2864. Nkemchoro
2865. Nkemdilim
2866. Nkemdirim
2867. Nkemefuna
2868. Nkemelu
2869. Nkemena
2870. Nkemere
2871. Nkemere
2872. Nkemjika
2873. Nkemka
2874. Nkenacho
2875. Nkenjibiri
2876. Nkenke
2877. Nkenobi
2878. Nkeobuna
2879. Nkeolisa
2880. Nkeonyeadinjo
2881. Nkeonyeasoa
2882. Nkeonyediriya
2883. Nkeonyeji
2884. Nkeonyelu
2885. Nkeonyema
2886. Nkeonyemelu
2887. Nkeonyemetalu
2888. Nkeonyeneme
2889. Nkerue
2890. Nkeze
2891. Nkolika
2892. Nkoloagu
2893. Nkume
2894. Nkume
2895. Nkwachi
2896. Nkwachuku
2897. Nkwado
2898. Nkwocha
2899. Nkwogbo
2900. Nkwoh
2901. Nkwoma
2902. Nkwonma
2903. Nkwonta
2904. Nkwuda
2905. Nlota
2906. Nmachi
2907. Nmachukwu
2908. Nmadinobi
2909. Nmajiaku
2910. Nmaku
2911. Nmanwanyi
2912. Nmaobi
2913. Nmawuagwa
2914. Nmawugo
2915. Nmawuko
2916. Nmeje
2917. Nmerika
2918. Nmeriogu
2919. Nmesoma
2920. Nmuoka
2921. Nmuomalu
2922. Nmuotalu
2923. Nmutaka
2924. Nnabenyi
2925. Nnabuchi
2926. Nnabufo
2927. Nnabuife
2928. Nnabuko
2929. Nnachebe
2930. Nnachetam
2931. Nnachetam
2932. Nnachi
2933. Nnadi
2934. Nnadiagbeke
2935. Nnadibuagha
2936. Nnaebuka
2937. Nnaegboka
2938. Nnaerika
2939. Nnajekwu
2940. Nnaji
2941. Nnajiofo
2942. Nnajiugo
2943. Nnalue
2944. Nnamah
2945. Nnamani
2946. Nnamani
2947. Nnanodu
2948. Nneamaka
2949. Nnediugwu
2950. Nneka
2951. Nnene
2952. Nnenna
2953. Nneoma
2954. Nnochiri
2955. Nnodim
2956. Nnodum
2957. Nnodumene
2958. Nnodumene
2959. Nnoli
2960. Nnorom
2961. Nnoruka
2962. Nnozirim
2963. Nnubia

2964. Nnunwa
2965. Nodebem
2966. Nodebemchukwu
2967. Nolue
2968. Nonso
2969. Nonyelum
2970. Nosike
2971. Nsidinanya
2972. Nsochukwu
2973. Nsoedo
2974. Nsonze
2975. Nsopulu
2976. Nsopuruchukwu
2977. Nsugbe
2978. Ntasiobi
2979. Ntasiobi
2980. Nwabala
2981. Nwabali
2982. Nwabekee
2983. Nwabialu
2984. Nwabialunozo
2985. Nwabiawa
2986. Nwabike
2987. Nwabike
2988. Nwabisi
2989. Nwabuafa
2990. Nwabuaku
2991. Nwabuaku
2992. Nwabude
2993. Nwabude
2994. Nwabudike
2995. Nwabudo
2996. Nwabue
2997. Nwabuebo
2998. Nwabuenyi
2999. Nwabuenyi
3000. Nwabueze
3001. Nwabueze
3002. Nwabufo
3003. Nwabugo
3004. Nwabugwu
3005. Nwabuife
3006. Nwabuko
3007. Nwabulu
3008. Nwabundo
3009. Nwabundu
3010. Nwabunie
3011. Nwabunike
3012. Nwabuno
3013. Nwabunwa
3014. Nwabunwa
3015. Nwabuoba
3016. Nwabuoke
3017. Nwabuoku
3018. Nwabuoku
3019. Nwabuozo
3020. Nwabuozuzu
3021. Nwabuozuzu
3022. Nwabuwa
3023. Nwabuzor
3024. Nwachebe
3025. Nwachekwa
3026. Nwacheobi
3027. Nwachie
3028. Nwachinemelu
3029. Nwachinemere
3030. Nwachinyere
3031. Nwachiri
3032. Nwachukwu
3033. Nwadiadi
3034. Nwadialor
3035. Nwadiashi
3036. Nwadike
3037. Nwadinkpa
3038. Nwadinobi
3039. Nwadiogo
3040. Nwadiogwa
3041. Nwadiufu
3042. Nwadiugwu
3043. Nwadiuko
3044. Nwadumeje
3045. Nwaebube
3046. Nwaebuka
3047. Nwaege
3048. Nwaeke
3049. Nwaele
3050. Nwaelu
3051. Nwaenekebe
3052. Nwaeze
3053. Nwaeze
3054. Nwaezeigwe
3055. Nwaezuoke
3056. Nwafichara
3057. Nwafili
3058. Nwafor
3059. Nwafuluaku
3060. Nwafusi
3061. Nwagba
3062. Nwagbaoso
3063. Nwagbara
3064. Nwagbara
3065. Nwagbo
3066. Nwagbologu
3067. Nwagbomkpa
3068. Nwagekwu
3069. Nwaguma
3070. Nwaguru
3071. Nwaigwe
3072. Nwaiwu
3073. Nwaizu
3074. Nwaizugbe
3075. Nwajei
3076. Nwajiaku
3077. Nwajide
3078. Nwajinka
3079. Nwajiobi
3080. Nwajiofo
3081. Nwajioha
3082. Nwajiuba
3083. Nwajiudo
3084. Nwajiugo
3085. Nwajuaku
3086. Nwaka
3087. Nwakaego
3088. Nwakaenyi
3089. Nwakaeze
3090. Nwakaibeya
3091. Nwakaife
3092. Nwakaike
3093. Nwakaile
3094. Nwakaire
3095. Nwakaku
3096. Nwakama
3097. Nwakamba
3098. Nwakamkpa

3099. Nwakanna
3100. Nwakanwa
3101. Nwakaobi
3102. Nwakaozo
3103. Nwakonam
3104. Nwakonobi
3105. Nwakor
3106. Nwaku
3107. Nwakuche
3108. Nwakude
3109. Nwakudo
3110. Nwakwelu
3111. Nwakwere
3112. Nwakwuru
3113. Nwala
3114. Nwalameje
3115. Nwalie
3116. Nwalue
3117. Nwalum
3118. Nwalusi
3119. Nwamadi
3120. Nwamaife
3121. Nwamaka
3122. Nwamalubia
3123. Nwamaoke
3124. Nwamara
3125. Nwamaunoh
3126. Nwamerie
3127. Nwametu
3128. Nwamkpa
3129. Nwamkpa
3130. Nwamodo
3131. Nwamono
3132. Nwamuno
3133. Nwana
3134. Nwanagu
3135. Nwanaza
3136. Nwanchie
3137. Nwando
3138. Nwandu
3139. Nwanedu
3140. Nwanegbo
3141. Nwaneko
3142. Nwaneli
3143. Nwaneli
3144. Nwanemaka
3145. Nwaneri
3146. Nwangele
3147. Nwangene
3148. Nwangige
3149. Nwanguma
3150. Nwangwu
3151. Nwanisobi
3152. Nwanjoku
3153. Nwanka
3154. Nwankiti
3155. Nwankiti
3156. Nwankolo
3157. Nwankwo
3158. Nwankwu
3159. Nwanna
3160. Nwanna
3161. Nwanneamaka
3162. Nwannedimkpa
3163. Nwannedinamba
3164. Nwannedinobi
3165. Nwannediuto
3166. Nwanochiri
3167. Nwanochiri
3168. Nwanodi
3169. Nwanoke
3170. Nwanokwara
3171. Nwanolue
3172. Nwanonenyi
3173. Nwanonenyi
3174. Nwanonozo
3175. Nwanoro
3176. Nwanoruo
3177. Nwanyanwu
3178. Nwanyibueze
3179. Nwanyikwe
3180. Nwanyinma
3181. Nwanynma
3182. Nwanze
3183. Nwaobosi
3184. Nwaochri
3185. Nwaodika
3186. Nwaoga
3187. Nwaogalanya
3188. Nwaogaraku
3189. Nwaogbo
3190. Nwaoha
3191. Nwaolum
3192. Nwaoluoma
3193. Nwaoma
3194. Nwaonu
3195. Nwaonwu
3196. Nwaopararocha
3197. Nwaopigbo
3198. Nwaorie
3199. Nwaorisha
3200. Nwaoziri
3201. Nwaozo
3202. Nwaozuzu
3203. Nwaozuzu
3204. Nwapa
3205. Nwapuruiche
3206. Nwasata
3207. Nwashili
3208. Nwasike
3209. Nwasike
3210. Nwato
3211. Nwatolue
3212. Nwatolue
3213. Nwatota
3214. Nwatu
3215. Nwaturuchukwu
3216. Nwaturuocha
3217. Nwaturuocha
3218. Nwaubani
3219. Nwaude
3220. Nwawelu
3221. Nwawike
3222. Nwawo
3223. Nwawo
3224. Nwawuaku
3225. Nwawuko
3226. Nwawuobi
3227. Nwazereho
3228. Nwazoluobi
3229. Nwazoro
3230. Nwazota
3231. Nwazue
3232. Nwazuluoha
3233. Nwazuluoke

3234. Nwazunafia
3235. Nwazunfia
3236. Nwazuonu
3237. Nwegbe
3238. Nwene
3239. Nwenekebe
3240. Nwenyi
3241. Nweze
3242. Nwezefunamba
3243. Nwigwe
3244. Nwizugbe
3245. Nwoba
3246. Nwobasi
3247. Nwobi
3248. Nwobochi
3249. Nwobodo
3250. Nwochie
3251. Nwodika
3252. Nwodo
3253. Nwofuluanu
3254. Nwoga
3255. Nwogbede
3256. Nwoge
3257. Nwogu
3258. Nwogwugwu
3259. Nwogwugwu
3260. Nwokafor
3261. Nwoke
3262. Nwokeabachie
3263. Nwokeabia
3264. Nwokebia
3265. Nwokebie
3266. Nwokebuobi
3267. Nwokedi
3268. Nwokedinobi
3269. Nwokejife
3270. Nwokejiobi
3271. Nwokeke
3272. Nwokemodo
3273. Nwokenodu
3274. Nwokeukwu
3275. Nwokezuike
3276. Nwoko
3277. Nwokolo
3278. Nwokoma
3279. Nwokorie
3280. Nwokoro
3281. Nwokoroma
3282. Nwokotota
3283. Nwokoye
3284. Nwolanma
3285. Nwole
3286. Nwolisa
3287. Nwolum
3288. Nwonwu
3289. Nworie
3290. Nworisha
3291. Nwosisi
3292. Nwosu
3293. Nwoye
3294. Nwoziri
3295. Nwude
3296. Nwudo
3297. Nwufo
3298. Nyeke
3299. Nyenke
3300. Nze
3301. Nzeabasili
3302. Nzeabata
3303. Nzeadachie
3304. Nzeadi
3305. Nzeadinjo
3306. Nzeako
3307. Nzechi
3308. Nzediaso
3309. Nzegwu
3310. Nzejekwu
3311. Nzejiofor
3312. Nzekwe
3313. Nzekwu
3314. Nzelu
3315. Nzenaso
3316. Nzenekwu
3317. Nzenwa
3318. Nzenweako
3319. Nzenweilo
3320. Nzenweokwu
3321. Nzeogwu
3322. Nzere
3323. Nzerem
3324. Nzeribe
3325. Nzerue
3326. Nzewi
3327. Nzewulu
3328. Nzimiro
3329. Nzota
3330. Nzubechukwu
3331. Obaeze
3332. Obagu
3333. Obah
3334. Obaji
3335. Obajulu
3336. Obanye
3337. Obasi
3338. Obasili
3339. Obata
3340. Obaze
3341. Obazie
3342. Obeagu
3343. Obele
3344. Obenata
3345. Obeta
3346. Obia
3347. Obiadachi
3348. Obiadi
3349. Obiaga
3350. Obiagboso
3351. Obiageli
3352. Obiagu
3353. Obiagwu
3354. Obiajulu
3355. Obiako
3356. Obiakoeze
3357. Obiakolam
3358. Obiakonwa
3359. Obiakouzu
3360. Obiaku
3361. Obialonye
3362. Obialor
3363. Obialr
3364. Obialuka
3365. Obialunozo
3366. Obiama
3367. Obianagha
3368. Obianaso

3369. Obianefo
3370. Obianeze
3371. Obianika
3372. Obianouka
3373. Obianudo
3374. Obianuka
3375. Obianuka
3376. Obianuko
3377. Obianumba
3378. Obianusi
3379. Obianuzo
3380. Obianwu
3381. Obianyo
3382. Obiaraka
3383. Obiaso
3384. Obiasoanya
3385. Obiasoegwu
3386. Obiasoeze
3387. Obiasogu
3388. Obiasomba
3389. Obiawuotu
3390. Obichebe
3391. Obichebelu
3392. Obichere
3393. Obichukwu
3394. Obidalor
3395. Obidaso
3396. Obidi
3397. Obidiadi
3398. Obidiaso
3399. Obidiegwu
3400. Obidigbo
3401. Obidigwe
3402. Obidike
3403. Obidimbu
3404. Obidindu
3405. Obidinma
3406. Obidiocha
3407. Obidiozo
3408. Obidiugwu
3409. Obiechena
3410. Obiechina
3411. Obiefoka
3412. Obiefula
3413. Obiefuna
3414. Obiego
3415. Obieje
3416. Obiekwe
3417. Obielum
3418. Obienu
3419. Obierika
3420. Obierika
3421. Obiesie
3422. Obieze
3423. Obighara
3424. Obigwe
3425. Obijekwe
3426. Obijiaku
3427. Obijiofo
3428. Obika
3429. Obikwelu
3430. Obikwere
3431. Obikwere
3432. Obikwesiri
3433. Obimdi
3434. Obimdike
3435. Obimdinachi
3436. Obimdinma
3437. Obimka
3438. Obimma
3439. Obinagha
3440. Obinani
3441. Obinaso
3442. Obinazo
3443. Obineche
3444. Obinedi
3445. Obinegbo
3446. Obinegbo
3447. Obinma
3448. Obinna
3449. Obinnaya
3450. Obinwa
3451. Obinwanne
3452. Obinweaku
3453. Obinweike
3454. Obinweuko
3455. Obinweze
3456. Obioha
3457. Obiolisa
3458. Obiora
3459. Obisike
3460. Obiukwu
3461. Obiwuko
3462. Obododike
3463. Obodoechina
3464. Obodoefuna
3465. Obodozie
3466. Obumneme
3467. Obumselu
3468. Obunadike
3469. Obunike
3470. Oburota
3471. Ochei
3472. Ochendo
3473. Ocheoha
3474. Ochia
3475. Ochiabuto
3476. Ochiagha
3477. Ochiawuto
3478. Ochie
3479. Ochiogu
3480. Ochirora
3481. Ochoifeoma
3482. Ochonma
3483. Ochuba
3484. Ochuenwike
3485. Odachikwe
3486. Odachiri
3487. Odachiri
3488. Odakpa
3489. Odeluga
3490. Odenigbo
3491. Odenigwe
3492. Odera
3493. Odiadi
3494. Odiakosa
3495. Odiari
3496. Odiazi
3497. Odiche
3498. Odidika
3499. Odiefe
3500. Odili
3501. Odilim
3502. Odilionye
3503. Odimegwu

3504. Odinakachukwu
3505. Odinamadu
3506. Odinamba
3507. Odinchefu
3508. Odinigwe
3509. Odinigwe
3510. Odinihu
3511. Odinkemelu
3512. Odita
3513. Odiukonamba
3514. Odobie
3515. Odoemela
3516. Odoemene
3517. Odogbo
3518. Odogo
3519. Odogwu
3520. Odoh
3521. Odom
3522. Odomere
3523. Oduagu
3524. Oduchi
3525. Oduchieme
3526. Oduchinma
3527. Oduenyi
3528. Oduga
3529. Odugo
3530. Odum
3531. Odumah
3532. Odume
3533. Odumegwu
3534. Odumegwu
3535. Odumodu
3536. Odunaka
3537. Odunukwe
3538. Odunukwe
3539. Odunze
3540. Offiah
3541. Ofiaeli
3542. Ofiaido
3543. Ofianeche
3544. Ofili
3545. Ofoamaeze
3546. Ofobie
3547. Ofobike
3548. Ofobiko
3549. Ofobueze
3550. Ofobundu
3551. Ofochebe
3552. Ofochukwu
3553. Ofodegwu
3554. Ofodeme
3555. Ofodike
3556. Ofodile
3557. Ofodire
3558. Ofodumeje
3559. Ofoebuka
3560. Ofoedu
3561. Ofoegbu
3562. Ofoegbunam
3563. Ofoegbusi
3564. Ofoelina
3565. Ofoesi
3566. Ofogbo
3567. Ofogbo
3568. Ofogbuilo
3569. Ofogbuo
3570. Ofojeme
3571. Ofojewu
3572. Ofojide
3573. Ofojike
3574. Ofokabie
3575. Ofokaja
3576. Ofokamji
3577. Ofokansi
3578. Ofokaoha
3579. Ofokara
3580. Ofokeze
3581. Ofolee
3582. Ofoma
3583. Ofomara
3584. Ofomata
3585. Ofonagoro
3586. Ofonta
3587. Ofonyili
3588. Ofonze
3589. Ofor
3590. Ofotoo
3591. Ofozoba
3592. Ofunne
3593. Ofunwa
3594. Ofuobi
3595. Ofuokwu
3596. Ofuonye
3597. Ogadinma
3598. Ogakwu
3599. Ogalanya
3600. Ogalonye
3601. Ogalum
3602. Ogaluonye
3603. Oganiru
3604. Ogazi
3605. Ogazie
3606. Ogbaji
3607. Ogbalu
3608. Ogbaogu
3609. Ogbapuluenyi
3610. Ogbata
3611. Ogbataku
3612. Ogbazi
3613. Ogbe
3614. Ogbenyeanu
3615. Ogbodu
3616. Ogbogbo
3617. Ogbogu
3618. Ogboli
3619. Ogbolu
3620. Ogboma
3621. Ogbonna
3622. Ogbonne
3623. Ogboro
3624. Ogbu
3625. Ogbuagu
3626. Ogbuefi
3627. Ogbuehi
3628. Ogbueze
3629. Ogbuh
3630. Ogbuji
3631. Ogbuka
3632. Ogbuluafor
3633. Ogbunamiri
3634. Ogbunka
3635. Ogbunuzo
3636. Ogbuti
3637. Ogechi
3638. Ogechukwu

3639. Ogele
3640. Ogeli
3641. Ogelue
3642. Ogemdi
3643. Ogemrue
3644. Ogene
3645. Ogenyi
3646. Ogerue
3647. Ogezue
3648. Ogidi
3649. Ogoamaka
3650. Ogobuchi
3651. Ogobugwu
3652. Ogochimerem
3653. Ogochukwu
3654. Ogodinma
3655. Ogodiugwu
3656. Ogoegbunam
3657. Ogoma
3658. Ogoneme
3659. Ogonna
3660. Oguagha
3661. Oguakwa
3662. Oguanya
3663. Ogubike
3664. Oguchi
3665. Oguchukwu
3666. Ogudelu
3667. Ogudire
3668. Oguebie
3669. Oguegbe
3670. Oguejiofo
3671. Oguelina
3672. Ogueri
3673. Ogugbo
3674. Ogugua
3675. Oguike
3676. Ogunnaya
3677. Oguoma
3678. Oguuno
3679. Ogwugwueloka
3680. Ohaam
3681. Ohaama
3682. Ohabiri
3683. Ohachu
3684. Ohadiegwu
3685. Ohadike
3686. Ohadire
3687. Ohadugha
3688. Ohadume
3689. Ohaebuka
3690. Ohaegbulam
3691. Ohaekwuotu
3692. Ohaeto
3693. Ohaeze
3694. Ohaezuba
3695. Ohaezue
3696. Ohaezue
3697. Ohaghara
3698. Ohagwa
3699. Ohajekwu
3700. Ohaji
3701. Ohajika
3702. Ohajiofo
3703. Ohajuru
3704. Ohaka
3705. Ohakaenyi
3706. Ohakwe
3707. Ohakwuo
3708. Ohakwuru
3709. Ohama
3710. Ohamadike
3711. Ohamaizu
3712. Ohamalu
3713. Ohamara
3714. Ohameze
3715. Ohanusi
3716. Ohanweze
3717. Ohanwike
3718. Ohanyilidike
3719. Ohanyiliofo
3720. Ohanze
3721. Ohaukwu
3722. Ohawueze
3723. Ohawuibe
3724. Ohawuike
3725. Ohawuile
3726. Ohaya
3727. Ohazuluike
3728. Ohazulukwu
3729. Ohazurukwu
3730. Ohazurume
3731. Ohazuwe
3732. Ohewuire
3733. Ohia
3734. Ohiaeri
3735. Ohiagu
3736. Ohiri
3737. Ojekwe
3738. Ojelubeolisa
3739. Ojelumba
3740. Ojemba
3741. Ojeogwu
3742. Ojiako
3743. Ojiaku
3744. Ojide
3745. Ojigwe
3746. Ojike
3747. Ojinaka
3748. Ojindu
3749. Ojinika
3750. Ojinike
3751. Ojinime
3752. Ojinkeonye
3753. Ojinwayo
3754. Ojiudu
3755. Ojiugo
3756. Ojogho
3757. Ojukwu
3758. Ojulumobi
3759. Okadigbo
3760. Okadigwe
3761. Okadiwe
3762. Okafor
3763. Okagbue
3764. Okah
3765. Okakim
3766. Okala
3767. Okalaogu
3768. Okam
3769. Okamegbumam
3770. Okamme
3771. Okanume
3772. Okaome
3773. Okaonye

3774. Okara
3775. Okeagu
3776. Okebuno
3777. Okechi
3778. Okechukwu
3779. Okegbe
3780. Okeke
3781. Okenanchi
3782. Okengwu
3783. Okenwa
3784. Okenwa
3785. Okenze
3786. Okeocha
3787. Okerafor
3788. Okere
3789. Okereke
3790. Okerengwo
3791. Okeze
3792. Okezie
3793. Okezie
3794. Okigbo
3795. Okikadigbo
3796. Okike
3797. Okiwe
3798. Okocha
3799. Okochi
3800. Okogba
3801. Okogbule
3802. Okoh
3803. Okoli
3804. Okolo
3805. Okolocha
3806. Okolue
3807. Okongwu
3808. Okongwu
3809. Okonji
3810. Okonjo
3811. Okonkwo
3812. Okonma
3813. Okonta
3814. Okorie
3815. Okorieagu
3816. Okoro
3817. Okorocha
3818. Okorodike
3819. Okoroigwe
3820. Okoroji
3821. Okoroma
3822. Okoromadu
3823. Okoromba
3824. Okoronkwo
3825. Okoronta
3826. Okororji
3827. Okosisi
3828. Okoye
3829. Okpai
3830. Okpala
3831. Okpalachi
3832. Okpalaeze
3833. Okpalanma
3834. Okpalannaa
3835. Okpaleke
3836. Okpalobi
3837. Okpaloka
3838. Okpalugo
3839. Okpara
3840. Okparachi
3841. Okparadike
3842. Okparaugo
3843. Okparaugo
3844. Okparocha
3845. Okpe
3846. Okpere
3847. Okpoko
3848. Okpueze
3849. Okuagba
3850. Okuchi
3851. Okuchukwu
3852. Okudo
3853. Okuegbe
3854. Okuwa
3855. Okuwuike
3856. Okuye
3857. Okwandu
3858. Okwara
3859. Okwaraji
3860. Okwatu
3861. Okwechieme
3862. Okwechime
3863. Okweizu
3864. Okwelume
3865. Okwesili
3866. Okwesilieze
3867. Okwo
3868. Okwuabotu
3869. Okwuadiazi
3870. Okwuagwu
3871. Okwuaso
3872. Okwuasoanya
3873. Okwuba
3874. Okwubelu
3875. Okwubie
3876. Okwuchukwu
3877. Okwudanego
3878. Okwudelu
3879. Okwudialor
3880. Okwudiashi
3881. Okwudiba
3882. Okwudike
3883. Okwudili
3884. Okwudima
3885. Okwuelinam
3886. Okwuesena
3887. Okwuesezia
3888. Okwueze
3889. Okwukaogu
3890. Okwukwe
3891. Okwumara
3892. Okwumelu
3893. Okwunalu
3894. Okwunari
3895. Okwunazo
3896. Okwundu
3897. Okwunna
3898. Okwunwa
3899. Okwuodo
3900. Okwuoha
3901. Okwuoha
3902. Okwuolisa
3903. Okwuoma
3904. Okwuonu
3905. Okwuosa
3906. Okwuowulu
3907. Okwurah
3908. Okwuselogu

3909. Okwusia
3910. Okwuta
3911. Okwuudo
3912. Olachi
3913. Olaedo
3914. Olanma
3915. Oleforo
3916. Olejeme
3917. Oleka
3918. Olekamji
3919. Olemere
3920. Olenmgbe
3921. Oli
3922. Oliaku
3923. Olie
3924. Oligbo
3925. Olikagu
3926. Olileanya
3927. Olili
3928. Olinze
3929. Olisabudo
3930. Olisaebuka
3931. Olisaemeka
3932. Olisakwe
3933. Olisakwue
3934. Olisama
3935. Olisanwe
3936. Olisanweokwu
3937. Olisaoma
3938. Oluchi
3939. Oluchukwu
3940. Oluedo
3941. Olueme
3942. Oluigbo
3943. Olumba
3944. Oluoha
3945. Omanukwue
3946. Omeaku
3947. Omeba
3948. Omede
3949. Omedo
3950. Omeh
3951. Omeha
3952. Omeifeaku
3953. Omeifeoma
3954. Omeifukwu
3955. Omeilee
3956. Omeje
3957. Omekannaya
3958. Omekaokwulu
3959. Omeke
3960. Omekwa
3961. Omelora
3962. Omelue
3963. Omeluebele
3964. Omeluogo
3965. Omeluoha
3966. Omem
3967. Omemgbojikwe
3968. Omemgbokwere
3969. Omenife
3970. Omeniru
3971. Omenka
3972. Omenkwa
3973. Omenma
3974. Omenma
3975. Omenuju
3976. Omenuko
3977. Omenwa
3978. Omenyelum
3979. Omenyiri
3980. Omeogo
3981. Omeokachie
3982. Omera
3983. Omezie
3984. Omezuru
3985. Omunuzua
3986. Onachi
3987. Onachukwu
3988. Onaedo
3989. Onaga
3990. Onah
3991. Onaji
3992. Onalife
3993. Onanma
3994. Onanwa
3995. Onebune
3996. Onejeme
3997. Ongaobiri
3998. Onochie
3999. Onochili
4000. Onochiri
4001. Onoh
4002. Onoja
4003. Ononauju
4004. Ononigwe
4005. Ononiwu
4006. Ononye
4007. Onoowu
4008. Onovo
4009. Onua
4010. Onuaguluchi
4011. Onuba
4012. Onubogu
4013. Onubueze
4014. Onuchukwu
4015. Onuegbu
4016. Onuekwujobi
4017. Onuekwuka
4018. Onuekwuke
4019. Onuekwusia
4020. Onugwai
4021. Onuigbo
4022. Onuigbo
4023. Onukaba
4024. Onukama
4025. Onukara
4026. Onukwube
4027. Onukwube
4028. Onukwubiri
4029. Onukwue
4030. Onukwuli
4031. Onukwume
4032. Onukwurunjo
4033. Onuma
4034. Onumadu
4035. Onumadu
4036. Onumba
4037. Onumonu
4038. Onunkwo
4039. Onunkwo
4040. Onunwa
4041. Onuoha
4042. Onuora
4043. Onuseluogu

4044. Onuzo
4045. Onuzurike
4046. Onwaneti
4047. Onweh
4048. Onweluzo
4049. Onwoegbuchlam
4050. Onwuachi
4051. Onwuachu
4052. Onwuagba
4053. Onwualu
4054. Onwuamadike
4055. Onwuamaegbu
4056. Onwuamaeze
4057. Onwuamaizu
4058. Onwuasoanya
4059. Onwuasouba
4060. Onwuatu
4061. Onwuatuegwu
4062. Onwuatuelo
4063. Onwuatuizu
4064. Onwuatundu
4065. Onwubelu
4066. Onwubie
4067. Onwubiko
4068. Onwubuya
4069. Onwuchekwa
4070. Onwudiegwu
4071. Onwudinjo
4072. Onwudiufu
4073. Onwudiwe
4074. Onwuegbuchulam
4075. Onwuegbuchunam
4076. Onwuegbuna
4077. Onwuegbuzia
4078. Onwuegenti
4079. Onwuejeogwu
4080. Onwuelingo
4081. Onwuelo
4082. Onwuemelie
4083. Onwuemena
4084. Onwuepe
4085. Onwugbenu
4086. Onwugbufo
4087. Onwughalu
4088. Onwughara
4089. Onwuha
4090. Onwukadike
4091. Onwukeme
4092. Onwukeze
4093. Onwukwe
4094. Onwuli
4095. Onwumechiri
4096. Onwumelu
4097. Onwumere
4098. Onwumere
4099. Onwunyili
4100. Onwunzo
4101. Onwuteaka
4102. Onwuzuligbo
4103. Onwuzulike
4104. Onwuzurigbo
4105. Onwuzurike
4106. Onwuzuruwa
4107. Onyeabo
4108. Onyeachonam
4109. Onyeagoro
4110. Onyeagwalukwe
4111. Onyeagwalukwe
4112. Onyeaku
4113. Onyeali
4114. Onyeama
4115. Onyeanusi
4116. Onyeanwuna
4117. Onyeaso
4118. Onyeazom
4119. Onyebalu
4120. Onyebalu
4121. Onyebeke
4122. Onyebiri
4123. Onyebuchi
4124. Onyebuenyi
4125. Onyechere
4126. Onyechizoro
4127. Onyedikachukwu
4128. Onyedike
4129. Onyedinachi
4130. Onyedinma
4131. Onyeduchukwu
4132. Onyedum
4133. Onyefuluchi
4134. Onyefuluchukwu
4135. Onyegbalu
4136. Onyegbaluko
4137. Onyegekwe
4138. Onyegekwu
4139. Onyeghara
4140. Onyegom
4141. Onyehuruchi
4142. Onyeibe
4143. Onyeife
4144. Onyeije
4145. Onyeike
4146. Onyeiro
4147. Onyeiwu
4148. Onyejabum
4149. Onyeje
4150. Onyejekwe
4151. Onyejeme
4152. Onyeji
4153. Onyejiaka
4154. Onyejiaku
4155. Onyejindu
4156. Onyejindum
4157. Onyejinka
4158. Onyejiofo
4159. Onyekaa
4160. Onyekaba
4161. Onyekachi
4162. Onyekachukwu
4163. Onyekaeze
4164. Onyekaibe
4165. Onyekamike
4166. Onyekaozuru
4167. Onyekaozuzru
4168. Onyekere
4169. Onyekonwu
4170. Onyekozulu
4171. Onyekporom
4172. Onyekwe
4173. Onyekwe
4174. Onyekwelu
4175. Onyekwena
4176. Onyekwere
4177. Onyekwere
4178. Onyekwere

4179. Onyekweta
4180. Onyekwue
4181. Onyekwuluje
4182. Onyekwuzia
4183. Onyema
4184. Onyemachi
4185. Onyemadike
4186. Onyemaechi
4187. Onyemaenu
4188. Onyemaizu
4189. Onyemaobi
4190. Onyemasi
4191. Onyemauche
4192. Onyemelukwe
4193. Onyemenam
4194. Onyemere
4195. Onyemesi
4196. Onyemete
4197. Onyemuche
4198. Onyemso
4199. Onyenachiya
4200. Onyenaucheya
4201. Onyenedum
4202. Onyeneke
4203. Onyenekwu
4204. Onyenka
4205. Onyenobiya
4206. Onyenoso
4207. Onyenso
4208. Onyenuforo
4209. Onyenweaku
4210. Onyenweizu
4211. Onyenze
4212. Onyeogadirima
4213. Onyeogu
4214. Onyeoha
4215. Onyeolulu
4216. Onyeomiko
4217. Onyeonyere
4218. Onyeso
4219. Onyesochukwu
4220. Onyesom
4221. Onyeudo
4222. Onyeukwu
4223. Onyewuchi
4224. Onyewuenyi
4225. Onyeze
4226. Onyezugo
4227. Onyezuluora
4228. Onyezuo
4229. Onyia
4230. Onyiaoha
4231. Onyiaoha
4232. Onyiauke
4233. Onyido
4234. Onyiliagha
4235. Onyiliofo
4236. Onyinyechi
4237. Onyioha
4238. Onyirimba
4239. Onyirimba
4240. Onyishi
4241. Onyiu
4242. Onyiuke
4243. Onyiyechukwu
4244. Opara
4245. Oparandu
4246. Oparaocha
4247. Opia
4248. Opidigbo
4249. Opiene
4250. Opkata
4251. Opuriche
4252. Opurum
4253. Oputa
4254. Oputa
4255. Orabike
4256. Orabile
4257. Orabuchi
4258. Orabueze
4259. Orabueze
4260. Oraduba
4261. Oradume
4262. Oraedu
4263. Oraegbu
4264. Oraekee
4265. Oraekwuotu
4266. Oraeto
4267. Oraezuba
4268. Orafu
4269. Orafugo
4270. Oragekpe
4271. Oragui
4272. Oraguzie
4273. Orajaka
4274. Orajekwu
4275. Oraji
4276. Orajiofo
4277. Orajiofo
4278. Oraka
4279. Orakeze
4280. Orakpee
4281. Orakwe
4282. Orakwelu
4283. Orakwube
4284. Orakwusia
4285. Oramadike
4286. Oramaeze
4287. Oramah
4288. Oramalu
4289. Oramasionwu
4290. Oranweike
4291. Oranweze
4292. Oranye
4293. Oranyeaka
4294. Oranyelugo
4295. Oraonu
4296. Orazuba
4297. Oriaku
4298. Oriaku
4299. Oriana
4300. Orijji
4301. Orizu
4302. Orji
4303. Oruche
4304. Orumba
4305. Osadebe
4306. Osaemeka
4307. Osaemena
4308. Osaji
4309. Osakwe
4310. Osealuka
4311. Osebuka
4312. Oseloka
4313. Osemeka

4314. Osinachi
4315. Osisioma
4316. Ositadinma
4317. Osoagbaka
4318. Osondu
4319. Osuagwu
4320. Osuala
4321. Osuchukwu
4322. Osueke
4323. Osuigwe
4324. Osuji
4325. Osungwu
4326. Osunkwo
4327. Osunmuo
4328. Osunwa
4329. Osuofia
4330. Osuoha
4331. Otaluka
4332. Otegbulu
4333. Otigba
4334. Otigbu
4335. Otitochukwu
4336. Otti
4337. Otuanya
4338. Otuawuibe
4339. Otubeleze
4340. Otubelu
4341. Otubelugo
4342. Otuonye
4343. Otuonyeadinma
4344. Ovute
4345. Oyiboka
4346. Ozioma
4347. Ozoaku
4348. Ozobia
4349. Ozobialu
4350. Ozobiara
4351. Ozobugwu
4352. Ozodo
4353. Ozoeme
4354. Ozoemenam
4355. Ozoemezia
4356. Ozoemezina
4357. Ozoene
4358. Ozoka
4359. Ozokwelu
4360. Ozongwu
4361. Ozonwa
4362. Ozoro
4363. Ozoude
4364. Ozougwu
4365. Ozowugwu
4366. Ozuah
4367. Ozuaka
4368. Ozube
4369. Ozueh
4370. Ozugo
4371. Ozuluonye
4372. Ozumba
4373. Ozuola
4374. Ozurumba
4375. Ozuzu
4376. Ralueke
4377. Rapulchukwu
4378. Riowachi
4379. Riowachukwu
4380. Sochukwu
4381. Soludo
4382. Somadina
4383. Somayina
4384. Somebina
4385. Somtochukw
4386. Sopuluchukwu
4387. Sopuruchi
4388. Sopuruchukwu
4389. Sorochi
4390. Tabansi
4391. Tagbo
4392. Tobechukwu
4393. Tobenna
4394. Tolisa
4395. Tomike
4396. Ubachukwu
4397. Ubadike
4398. Ubah
4399. Ubahakwe
4400. Ubajaka
4401. Ubajiaku
4402. Ubaka
4403. Ubakanma
4404. Ubakanma
4405. Ubakonam
4406. Ubaku
4407. Ubalue
4408. Ubalum
4409. Ubangwu
4410. Ubani
4411. Ubanwa
4412. Ubaorakwe
4413. Ubaruru
4414. Ubazue
4415. Ubesie
4416. Ubezuonu
4417. Ubiji
4418. Ubochi
4419. Uboma
4420. Uboma
4421. Ubosinwanne
4422. Ucha
4423. Ucheabaka
4424. Ucheabuotu
4425. Ucheagwu
4426. Ucheakolam
4427. Ucheanyo
4428. Uchebuizu
4429. Uchechi
4430. Uchechukwu
4431. Uchedike
4432. Uchefuna
4433. Uchegazie
4434. Uchegbulam
4435. Uchegbunam
4436. Uchemadu
4437. Uchendu
4438. Uchenna
4439. Uchenwa
4440. Ucheolisa
4441. Ucheoma
4442. Ucheonye
4443. Ucheora
4444. Udaegbe
4445. Uddoh
4446. Udeagbala
4447. Udeagbulam
4448. Udeagha

4449. Udeagwu
4450. Udeaja
4451. Udeakpu
4452. Udeaku
4453. Udealor
4454. Udeani
4455. Udebuana
4456. Udechukwu
4457. Udedike
4458. Udegbunam
4459. Udekwe
4460. Udekwu
4461. Udelue
4462. Udemba
4463. Udemezue
4464. Udengwu
4465. Udengwu
4466. Udenkwo
4467. Udenmuo
4468. Udenna
4469. Udennaka
4470. Udensi
4471. Udenwa
4472. Udenyili
4473. Udenze
4474. Udeogaranya
4475. Udeogu
4476. Udeokwu
4477. Udeonicha
4478. Udeora
4479. Udeorji
4480. Udeoye
4481. Udeozo
4482. Uderah
4483. Udeze
4484. Udezue
4485. Udezuligbo
4486. Udezurigbo
4487. Udoamaka
4488. Udobialu
4489. Udobundu
4490. Udochi
4491. Udochukwu
4492. Udodi
4493. Udodinma
4494. Udodiri
4495. Udoeze
4496. Udogu
4497. Udoji
4498. Udoka
4499. Udokama
4500. Udokwu
4501. Udokwu
4502. Udolisa
4503. Udondu
4504. Udonkwo
4505. Udonna
4506. Udoye
4507. Udozo
4508. Uduaku
4509. Uduamaka
4510. Uduaro
4511. Uduchukwu
4512. Ududike
4513. Uduego
4514. Uduka
4515. Udumaga
4516. Udumah
4517. Udumeje
4518. Udunwa
4519. Udunwanne
4520. Ufele
4521. Ufere
4522. Ufie
4523. Ufoagu
4524. Ufoaja
4525. Ufoaku
4526. Ufochukwu
4527. Ufodike
4528. Ufoegbunam
4529. Ufoeze
4530. Ufoma
4531. Ufomadu
4532. Ufondu
4533. Ufooma
4534. Uforah
4535. Ugbaelu
4536. Ugbaja
4537. Ugbala
4538. Ugboaku
4539. Ugbobuaku
4540. Ugboedo
4541. Ugbonyamba
4542. Ugeagbala
4543. Ugeagha
4544. Ugechi
4545. Ugechukwu
4546. Ugedike
4547. Ugeh
4548. Ugehnwa
4549. Ugelem
4550. Ugelenma
4551. Ugeloma
4552. Ugemba
4553. Ugeme
4554. Ugenyi
4555. Ugeoma
4556. Ugeozo
4557. Ugha
4558. Ughaenu
4559. Ughamba
4560. Ughanmadu
4561. Ughanne
4562. Ugoabata
4563. Ugoacha
4564. Ugoagbala
4565. Ugoagu
4566. Ugoanyanwu
4567. Ugocha
4568. Ugochaa
4569. Ugochi
4570. Ugochukwu
4571. Ugodibia
4572. Ugodike
4573. Ugoebelu
4574. Ugoenyi
4575. Ugoeze
4576. Ugoezue
4577. Ugogiofor
4578. Ugoha
4579. Ugokwe
4580. Ugomba
4581. Ugonabo
4582. Ugonaorji
4583. Ugondu

4584. Ugonma
4585. Ugonna
4586. Ugonwa
4587. Ugonwa
4588. Ugonwafo
4589. Ugonwanne
4590. Ugonwata
4591. Ugonze
4592. Ugooma
4593. Ugoozo
4594. Ugorji
4595. Uguru
4596. Ugwah
4597. Ugwnwanne
4598. Ugwoke
4599. Ugwu
4600. Ugwuaja
4601. Ugwuani
4602. Ugwuanya
4603. Ugwuanyi
4604. Ugwuchi
4605. Ugwuchukwu
4606. Ugwudike
4607. Ugwuegbu
4608. Ugwuegede
4609. Ugwueze
4610. Ugwuibe
4611. Ugwujimba
4612. Ugwuka
4613. Ugwumadu
4614. Ugwumba
4615. Ugwunna
4616. Ugwunwa
4617. Ugwunwanyi
4618. Ugwunze
4619. Ugwuocha
4620. Ugwuoke
4621. Ugwuozo
4622. Ujah
4623. Ujunnwa
4624. Uka
4625. Ukaatu
4626. Ukabiala
4627. Ukachi
4628. Ukachukwu
4629. Ukadike
4630. Ukadinma
4631. Ukaegbu
4632. Ukaiwe
4633. Ukamaka
4634. Ukatah
4635. Ukeje
4636. Ukejianya
4637. Uketui
4638. Ukoha
4639. Ukonu
4640. Ukonwa
4641. Ukpabia
4642. Ukpai
4643. Ukpoeze
4644. Ukwachi
4645. Ukwadike
4646. Ukwujiagu
4647. Ulasi
4648. Ulinma
4649. Uloaku
4650. Ulochi
4651. Ulojiofo
4652. Uloma
4653. Uluaku
4654. Ulunma
4655. Ulunwa
4656. Uluozo
4657. Umeadi
4658. Umeagbunam
4659. Umeaku
4660. Umealor
4661. Umeamadi
4662. Umeasiegbu
4663. Umechukwu
4664. Umedialor
4665. Umedike
4666. Umefo
4667. Umeji
4668. Umejiaku
4669. Umejiaku
4670. Umejiofo
4671. Umeliora
4672. Umelue
4673. Umemezia
4674. Umenwa
4675. Umenyi
4676. Umenyilora
4677. Umeobi
4678. Umeokachie
4679. Umeolias
4680. Umeora
4681. Umeorah
4682. Umerah
4683. Umesie
4684. Umenyi
4685. Umeze
4686. Umezinwa
4687. Umezioha
4688. Umezue
4689. Umezue
4690. Umezuoke
4691. Umezuruigbo
4692. Umunna
4693. Umunnaji
4694. Umunajiofo
4695. Umunnaka
4696. Umunnakwe
4697. Unachukwu
4698. Unaegbu
4699. Unaegbu
4700. Unaigwe
4701. Unaka
4702. Unanwa
4703. Unegbe
4704. Unegbu
4705. Unoaku
4706. Unobuife
4707. Unoma
4708. Urechi
4709. Uredi
4710. Urenma
4711. Urenwa
4712. Uru
4713. Uruaku
4714. Urunwa
4715. Utah
4716. Utazi
4717. Utoaku
4718. Utodinobi

4719. Utondu
4720. Utondu
4721. Utonwa
4722. Utonwanne
4723. Utouwaegbulam
4724. Uvuka
4725. Uvute
4726. Uwaamaka
4727. Uwabunkeonye
4728. Uwachi
4729. Uwadi
4730. Uwadiegwu
4731. Uwadimbu
4732. Uwadiuba
4733. Uwadiufu
4734. Uwadiugha
4735. Uwaebuka
4736. Uwaechue
4737. Uwaegbulam
4738. Uwaekwuotu
4739. Uwaesika
4740. Uwaezuike
4741. Uwaezuoke
4742. Uwagbahim
4743. Uwakanma
4744. Uwakolam
4745. Uwakwe
4746. Uwala
4747. Uwalaka
4748. Uwama
4749. Uwandu
4750. Uwaoma
4751. Uwasirike
4752. Uwawuako
4753. Uwazurike
4754. Uyaenu
4755. Uyaigwe
4756. Uyandu
4757. Uyanmadu
4758. Uyanne
4759. Uyanwa
4760. Uzoabaka
4761. Uzoabasi
4762. Uzoafia
4763. Uzoaga
4764. Uzoagbala
4765. Uzoahia
4766. Uzoaku
4767. Uzoalor
4768. Uzoamaka
4769. Uzoamara
4770. Uzoaru
4771. Uzochi
4772. Uzochikwara
4773. Uzochukwu
4774. Uzodike
4775. Uzodima
4776. Uzoebube
4777. Uzoechina
4778. Uzoego
4779. Uzoegwu
4780. Uzoejinwa
4781. Uzoeto
4782. Uzoewulu
4783. Uzogo
4784. Uzoigwe
4785. Uzoije
4786. Uzoka
4787. Uzokwe
4788. Uzoma
4789. Uzondu
4790. Uzonkwa
4791. Uzonna
4792. Uzonwa
4793. Uzonwanne
4794. Uzoogo
4795. Uzougo
4796. Uzoukwu
4797. Uzoulu
4798. Uzowulu
4799. Uzu
4800. Uzuaga
4801. Uzuagu
4802. Uzuako
4803. Uzuakpundu
4804. Uzuakpunwa
4805. Uzuchukwu
4806. Uzuchukwu
4807. Uzudike
4808. Uzuebie
4809. Uzuegbunam
4810. Uzuego
4811. Uzuegwu
4812. Uzujiaku
4813. Uzukwu
4814. Uzunakpunwa
4815. Uzunwa
4816. Uzunwoke
4817. Uzuwuru
4818. Wabara
4819. Wachukwu
4820. Wobasi
4821. Wogu
4822. Wokejide
4823. Wokocha
4824. Wokoma
4825. Yagazie
4826. Zamoku
4827. Zebechukwu
4828. Zebeilo
4829. Zebenjo
4830. Zebeugha
4831. Zebeolisa
4832. Zebeonye
4833. Zelibe
4834. Zelunjo
4835. Zerechi
4836. Zeribe
4837. Zimako
4838. Zimuzo
4839. Zobem
4840. Zojide
4841. Zomam
4842. Zonyelum

NOTES

Motivation

1. Nnamdi Azikiwe: West African Pilot Group of Newspapers
2. Holy Bible: *The Book of Hosea Chapt. 4 v.6*
3. Dr. Emman Kwegyir Aggrey: *Convocation Speech*, 1914.

Chapter 1

1. Ndubisi Nwafor: *Ph.D Theses, University of Ibadan*, 1991
2. Mathias Ugochukwu Ekeanyanwu*: Interview with Ndubisi Nwafor*, 1982.
3. Prof. E. Isichei: *A History of Igbo People,* 1976
4. G.T. Basden: *Niger Ibos,* 1966.
5. Herskanin: *University Term Lectures, University of Hamburg*, 1978
6. Hersen Berrg: *Ethnic Migrations*, 1977
7. Z. C. Obi: *Interview with Ndubisi Nwafor*, 1979
8. Herbert Cole & Chke Aniakor: *Museum of Cultural History*, 1984
9. Marshall Cavendish: Peoples of Africa, 2001

Chapter Two

1. Justice Sowemimo: *Federal Supreme Court Gazette*, September 11, 1963
2. Opia, Eric A; "Why Biafra?"; Leswing Press, 1972.
3. The Aburi Accord: Accra Ghana, 1967
4. Achebe: *Things Fall Apart*, 1994
5. Opia, Ibid

6. Chief Olu Sau: *Nigerian Punch Newspaper*; October 20, 2008
7. Northern Nigerian Government Gazette, Kaduna, 1964

Chapter Three

1. Marshall Covendish: Ibid
2. Ola Rotimi: *Kurunmi,* 1971
3. Chief Bellgam Pepple: *Eastern Nigerian Outlook*, February 15, 1958
4. Dr. Eze Akanu Ibiam: *Letter of protest to Her Royal Highness*, 1967
5. IITA International Demographics; 1989
6. The Catholic Observer: October 2003.

Chapter Four

1. Achebe; Ibid
2. George Orwell: *Animal Farm*
3. Achebe; Ibid

Chapter Five

1. Achebe; Ibid
2. Dr. Afam Ebeogu: *The Social Drama of Igbo kola Culture*, 1988

Chapter Seven

1. The Holy Bible: Gen. 1 v 28
2. Ibid, Psalm 127 v 3-5.

Chapter Nine

1. Dr. Igwe: Ahajioku Lectures, 1988
2. Dr. Igwe, Ibid
3. Dr. Igwe, Ibid

Chapter Twelve

1. Churchill, London Times, March 1969
2. Israel Nwoba: "*The Three Night Wizards*"

Chapter Thirteen

1. Shakespeare : *"Twelfth Night" Act 2 Sc. V*
2. Achebe: *"Things Fall Apart"*
3. Odumakwu Ojukwu: *"Ahiara Declaration"*, 1967
4. Prof. Sylvanus Cookey: *Interview with Henry Chukwurah SunNews*, Feb. 27, 2012
5. Odumekwu Ojukwu: "Principles of Biafran Revolution", June 1969
6. The Holy Bible: Exodus chapter 14 vv. 10-12
7. Prof. Sam Aluko: Interview with Duro Adeseko: *"What Ojukwu told me—Before, during and after the war."*
8. Shakespeare: *"Julius Caesar" Act 4, Sc. 3*
9. The Holy Bible: Psalm 118 v.22; Matt. 21 v. 42
10. Odumekwu Ojukwu: Ibid
11. Dr. Akanu Ibiam, Ibid